The Noiseletting:
Hijinx, Hard Knocks and Wisdom from Life Inside the Music Industry
Byron Fry

Print ISBNs
Amazon print 9780228633280
Ingram Spark 9780228633297
Barnes & Noble 9780228633303
BWL Print 9780228633310

BWL Publishing Inc.

*Books we love to write...
Authors around the world.*

http://bwlpublishing.ca

Copyright 2024 by Byron Fry
Editor JD Shipton
Cover artist Michelle Lee

All rights reserved. Without limiting the rights under copyright reserved above, no part of this publication may be reproduced, stored in or introduced into a retrieval system, or transmitted, in any form, or by any means (electronic, mechanical, photocopying, recording, or otherwise) without the prior written permission of both the copyright owner and the publisher of this book

Dedication

To Veronica

Thank you for being the one who finally showed me that I can be accepted as I am.
You make my life feel beautiful.

To Britt

Thank you for being such a splendid next generation,
and for teaching me what true show-up looks like. I admire you to no end.

To Jesse

Relax. I'll take you on a walk just as soon as I'm finished here.

Acknowledgements

Thanks to:
Jude Pittman, for the willingness to open the door for a relatively unproven author, and for the words of encouragement;
J.D. Shipton, for the fresh editorial perspectives and patient guidance through the logistics of getting things from manuscript to world;
Randy Fry, for the priceless and concise clarity regarding what not to do as a writer, delivered in blatant enough terms for even his little brother to grasp; and

Jay Lang, for having said so many bewilderingly great things about my writing over the years, for having led the way into authorship by such inspiring example, for encouraging me to write this book—any book—and for having introduced me to Jude, J.D. and the rest of the crew at BWL.

Endorsements

"This book is essential for artists at any stage of their careers. Whether you're an industry veteran or a newcomer, this frank examination of the music world's funny yet brutal realities offers valuable insights and plenty of entertainment. Byron Fry's journey reveals unfiltered, powerful truths about life as a musician, making it a crucial read for musicians and non-musicians alike."
- Jay Lang, BWL bestselling novelist, brand ambassador, content leader and literary columnist for V13 Media

"Not only is Byron a killer, versatile musician, and my favorite kind of guitarist (the shredder!), he is one of the most perspicacious thinkers I've ever run across. So if there's anyone to tell the story of life as a road-and-session musician, he's your guy for the real inside scoop, which I guarantee you will be as funny as it is horrifying, about an ultimately strange and rewarding life."
Angela Carole Brown Vocalist, Recording Artist, Visual Artist, Author and Winner of the North Street Book Prize in Literary Fiction

"Byron Fry can play any style and always made time for my projects. The two things I could always count on."
Barry Coffing, Producer, Composer, #1 Hit Songwriter and Emmy Loser

"My father used to share some very colorful

stories about the guys in the Sinatra band, the Wrecking Crew and Zappa, but he got a kick out of hearing me tell him about guitar virtuoso Byron Fry rock climbing an ancient church in Estonia, tuning his guitar to a passing plane and switching from hard rock to fusion to country to jazz ....within the same guitar solo!"
Bill Rotella, Singer / Songwriter / Coolest Bandleader Ever

"Byron Fry is proof positive that it is possible to not just survive, but thrive in the music industry over decades...IF you have the work ethic, tenacity, and multi-faceted virtuosity as he does. This book is a must-read for the inspiration!"
Chris Stevens, Percussionist, Spearhead / Band Director / Sensei of the Prizewinning Long Beach Polytech H.S. Big Band / Force of Nature, Builder of Futures

"Experience the journey of true creativity through music and his writings."
Christine Day, Vocalist, Contractor for Music, Film and TV

"Byron is THE real deal. Every single time we've met or talked, I seem to learn something from him. He's always able to open a door that I've not seen. Read this book and see for yourself..."
Erkka Korhonen, Multi-Platinum Record Producer, Arranger, Guitarist

"I've been nominated for a Grammy and a Golden Globe, and have worked with some of the finest musicians in the world. I put Byron in that category. He's pitch-perfect in everything he does...working with him was a real pleasure. He is always spot-on."

Frank Stallone, Hit Recording Artist / Songwriter, Actor

"Knowing Byron's brain, this book is going to be a must-read, true encounters of a musical genius."
Gary Ponder, Blindingly Articulate Drummer / Musician with Gary Wright, Maureen McCormick

"Byron is a very creative and musical composer / arranger / producer, as well as a good speaker and humorist. He's helped me on thirteen very different pieces I've written—jazz, blues, rock, fusion, flamenco, soul, funk and movie soundtrack materials—providing tracks on electric, steel acoustic and nylon acoustic guitars and bass. It's a pleasure working with him and he always makes my material work smoothly and sound better."
Jack Jacobsen, Keyboardist with Huey Lewis, Van Morrison and Tommy Tutone

"Having been party to, and/or privy to, a significant portion of Byron's lifelong journey through the labyrinth of the music industry, I have watched him navigate his way through times that were good and times of struggle. But through the years, no matter the circumstance, his standards in music have never wavered. Nor will they ever, because he holds music itself as a steady, unsullied North Star."
James Hurley, Singer-Songwriter, Indie Recording Artist, Guitarist, Generator of Cogence

When Byron asked me to join his project, I of course said yes and knew I was gonna love it. One of the early-on drum charts Byron sent me contained the following verbal direction over a few bars of slash marks: 'drum fill that could sterilize a buffalo from 300 yards'. What's not to love?"

Jay Setar,
Freelance L.A. Drummer / Epicenter of Weaponized Sound Waves

"Definitely overdue, Byron brings you through the trials and tribulations of being a world class arranger / guitarist / musician in today's musical landscape. Where excellence is oft overlooked, you won't be able to put it down!"
Mark Corradetti, Bassist in Allan Parsons' talent stable

"Byron has performed and recorded with many 'name' musicians and produced hundreds of songs in his home studio. He even composed and conducted a three-movement symphony. I trust that many aspiring musicians will reap huge benefits from these valuable insights gleaned from a long and successful musical career!"
Mark Varney, Producer of iconic albums featuring Allan Holdsworth, Frank Gambale, Brett Garsed and Shawn Lane

"Byron Fry is a world class player and musician, period! Plus a very kind, caring and 'real' intelligent person, and a solid stand-up fellow."
Thomas Nordegg, Mad Genius Guitar Tech and Inventor of Technologies behind Steve Vai, Frank Zappa, Dweezil Zapppa, Yngwie Malmsteen, Jimmy Page, etc.

"Byron lifted my creativity to levels I never imagined, using a lifetime of musical experience. I'm so glad he wrote this book to share that experience with everyone."
Steve Kramer, Songwriter / Executive Producer

Forward

Like most blood clots in the gooey mess of the music industry, I'm not a household name. But I'm known among some noted corpuscles in the hallowed and storied arteries of Southern California's musical anatomy, and hopefully that counts for something.

I've written this book to be a fun and informative read, geared for the general public as well as those afflicted with the genetic psychosis that makes us musicians. I've tried to remove the bark from the tree as completely as possible without getting tarred and feathered, sued by stars or disavowed by family, in hopes of showing you what it's actually like to live life in the music industry—not the glitzy, glamorous thing most of the world sees in Hollywood's far-flung depictions, but the actual animal. It's far more interesting, more dangerous, more difficult, more intense and more rewarding; the truth harder to believe than the fiction. It's more full of laughter and tears, absurdities and irony, darkness and incredibly bright, golden moments than anything that TV or film could ever convey.

What this book is *not* is a bunch of glittery Hollywood hype and hoopla. There's inevitably what looks like namedropping, but only when it's pertinent. To illustrate things, there are stories from gigs in different genres, cultures and countries, from biker bars, juke joints and hotel lounges to major tours, live international TV broadcasts, orchestral performances, and motorcades.

So far, over the unlikely course of my career, I've worn a disturbingly high number of hats. The stories in this book, as fun as I hope they are, provide useful and hard-won lessons from those contrasting experiences:

Commissioned orchestral composer, rock and roller, jazzer, contract artist for the State of California, studio guitarist, cruise ship musician, soul / R&B rhythm section player and vocal crooner, commissioned big band composer, top 40 musician, funk musician, clinician, quasi-actor, high-profile touring player being chased by autograph houndettes, classical pianist, arranger / producer, music professor, signed recording artist, blues guitarist, transcriber, country/western producer, film and TV composer (racing deadlines), tuxedoed guitarist in wedding bands, faux-flamenco hero throwing down flurries of too many notes in Malta, a guitar-playing Frankenstein, and the guy on screen playing guitar to a TV broadcast viewership larger than the Super Bowl as my amps blew sky-high.

At this point I've played gigs, concerts, shows and sessions of every type, in every setting not under water or on the moon. Many have been high profile, the majority haven't, but at the end of the day every gig is just a workaday situation. Every story herein carries experiences, tips, perspectives and information that I hope will be eye-opening for non-musicians, and useful for those who are treading this cockroach-infested, rhinestone-encrusted, dangerous, and incredibly, heartbreakingly beautiful path.

Training is the most fundamental aspect of every musical career—sorry, it's not posing in front of cameras and being fawned over by fans on a diamond-studded red carpet—so the book will spend just a little while lending a headlamp to anyone wanting to navigate the dark and cryptic murkiness that is musical training. Otherwise, it loosely follows the chronology of my experiences so far, from training to my broken and bumpy trajectory climbing up from the bottom ranks to whatever dubious position it is that I currently occupy. Many of the oddest, funniest, darkest and most valuable lessons have come from the most humble gigs.

Every musical career is a hard road, and leaves little room for dealing with personal battles, so I've included some of mine—from physical setbacks to financial woes to parenthood—to illustrate how it's not only possible, but vital for a musician to adapt, overcome, restrengthen, and move forward.

Please believe me when I say: Some people are infected at birth with the musical virus. Science, society, and our families are a long way from understanding it, and those of us who are truly infected will die if we do anything else with our lives. If that's you or a loved one, my hope is that this book will help you comprehend the improbabilities to come, and prepare for them. Good luck and bon voyage.

Table of Contents

Chapter 1 15
Chapter 2 20
Chapter 3 26
Chapter 4 39
Chapter 5 43
Chapter 6 47
Chapter 7 55
Chapter 8 62
Chapter 9 69
Chapter 10 74
Chapter 11 87
Chapter 12 92
Chapter 13 100
Chapter 14 106
Chapter 15 111
Chapter 16 119
Chapter 17 138
Chapter 18 146
Chapter 19 157
Chapter 20 162
Chapter 21 168
Chapter 22 178
Chapter 23 183
Chapter 24 190
Chapter 25 198

Chapter 26 209
Chapter 27 214
Chapter 28 243
Chapter 29 247
Chapter 30 250
Chapter 31 253
Chapter 32 260
Chapter 33 274
Chapter 34 280
Chapter 35 287
Chapter 36 299
Chapter 37 304
Chapter 38 312
Chapter 39 317
Chapter 40 324
Chapter 41 327
Chapter 42 353
Chapter 43 356
Chapter 44 363
Chapter 45 368
Epilogue... 373

Chapter 1
Headwaters

The screaming mob of girls chased me relentlessly, splitting up so that some could cut me off from the line that the others had me running down. They were as organized as a hunting pack of wolves, if wolves hunted in packs of thirty. They could spell each other, but there was only one of me. I had to keep moving.

Finally, gasping for breath and legs starting to fail, I found myself first cornered then pinned down at home plate in the baseball diamond of Parson's Elementary School in Castro Valley, California. I was eight years old, it was recess on a beautiful spring day and unbeknownst to me, just before the recess, my third grade teacher had switched the classroom intercom mic on, so that my show-and-tell performance of "Wild Thing" by The Troggs (singing and playing my Harmony archtop guitar) had been broadcast to the entire school through every classroom's PA speaker.

Suddenly to them, I was something more than me.

Lying helplessly on the ground at the bottom of a pile of wild, screaming and giggling space aliens, I felt a mysterious intoxication as they started to rip off my shirt, mimicking what the mob of women did to Paul every Saturday morning in the opening credits montage of The Beatles Cartoon.

Before that day I was the notorious outcast, literally the solitary long-haired kid in a redneck town of 45 thousand. Being the center of attention had never been enjoyable. Now I had been shown some sort of—what? Acceptance? Adulation? What was this weird thing? I was smart enough to know it wasn't real friendship, but one thing I was certain of:

It was nice.

The next instant, the girls abruptly lost all interest and moved off toward the next thing like I didn't exist (there was a good lesson for me there, had I been old enough to grasp it), and while my shirt survived, it was a headier experience than my eight-year-old brain knew what to do with. While I was in the middle of that experience, I found myself living the story with one part of my mind while narrating it with another: *"No shit, there I was, being chased by thirty girls!"* This splitting of consciousness became sort of a habit.

I remember dusting myself off and thinking—no, knowing—that this was it: Music would be my life.

I had already suspected though, as did my mom, my dad and my two older brothers. I was the only one of us who ultimately had no choice in life but music, but the whole family was musical. Mom played violin in string quartets, my older brothers had a great acoustic duo in their junior high and high school years called The Wayfarers, and Dad had a rich and wonderful baritone voice. But we all knew I was helplessly musical, from infancy.

I was five when my family duped me into performing on stage for the very first time. I had no idea what was going on. They just gently pushed me out from a mysteriously dark area in the back of a building onto a flat wooden surface with the brightest light that I had ever seen, shining right into my eyes. Other than that light, it was so dark that nothing else existed. The brightest light, the darkest dark, and eerily silent: not so much completely quiet as completely hushed. I felt like I was standing on a big microscope slide, and the light was a giant eye staring at me.

I had been told to play my ukulele and sing "Blowin' in the Wind" by Dylan, a song I liked despite not fully understanding its meaning. I played and sang the song. When I finished, I was horrified when right in front of me, between me and the light, at least fifty people suddenly exploded into uproarious shouting, cheering and clapping. I remember running off stage as fast as I could.

While receiving congratulations and pats on the head backstage afterwards, my oldest brother's best friend Leonard H. took me aside and gave me a five dollar bill. He looked me right in the eye and said, "This is for doing a good job. Don't ever forget this." I never have.

All these years later, through the thousands of gigs and shows, the tours, the records, the uproarious laughs with brothers and sisters of The Craft, the dark fights for life, the standing next to greatness in The Fleeting Golden Light—through all of it—I've never been able to pinpoint where I end and my musical processes begin. I might as well try to point to the boundary between myself and my right knee, or between my skull and my thoughts. Screaming females aside (whatever that's about), in all seriousness my relationship with music is not so much a relationship as it is simply me. Most musicians feel the same way.

I strongly suspect that there's a neurological condition that makes people like me the way we are, so that we *have to be music* and *music has to be us*, or we die. There is no choice of career or lifestyle...it's like the Achilles character in the film "Troy" played by Brad Pitt, when he's asked why he chose to become a warrior. His reply is "There was no choice. I was born, and this is what I am."

Maybe science will figure it out someday.

I'd be a musician now regardless of whether or not I'd been pinned down by 30 giggling girls at age eight, but suffice to say it probably helped grease the wheels. I've still got a picture of that old Harmony archtop...it was a Christmas gift. It cost my dad $70 in a Montgomery Ward catalogue, had strings about the same gauge as transcontinental telephone cables, and action so high the strings and frets were in two different zip codes. Playing that beast from age seven to ten was a real character builder, and laid a foundation of hand strength that would serve me well.

* * *

Playing guitar is demoralizingly hard when you begin. The strings hurt and can cut into your fingers, the hand position is so weird it feels like the universe is pranking you, you have to press the strings with muscles you haven't developed yet and a hand that's turned upside down, and you have to do it with laser-guided accuracy.

There's a peculiar clarity to the memories of life-changing moments, and I remember the first chord I ever played on guitar like it was yesterday. My big brother Randy showed it to me one sunny afternoon when I was five. He was eleven—a big kid—and I had finally pestered him into agreeing that I was big enough to graduate from ukulele. In retrospect, it's clear now that the uke was a beguiling gateway drug that inevitably led me toward guitar and this life of debauchery and dubious undertakings in the company of such incredible talent, all of us helplessly circling the musical drain while experiencing amazing things in amazing places. But we couldn't have known the risk so far upstream, in the summer of '63, when Randy showed me my first actual guitar chord. It was like my first hit of the new drug.

I still remember the texture of the blue cloth couch we were sitting on in the living room by the back door, I remember the door was open and a diagonal shaft of warm sunlight was streaming in, and I still remember the impossible awkwardness of trying to play that damned E Major, and thinking "He's pulling my leg. This is impossible, playing guitar CAN'T really be this hard." It was a classical guitar, about the same size to me at five as an upright bass is to me now.

That I didn't turn my back on guitar then and there for all time is testament either to my moxie or my poor judgement, I've never known which. And though it felt impossible at first, I kept right on playing—because the better I got, the more fun it became. It had nothing to do with discipline, it was more like playing frisbee or riding my bike: just one of those fun things I always did growing up.

Its grip on me continually tightened, with an inexorable force as impossible to resist as gravity. By age eight, the guitar had become an appendage of my body.

Now, all these decades later, I've spent my life guitaring my way around the industry and the planet, working at times with some good names, getting the call for some of the more technically challenging gigs in the tall grass, and critical acclaim from luminaries in the guitar fusion genre. The point is this: I'm not especially gifted. I did get an early start—I have no memories that predate music in my life—but basically the truth is that I'm not freakishly talented. So if I can do it, you can too. If you have that voice in your head telling you that playing music (on any instrument) is too hard, don't listen to it. It's bullshit.

Chapter 2
Choosing a Horse

Lest you think my life or this book is all about the guitar, I should confess that I started on piano. Not only that: professionally, I'm really all about composing, arranging, orchestrating and producing, as I encourage every musician to be. If all I could do was play guitar, my starved carcass would've been discovered in a pile of refuse under a freeway overpass by someone fixing a flat tire, long ago. That's a tip for anybody thinking of becoming a guitarist: Throw a rock anywhere in Los Angeles and you'll hit five of us, at least one of whom will be pretty good. Playing is all well and good, but the music you write and/or arrange is what can change your career, your life and the world.

What if Beethoven had just been a pianist? Lennon and Dylan just guitarists? We tend to regard iconic music like it's a part of the natural world, like Yosemite Valley or the moon, because it's written so perfectly it just feels inevitable. But it's really not that way at all. There was a moment when Beethoven's Fifth Symphony didn't exist. A guy, just like us, sat down and transcribed what the universe was pointing out to him as the most obvious thing to do at that time. Then, because that guy put that pen to that paper at that time, it existed: A piece of music so perfect and iconic that it will last at least as long as the human race. For all we know, longer. It's hard sometimes to believe that it's not magic, but it's not. It's just a really fine set of skills.

Playing is fine, it's prerequisite. At a certain level, having world-class chops is the cover charge that gets you into The Room. But being hired as a player, you're just pounding nails as a laborer on the job site. On the other hand, being the composer or arranger or producer is like being the supe, or the architect. I'm not talking about getting a DAW (Digital Audio Workstation), editing some loops and calling yourself a "composer". I mean actually learning the skill sets of composing, arranging, orchestrating and producing. There's a lot to it, sure. But it's very doable, I promise.

Until you try, you really can't know what voice or what power might be inside you. For all you know, you'll make a massive contribution to our collective voice. Plus, if you get the right kind of work, you're pissing in tall cotton and farting through silk.

* * *

The currents of political and logistical power in music radiate outward from the keyboards. It's like some kind of law. If you need to get your bearings in a working situation, or if you're just watching a show and wondering who's calling the shots on stage, Command HQ is usually the keyboard rig.

Keyboardists tend to be the boss on the job because keys are by far the easiest to write and direct from. Every human should play some piano, whether they're even musical or not. It's the best interface between the human brain and harmony, so it's an understandable tradition that the keyboard player is more or less automatically the MD (musical director) on a gig, regardless of his or her actual qualifications.

My Mom was fond of saying that she started my ear training before I could walk, sitting at the piano with me in her lap. And I remember climbing up onto the bench alone when it was chin-high to me every day, exploring the relationships between notes, eventually finding chords, then scales, then different arpeggios. I had no idea what I was doing. I just went exploring for what sounded good.

At age nine I started piano lessons with a friend of my mom's in Berkeley named Gloria Dolan. She was an acclaimed Bay Area concert pianist, and had two grand pianos dominating her living room, arranged back-to-back so that we could sit facing each other.

Her house was a peaceful and quiet space. This was in stark contrast to a mile or so southeast, where Berkeley's ever-present demonstrations on Tele (Telegraph Avenue) and in the Sproul Hall plaza were being cracked down upon, triggering what became a daily routine of full-blown riots. The other four days of the week after school I'd make my way up Dwight Way to Tele, where National Guard helicopters sometimes made like crop dusters, teargassing protesters in coordinated attacks with lines of police in riot gear wading in and bashing skulls with their clubs. Being around all that never felt normal exactly, but I got used to it.

On Wednesdays after school I walked the other direction, to Gloria's house. It was like a peaceful retreat.

The first thing she did at our first lesson was to test my ears:

"Okay, I'm going to play a note and I want you to play it back to me."

She did, I did.

"Okay, I'm going to play a few different notes and I want you to play them all back to me."

She did, I did.

"Okay, now I'm going to play some chords. See if you can play them back to me."

She did, I did.

Then the air in the room seemed to change. She paused a beat, just looking at me with an eyebrow raised. "Byron, do you know what perfect pitch is?"

"No."

"It means you know what every note is, by ear. You have perfect pitch, and that's a very special thing. I think we should build on that."

Now, if you're a musician reading this you're rolling your eyes and saying "Ohgawd, he's *perfect pitching* us."

And I get it, really I do. People with great ears tend to make it clear that they have that going on, and it's probably irritating. There's a joke about it:

Q: How do you know when someone has perfect pitch?

A: They'll tell you.

Nonetheless, it's important information. Even in upper echelon circles and larger ensembles, there aren't that many people in the room with great ears, so being known for perfect pitch is undeniably a good thing in this, the most competitive industry on Earth. More importantly, anyone with ears like mine is a great troubleshooter to have around.

Any good biologist will tell you the main sense for most species on this planet is sight, but with music, it's hearing. Training your ears is the most important of *the three pillars*, the other two being your chops on your instrument and your cognitive understanding.

Perfect pitch isn't some freaky thing you're just born with; that's bullshit. It's true that there's such a thing as aptitude, and getting an early start is great, but I've taught several people to develop perfect pitch. It's sort of a parlor trick, you'd be surprised. So don't think you can't develop great ears. That's also bullshit.

I owe Gloria Dolan a great debt of gratitude, because being a mom, she was intuitive enough to see that I was a wild child and lacked the patience for doing things the normal way (spelled: responsibly), so instead of making me learn to read music and losing my interest, she taught me by ear. I studied from her for 5 years, developing technique and skill until I was playing Chopin's Minute Waltz, and here's the thing and why she was so awesome: She always set the music in front of me on the piano, so that I had it there to refer to and to keep track of things. And she actually did teach me to read, in little bits. It gradually added up.

Without my knowing it, her devious tactics were making me quasi-literate, despite my baser instincts. She's one of several great teachers to whom I owe everything, my brother Randy being the very first to encourage the flow, way up at the headwaters.

* * *

The passion that I felt for music in my early single digits expanded and gained power, like a crowning lava plume under a volcano. At age ten, I got my first electric solidbody guitar. It was a used Fender Jaguar that cost $175 at Leo's in Oakland. Wherever it is now, if it's in one piece it's worth about ten grand. My folks borrowed a Vox amp for me from some friends, and I started a rock trio of ten year-olds with my school buddies Brian Abbott on Bass and Carl somebody on drums. We played an ad-hoc collection of current hits almost every day in the big multipurpose room at Walden elementary school in Berkeley. We took liberties with Sly Stone, lacerated Otis Redding, pounded CCR and flailed at almost every song on Cream's Disraeli Gears album. In the middle of 1968 Berkeley, surrounded by the daily violence of political upheaval and the incredible musical renaissance that was busting out all over, playing with my buddies gave me the same sensation I got when I caught a big wave body surfing. I could feel the ground swell, and I knew I was on to something. That lava dome was developing a pulse and prehensile appendages.

By age fourteen, when I wasn't with my non-musical hometown tribe of best buddies—a suspicious pack of longhaired, half-feral wildlings marauding the East Bay like coyotes—I was getting so engrossed with piano and with guitar that it was clear: I was riding two different young stallions with a foot on the back of each, and they were both gaining muscle, speed and momentum.

Something had to give. I had to choose a horse. Piano was, to me, something on which I could recite. Guitar was something for jamming, expressing myself and having a good time.

I remember my oldest brother Gary talking to me about it in the kitchen one day and saying in no uncertain terms, "Byron, keyboardists are the musical directors, composers and producers. Be a keyboardist, goddammit. You'll have a much more solid future and career than if you become a guitarist."

Naturally, I chose guitar.

Chapter 3
Dojo by the Bay

The most apt word to describe how I attacked chop-building on guitar, having turned my back on keyboards, is "possessed".

I bought a cheap Telecaster knockoff from a friend, made by National. I called it my "sacrificial neck", and sawed through the frets developing my vibrato and bends: half step, full step, minor third and major third, pushing bends with and without vibrato on the 3 small strings, pulling on the big ones, all of that multiplied by my four fingers. Basically, every kind of bend and vibrato I could possibly find myself playing was systematically arranged into a workout routine. Those frets were reduced to metal shavings in under a year, I had my bends and vibrato, and I hadn't destroyed the neck on my gorgeous Les Paul Black Beauty.

Frau Metronome and I would begin a stormy relationship that year as well. I painted a picture of her in my mind that I see clearly when I shed (shed: short for woodshed, meaning practice): The Frau appears in my mind as a burly, big-boned overweight Austrian battle axe with a lower jaw that juts out like a bulldog, bushy eyebrows like Leonid Brezhnev and big moles on her face, carrying a big stick that she whacks me with when I fail to play things in sync with her. She's an unforgiving, vindictive witch whose itinerary is to let me get away with nothing but absolute perfection. But when it's good, she changes into a gorgeous and graceful smiling thing and oh, how we dance. I discovered so many polyrhythms (layering one rhythm over another) with her. Two against three, three against four, four against five and other temporal collages. The most interesting ones would never pack a dance floor, but musicians who are wired to love oddball rhythms don't typically care about dancers.

I had gotten an incredibly nice Guild D25 steel string acoustic guitar for Christmas at age twelve. My parents gave me a heads-up months beforehand, and I was allowed to search the entire Bay Area for the right axe. I rode public transit to hit every music store in the nine counties, and it came down to either that Guild or a gorgeous old Martin, both of which happened to be in the vault below Leo's. After agonizing for a couple of weeks, I chose the Guild. It cost $250, which was a lot of dough in 1970 for parents who worked in academia. To this day, it's my most coveted axe. It's also one of the most recorded guitars I own, and one of two that I'd run through an inferno to save.

With that Guild, I discovered that when you're really locked in with Frau Metronome, you can make her sound disappear entirely. I still love to do that. I imagine that old Austrian witch with duct tape over her bewhiskered maw.

Independence exercises for the left hand digits became (and still are) a major part of my regimen. I have an intense and productive regimen, with which I torture and demoralize guitarists who are unfortunate enough to study with me.

For those not on a musical path it can be alienating to see a loved one become a non-communicative pile of protoplasm, perpetually hunched over an instrument like some drooling subhuman ogre, literally oblivious to their immediate environment. For all purposes of interaction, we might as well be unconscious or OD'd on barbiturates. It's tough on relationships with non-creatives, unless they are of the supremely accepting and forgiving sort.

Luckily for me, I lived with my Dad during my teens, and he was one such human— oddly patient with the noise, and with how tuned out I was when I was playing. Sometimes he'd get frustrated when he really did need to talk to me, but otherwise he was very cool about it. Looking back, it's clear that he was far more patient with my invading his space with racket than I would be if the tables were turned.

* * *

I should illustrate my somewhat unmoored mental state where personal safety is concerned, because it's had an effect on my life, hence my career, hence this book. Like most red-blooded males, my first few decades were a fine study of seeing just how far I could push things and survive. Whether cliff jumping and counting the seconds before I hit water, getting the most gigantic air I could on a pair of skis, or taking a fall off a crag at age 14 when a deliberate stunt 45 feet off deck went badly (I stood up dusting myself off and laughing—ah, the rubber joints of youth), I had an enthusiasm for tempting fate that raised eyebrows all around me. It made me feel more alive in my time, and my parents old before theirs.

Every neighborhood has that one kid who everyone is sure will be dead before they reach twenty one, killed by their own antics. I was that kid. I'm gratified to have survived my adolescence; it chagrins me that I no longer bounce, and have to be careful.

High-speed drifting out Redwood Canyon in the East Bay was a rite of passage, and a thing I loved to do in my jalopy. Granted, a beat up '62 Chevy Nova wagon with a straight 6 and three-on-the-tree trans isn't the first thing that comes to mind for that kind of thing, especially with used tires showing two layers of thread, and a drop of hundreds of feet on the outside of half of the curves, with no guard rail. But we make do with what we have on hand.

Palomares Canyon was (and no doubt still is) a great road for testing the limits. Nine miles of S-curves, high-speed straights, hairpins and decreasing radii turns with reverse camber and oak trees on the outside, she's an unforgiving mistress who killed plenty of us in my hometown during my high school years.

My buds and I, out joyriding Palomares in Ray B's grandmother's VW fastback before we were legally licensed to drive, got the notion one day that it would be an especially good idea to take turns lying on the roof holding the side rails while whoever was behind the wheel tried to throw us off to our deaths. Nobody died, but I came close once when my best friend Kevin W got the inspired notion to suddenly stomp the brakes at high speed. I was launched forward over the windshield and was headed toward the pavement directly in front of the front wheels, and only by doing a cat-like midair 180 and grabbing the edge of the hood at the bottom of the windshield did I avoid going under the tires.

* * *

So that's the guy I was when, at sixteen, I met Richard W...a delightfully good drummer my age who shared my love of odd meters and creating the most progressive and challenging music possible. My love of "prog" dates back to my big brother Gary innocently giving me ELP's "Tarkus" for Christmas when I was twelve, and King Crimson's "Starless and Bible Black" when I was fifteen. In his defense, he couldn't have foreseen the monster he'd be loosing on the world. And meeting Richard—a like-minded miscreant willing to throw down as aggressively as me in the pursuit of The Great Unlikelihood—was a timely co-sign to my new mental disease. We immediately became close brothers and played for hours every day, in a space that differed from the norm as much as the music we played.

We had been looking for a place to spray our nonsensical noise into the universe, where we wouldn't disturb anyone and no one would disturb us. Ideally, it would be a place where we could safely leave our gear set up (called a "lockout rehearsal space" in normal jargon). A set of drums and a Fender Bassman 100-watt amp with a 4X12 cabinet (four 12 inch speakers), both being played by out-of-control adolescent hooligans, is a big noise. We knew we needed to be out of the way of things.

After searching local facilities high and low, and unable to afford anything normal, we looked to more and more unconventional spaces. For weeks we searched the East Bay and found nothing. Then one day Rich and I were out by the mudflats of The Bay, rummaging through the rust in junkyard row for some Chevy Nova part or other, when we noticed something.

Verging on the mudflats a couple of hundred yards north of us—between Junkyard Row and the dump—was the only house for half a mile in any direction. It was so rundown and ramshackle, it defied the laws of physics just by standing. It was on the last few acres of grasses before the actual mud of the tidal flat...it looked like a high enough tide would wipe it right off the map.

Rotting on the boggy land about 35 yards from the house was an old 40-foot semi trailer on five-foot tall stacks of wooden blocks, no wheels. We went and took a closer look. It was old, rusted and rickety, and there were bullet holes in the sheet metal. But the doors, walls and floor all looked intact.

"It's perfect!" we both said.

We went up to the front porch and knocked on a screen door that was about to fall off. After a short conversation with the sweet old drunk who lived there, we had a rehearsal space and his permission to run a chain of extension cords across the ground to the trailer from his house for power. We offered to pay for the electricity, but he said not to worry about it. I have no idea how many building codes we were violating, but those were different times, and nobody paid much attention to things this far out by the mud. That was kind of the whole point.

Shortly after that we were joined by Gregg Dugger, a phenomenally talented guitarist who could absolutely shred right or left-handed, on a guitar strung either way. That's four different ways this guy could throw down, which freaks me out to this day. We had way too much fun playing for hours every day in that trailer, cutting our teeth, shaking the bugs out of the groove-building process. It was a priceless Dojo for all of us at the time.

The three of us would sometimes grab a bassist and play at weekend keggers or backyard jams. The usual repertoire among East Bay adolescent musicians was progressive rock and funk, which is another reason I'm lucky to have been raised when and where I was. Songs off of Jeff Beck's Blow By Blow and Wired albums were our favorite racetracks at those parties.

After a bit, Rich and I decided that Gregg was too rock and roll, and in a shamefully high-nosed bit of elitism, kicked him out of the "band". Looking back on it, we had no realistic basis for doing what we did; none at all. Gregg was invested, he was sweet, he was madly talented, and I've regretted that move ever since. That band would ultimately go nowhere anyway, of course—we were playing what would be called "math prog" today. And we hurt Gregg for no reason. It was a harsh lesson for every one of us. Live and learn.

We did eventually repair relations with Gregg, and made another band with a great singer / frontman named Van Ortega. We played rock covers, mostly Zeppelin and Deep Purple, but also some Queen. It was good times. And if I'm being honest, it's a good thing that I played some Rock at that point, to ground me a bit and bring me in from exploring the outer reaches of quantum unlikelihood.

I did some research and found Gregg decades later, and called his number. We got caught up on each other's news. He'd been a guitar teacher in the East Bay for many years, playing his classical solely for himself in his bedroom, because having to perform detracts from the quality of his practice and his chops. This is exactly what Byrd (Charlie Parker) said at one point...he who is credited with unlocking the technical nuts and bolts of modern harmony, and arguably the best alto player who has ever lived.

I think it was Herbie Hancock who said that the best players in the world aren't playing out, they're playing in their bedrooms, and we'll never know who they are. I fully agree. I can't say from recent firsthand experience how good Gregg Dugger has gotten on guitar, but I'm fairly confident he's one of the most horrifying monsters on the face of this planet. Call it an informed guess.

Rich and I would go on to be roommates in Tahoe at 18, spend time playing together in L.A. in our early twenties on Motown sessions, and playing live behind the likes of Maxine Nightingale and I can't remember what else. But it's the snot-slinging fun we had playing that weird stuff in that beat-up old 40-foot trailer on stilts that always makes me smile. It laid a good part of my foundational skills as a rhythm section player, and it shaped my thinking about writing and arranging for drums.

Even after all the training I've had, what I learned out there on the mud is a big part of how I think. I can still smell the fruity stench of the dump and the salty mud, and hear the seagulls arguing amid the grunts of Caterpillar D9s shoving around piles of garbage.

***

Around this time, my good friend Kevin W's big brother Dave took the notion of being my manager for about fifteen minutes. He had managed some Bay Area bands in the 60s, and to hear him tell it, he was connected to this singer, that promoter, the other dignitary, and luminary mover-shakers all up and down the Bay Area music scene's august spectrum. He was full of stories of his adventures through rock and roll's seedy underground, which I took to be liberally embellished. No matter, the yarns were harmless and entertaining, as was Dave.

He knew a singer from the circuit "back in the day", who was very well-connected and had been cast as the lead (and only) role in a one-man play off Broadway in The City, called "Back's Tracks". Dave talked me into driving the two of us across the Bay to check it out. What the hell, I wasn't doing anything else that night…might as well go watch a singer experiment with acting.

That night, Dave and I headed over to the City, got to Broadway and parked, then walked a few blocks through an environment that was part theater district, part brothel and part carnival. Here was a street whose displays were dedicated to the marketing of carnal pleasures, which one might reasonably expect to be presented with some kind of beauty, some kind of gracefulness, but whose garish and tactless facades had all the sexy allure of a rodeo clown wearing fake boobs, false eyelashes and Halloween candy lips.

We wandered past barkers in front of strip joints, neon signs depicting naked women, drunks passed out on the sidewalk in puddles of piss in front of liquor stores, bordellos with ladies-of-the-night posing in the front window in lighting intended to be sexy, but whose reds, greens and purples gave them more of a macabre eeriness than anything else. We walked under a long-standing marquis encircled in blinking lightbulbs announcing "CAROL DODA - THE PERFECT 36". This was the well-known monicker by which she was known to adolescent males of every age throughout the bay's nine counties, thanks to her station ID voice-over for the cable channel of that number. Her booking at that theater had lasted so long, it was widely regarded as a historical landmark. We weaved on through streetwalkers, pimps, beat patrolmen, junkies and dealers until we got to the "off broadway" theater's cross street, found the theater, bought tickets and went inside.

Edwin Mahoney's portrayal of an aging, has-been rock star was actually really good, as was the play. It was the kind of thing that critics would probably pan, critics not being musicians. But I dug it. And the task of holding an entire stage, audience and storyline, single-handed, wasn't lost on me. That was one hell of a challenge for somebody new to acting, and he owned it in good form.

It was after the performance as the crowd was milling about that we both noticed Bill Graham, the visionary concert promotor for the entire West Coast and in no small part the entire country—for all of rock and roll, if I'm being realistic—and one of the Bay Area's greatest treasures. He was standing in the middle of the theater as people filtered out, dressed very expensively and wearing an even more expensive-looking, totally silent super model on his arm while he talked to Edwin and his silent supermodel. Dave got up his courage and dragged me along to make an introduction. Dave had all the debonair of a junkie panhandler, but he got things done.

"Heyman, excuse me Mister Graham, I'm sorry to intrude but you might remember me I'm Dave W., I used to manage Bogus Thunder, do you remember? We played the yadda yadda festival and I think you're just the best thing that ever happened to the music scene here in the Bay, and I'd just like to say that it would be a huge honor, if it's okay, to introduce you to an up-and-coming star, this kid plays his ass off and he's gonna be something, so I thought you should meet him..."

When Dave started speaking, Bill's face looked a bit startled at the intrusion, then changed to mildly irritated, then eventually to a look of tired resignation to hear him out. He quickly looked me up and down—a sixteen year-old kid just barely old enough to have acne—and gave me a quick look that seemed to question the pairing of Dave and myself. I replied with an eyebrow shrug. He cracked a half-smile. Edwin looked miffed that we'd barged in on his time with Bill Graham. Dave finally got to the part where he said, "Mr Graham, this is Byron Fry. He's gonna..."

Bill Graham's eyebrows went up. "Byron Fry?" he said, "Is that your real name?"

"Yes", I said.

"That's a good name! How about giving me your phone number."

My eyebrows went up. "Of course!" I said, thinking "No shit, there I was, talking with Bill Graham and he asked for my number!"

He wrote it down, then said "Now if you'll excuse us, Eddy and I have some important business to discuss."

We graciously bowed out. As awkward as it was, Dave had indeed gotten it done: I left that theater in a world where Bill Graham knew my name, thought it was a good name, and took my number. I was certain that nothing would come of it—he hadn't heard me play or do anything, so he had no reason to call. But it was still a cool experience. And Dave had managed to simultaneously impress and embarrass me—no mean feat.

A couple of weeks later, I arrived home one afternoon and my dad said "Hey bud, you got a phone call from a Mick Brigdon. Said he works for a Bill Graham Presents."

"WHAT?!?"

"Something about needing a last-minute opening act for somethi..."

I launched from the front door and flew over the couch like superman, grabbing the phone off the end table from midair, did a tuck-and-roll on the living room carpet and called the number. Alas, Mick wasn't there and I wound up leaving an overly-exited message with a confused secretary, and that's as far as any of that ever went. Had the offer still been on the table, I have no idea what I would have put together...a collection of teens experimenting with progressive odd-meter fusion? Probably just as well I didn't get the opportunity. But it would have been interesting to try.

Not long after, "Mahoney" had been shortened to "Money" and you can figure out the rest.

* * *

It was about this time that my brother Randy and I started to play as an acoustic guitar / vocal duo. We played Grog & Sirloins, Rusty Scuppers, Rusty Pelicans and the like all around the Bay. I couldn't legally play bars yet, but restaurant / bars were okay. We did a live performance at a local radio station in Berkeley—I don't remember its call sign—and that was the first time I ever heard myself on the radio. I was expecting to break out in goose bumps listening to the recording, but it was oddly anticlimactic.

Here's the thing about doing a live broadcast from a radio station: Whether it's terrestrial, satellite or 'net, you have no way of knowing the size of your listenership. Nobody's there—just you, the DJ and the techs—so it always feels like the size of your audience is zero. Hearing yourself on the radio, oddly, is not much different.

Randy is by far the one with the most native musical talent in the family. As a kid, he could absent-mindedly hum a melody and whistle harmony to it simultaneously (try doing that sometime) while concentrating on whatever unrelated task his hands were doing. He still can, if I ask him to. He was a songwriter at the level of Leonard Cohen or Dylan...I assume he's still got that going on too, if he ever wants to pick up The Pen again. His chops as a finger-style acoustic guitarist were seriously good, and he's the closest thing I ever had to a guitar teacher. The foundation of right-hand finger-style technique he showed me way up at the headwaters has served me well.

After living hand-to-mouth on the singer / songwriter circuit for about a decade, he summarily turned his back on music, got into computer programming school, and within about two years of graduating he bought a house on a hill in Pebble Beach up by 17 Mile Drive. I'd like to say he never looked back, but I know it haunts the man.

* * *

That's how a teenaged prog/fusion head wound up playing singer-songwriter stuff on acoustic guitar, and it's part of a much larger and more important point about music.

To set this up, I should explain that I'm not just a prog / fusion (progressive jazz / rock fusion) head. Like most working cogs in the machinery of the LA music industry, I'm not just an any-one-thing. I grew up listening to, and loving, an extremely wide spectrum of music, ranging through every kind of Classical, Jazz, R&B, Motown and Funk, Folk, Rock, Blues, Acoustic stuff, Salsa, Bossa Nova, Samba, Ravi Shankar, 60s-era Bay Area jam bands like Jefferson Airplane and The Dead...and yes, Prog and Fusion of every kind, too. The time, culture, house and family I grew up in were a roiling, boiling cauldron of musical diversity. My musical tastes are the happy result of that, as is my diversity as a musician.

The Bay Area was a wonderful fountain of live concerts as well, featuring the top talent in every one of those areas. I drank deeply, right from the fountainhead. I saw some legendary shows.

Whether you play music or not, here is why this matters to you, and what I always tell people at clinics, workshops and master classes: If you have a favorite genre, that's cool. But if you think you don't like some genres simply because they're those genres, you need to lose that.

Music can only be good or bad based on whether it's good or bad. Genre is the least relevant factor in assessing the quality of music. I can say this with some authority, having made much of my living for lo, these many years gone by, as an "arranger". That's code-speak for dressing up pieces of music in whatever clothing is needed for a specific application, live or in the studio.

And I can say this: The stronger a piece's basic bones are—the melody, the root motion, the chords, the bass line and the lyrics (if applicable)—the more radical the changes can be thrown at it in arrangement and production. A well-written piece of music can be presented to the world as any genre. Bad writing simply can't. So look to the quality of the ideas, not what culture the music is from, or who else likes it, or what kind of sonic clothing it happens to be wearing in order to be presented to whatever market. Take down your fences and lose your mental horizons, and not just in music. Ultimately, it is only the quality of our ideas, and how well we implement them, that will determine how good they are...and how tall we as a species can stand up beneath the stars.

Chapter 4
Training Tries to Get Real

Birth, school, work, death.

As in many countries, that's the most likely life schematic for an American. To my credit, I perceived this clearly by about halfway through high school and made plans to dedicate a couple of years between high school and college to getting my ya-yas out. It was evident to everyone around me by then that I had some extra ya-yas to deal with, and it seemed like the best plan was for me to handle it while I was still young enough to bounce, and strong enough to put the time to good use. Nobody argued the idea, not even my Dad.

The first such year was spent in South Lake Tahoe, working as a cook and playing guitar with either the stereo or Richard W, whichever was most readily available at the moment. I also had an acoustic guitar / vocal duo with Gary Epps, a local ski bum and musician who was actually a really strong guitarist, and we pushed each other's chops. We scored a steady gig at an upscale local restaurant, which paid pretty well and fed us far swankier cuisine than untamed late-adolescent mongrels like us could ever have encountered otherwise.

I had good vinyl and a decent stereo. Playing to records can be a powerful practice tool, and I played along with some great musicians on some great albums: Genesis, Jeff Beck, Jean-Luc Ponty, Return to Forever and the like. Playing to the stereo is great ear training, chop-building, and great practice finding a part that fits in nicely.

The main reason for choosing Lake Tahoe had been to fully experience the lifestyle of a ski bum, which had been a bit of unfinished business between me and the universe since my pre-teens. Alas, having finally moved to Tahoe and gotten a pad and a job, I had a spectacular flying spill my third day on the slopes at Kirkwood, landing on my head and injuring my C-spine, and that was all she wrote for skiing that year. Fortunately I hadn't bought the season pass, and I still had my guitars. So outside of work hours I kept honing my chops, and started taking stock of California colleges with strong music departments.

Training is by far the most fundamental and influential aspect of any musical career, so what follows is an important read for any who are interested in walking the impossibly beautiful, vermin-infested path that is music.

* * *

The following Fall semester I made my first run at higher education as a music major at a community college in Palo Alto. Sadly, despite having a great electronic music program and a superb concert choir, the theory itself was a bunch of tripe—and this is where I impart a cautionary tale for anyone interested in learning how music goes together:

Harmony / theory-wise, the vast majority of musical curricula on planet Earth is taught according to conventions and traditions from the 1700s, via language so obfuscated and opaque, it's impossible for many of us to even use it as a vehicle of learning. Not only that, but the tenets involve rules that JS Bach is professed to have used when composing, but actually didn't. This is almost entirely a consequence of the "grad-becomes-professor academic feedback loop", and accreditation committees that require schools to limit modern curricula to that of three hundred years ago. Here's an example of how theory is taught in most places, compared to how simple it can be to teach and learn:

First, the old way. Let's say you're just getting acquainted with music theory. The teacher tells you that C is tonic, D is supertonic, E is mediant. What does that suggest F must be? You have no idea, of course. That's the language they use in many places.

Now on the other hand, let's say I tell you that C is one, D is two, E is three, so F must be what? You know it's gotta be four. There's a lot more to it than that of course, but that's the basic system. Music is, at its core, a fairy simple nuts-and-bolts system of alpha-numerics. That's how easy it can be to learn music theory. Even without the opaque lingo, the rules they say Bach lived by are malarkey too. I was in the concert choir concurrently with the theory class at that school, and just by chance we were rehearsing an incredibly beautiful Bach motet at the same time I was being asked to swallow the puddin'-headed premises in the theory textbook. I took it as long as I could, but a man's got his limits and the day finally arrived when mine were reached. I had to say something, or the rest of the class would be worse off for my silence.

I showed the theory teacher the score for the Bach motet, pointing out where Bach himself had violated every rule we were being taught, several times, literally right there in black and white. In fairness, it probably wasn't the best idea I ever had to show her that right in front of the entire class. One speaks truth to power at the right place and time. Live and learn.

But to put this into perspective, just for gits and shiggles let's say that science operated with the same agenda of maintaining a stringent status quo from the 1700s in higher education. Where the hell would we be? Music is nothing to me if not exploration. Every musician I admire—every single one, including Bach—has pushed the envelope of what was understood and what was thought of as possible. For music education to be mired in the distant past the way it is, and for that to be the accepted norm at such high levels of administration, is not just inexcusable: It's a crime against students everywhere and the art of music Herself.

So if you're eyeballing schools, or formal musical training of any kind, here's the tip: Choose carefully. One good thing you can do is to ask someone from the LA studio scene where to learn. Here, we commonly have movie dates in the big sound stages with over 120 expensive union cats on the clock, and every single minute costs a small fortune. There is ZERO time or tolerance for obfuscated language, or people who don't understand the functional nuts and bolts of what's going on. There's no better proving ground on planet Earth, no place that has more money on the line daily, or that requires practitioners of The Craft to have a clearer understanding of music, than right here in LA.

Prior to the moment I showed the theory instructor how full of shit the textbook was, I was the top student in class and she had me tutoring others. After that, she dropped my grade. I got a sour taste in my mouth and bailed on that particular college, which opened up my dance card for the next effort at getting my ya-yas out.

This time I opted for a year in San Diego—a town with a culture perfectly suited for such an enterprise.

Chapter 5
Sun, Shine on Me

The iconic melody of Europa soared out of my amp like it had a life of its own, over the heads of everyone on the beach, through the columns of barbecue smoke, past the seagulls, across the ocean to the horizon, winging on towards the sun. It was Fourth of July in San Diego, the beach so crowded you almost couldn't see any sand. From the back deck of the beach house where we were set up, I was looking out over a human carpet glistening with beer, suntan lotion, bikinis, beach bikes, umbrellas, children running wild and parents yelling themselves hoarse trying to keep them close. It was a gorgeous, sunny Independence Day celebration. The sea of bodies stretched farther than I could see up and down the beach, and the couple of thousand who were within earshot of our PA were cheering me on the extra long sustained notes. "No shit, there I was, playing Europa to a whole sea of people on the beach..." It was the largest crowd I had played for to date. I was twenty.

When we ended the song and a couple of thousand people cheered, it was an electrifying sound and feeling. It was my first time receiving that particular flavor of validation, like I had proved something to the universe and could say "See? I can be good at this, I told you" to every voice who had ever doubted it, including the one in my head.

I was playing with a great crew I had met and started hanging with not long after moving to town. They were a gregariously friendly, fun band of buddies who liked to mess around making noise on the weekends. They were popular socially, so I got introduced around a new cadre in good form. Even though we were playing weekend house parties and not clubs or theaters, we had a following of pretty girls. Life was good.

Pete and Dave Lynch were twins of Irish descent, coincidentally also from the East Bay. Their dad had some dough and had set them up with a pretty serious PA system, which is how all those people had heard us holding forth on the beach. Pete ran sound, Dave was a good strong drummer and still is. He's up by Portland these days. Henry was a sweet, unassuming guy who sang and played rhythm guitar, Billy was a big, large-boned guy who looked so much like a bass player, he would've had to be a linebacker in the NFL or a WWF wrestler if not for bass. We had a blast hanging out.

Pete, Dave, a plucky guy named Jeffro and I all wound up renting a large 4-bedroom house together in Claremont, where the parties we threw are now the stuff of legend. That also got me out of my cousin Russ's apartment, which he no doubt appreciated.

Jeffro was a fellow adrenaline junky, so we naturally hit it off. A wiry guy with long hair, he didn't play an instrument but his attitude was a hundred percent rock and roll at all times. He got me a job cooking seafood at the family restaurant where he was a sous chef in La Jolla, and we commuted on his Yamaha 500 dirt bike, weaving through traffic like banshees: a quick blur with a long trail of yellow hair.

Dave and Pete's PA—the mixing board, the amp rack, monitors and mains (speakers)—needed a place to live when not in use. I didn't have much in my bedroom besides a mattress on the floor, my guitars and my amp, so when they asked to store it in my room, I agreed...as long as I could use it as my stereo. What I was suggesting was about like using a firehose as an eyedropper. We all immediately agreed it was a great idea, if only out of scientific curiosity: Was it possible to deploy such large weaponry in such a small space without destroying the house and my ears?

It was comically massive in the tiny bedroom: Built for spaces that hold over a thousand people, each of the two mains had a big JBL horn on top of a dual 15" speaker cab, and with the board sitting on top of the amp rack in the middle, it was the exact width of one of the walls and stood out four or five feet into the room. It looked like a weaponized, blown 427 Cobra motor stuffed into a tricycle. It was so hilariously inappropriate for the space it occupied, it could only be described as perfect. I plugged my turntable into the board, plugged my guitar into my trusty Bassman 100 and 4X12, and I was off to the races. The UK album had come out by then, so I added that to my workout routine, along with the Romantic Warrior album by Return to Forever. There were plenty of sections I couldn't play, but that didn't stop me from throwing myself at it. It was fun practice.

My cousin Russ and I had done plenty of chop-building too, when we were rooming together in his apartment. He's a fellow guitarist—a really good one—and we've been close since babyhood. He's native to Oklahoma, but spent several years in Cali. We had some great times in that tiny pad of his in Pacific Beach, mostly jamming on acoustics, cutting heads (trying to outdo each other) and having fun. We saw some great shows at the San Diego Roxy: Metheney's first tour, John McLaughlin, Jan Hammer, Dixie Dreggs...it was a great time to be twenty, living in San Diego and learning The Craft.

On my 21st birthday we held a massive bash at the house. My Dad drove all the way down from the Bay to be there (EVERYBODY loved my Dad, everywhere he went). It was truly a bash for the books.

And with that milestone reached—contrary to all likelihood and expectations, and despite my best efforts—I had survived to manhood. As the party wound down, I sensed a shift in the wind: the end of a chapter. As much as I loved hanging out with my San Diego tribe, we all knew my presence there was temporary. It was getting to be That Time.

I left San Diego and my buddies not long after, to resume my pilgrimage for the right musical training. It hurt to leave; they were such a great crew and we were such tight brothers by that point. It always puts a smile on my face to rifle through my memories of those times, some of which aren't fit for print. Suffice to say that my 20th year was some serious fun, I didn't break my neck, and I did indeed get some ya-yas out.

Chapter 6
Training Gets Real

It was a time of impossible growth—tears, laughter, yelling, loving, people getting thrown up against the insurmountable and discovering they actually had the training to handle it, lives being shaped, skills being built, futures being cast from the Great Puppeteer's crucible full of molten potential as he chuckled. And through it all, ceaseless music. Some of the finest studio musicians in LA were in The Room every week, playing dubious charts scribbled by sleep-deprived students learning The Craft.

It all happened on Ventura Boulevard in Studio City, a block or so east of Coldwater, in a humble two-story office building whose only remarkable feature is how unremarkable it is. There's currently a dry cleaner occupying what once was, to me and many others whose lives were changed there, sacred ground. A Temple, The Holy Land, Mecca, Houston Control, take your pick. I can't pass that building without genuflecting a few times, mentally at least. It used to be DGMW, or Dick Grove Music Workshops...a comically humble name for such an incredibly powerful music school.

My first time going inside was for a face-to-face appointment with Dick Grove, the man who would ultimately give me the keys to the kingdom. I had hitchhiked down to LA from The Bay the day before with a backpack and my Guild D25 acoustic, the very image of a tousle-headed kid with a dream. Arriving late at night, I had rolled out my bag and crashed in the weeds hidden from view under a billboard, about a block east of the school. When morning came I ate my first of what would become many meals at Twain's coffee shop, cleaned myself up in the bathroom, walked across the street to DGMW, and went upstairs to meet The Man.

He was warm, but very direct and blunt—a manner of communication I quickly came to appreciate—and after a few placement test questions, he put me into the first-year program, called "PREP". A month or two prior, the same questions had placed me halfway through the second year at Berklee School of Music in Boston. It was obvious to me I was in the right place: Average class size was tiny, the teachers were top-feeders in the industry whose names are royalty: Sammy Nestico, Russ Tuttle (staff guitarist at Columbia), regular clinics from gods like Henry Mancini, Lalo Schiffrin, Tommy Tedesco, and on and on. But the real power under the hood was Dick Grove himself, the curricular genius who put it all together and made it all happen for us.

They taught in the plain nuts-and-bolts English of getting stuff done, which I discovered to be the way folks talk in the industry hereabouts. There's neither time nor patience for the academic pretentiousness of twenty-five cent Italian or Greek words—we had deadlines to meet and work to do, starting the first day of school. It was so right and so refreshing, I constantly wanted to holler "YES!!" at the top of my lungs. They never sold us out, we got no breaks that we wouldn't get in the real world, but the curriculum was so well-ordered that we always had the knowledge we needed to handle what was dumped on our plates.

We were being prepared in no uncertain terms for how tough the industry is: language and lessons were both blunt. Stories were scary, or hilarious and scary. And we got it. Things were made so abundantly clear that "your dog could understand it", as Dick used to say. The harmony curriculum was the central pillar of the school, and the revolutionary way he presented it was truly the cure for the educational cancer that pervades music programs everywhere. Though the school has sadly passed from this earth along with Dick Grove, there are a handful of pilgrims keeping that curriculum alive through their own teaching. I'm one.

Not far into that first year in LA, I got my first real recording session. It was for Cecil Shaw on Motown records, at Can Am studios in the Valley. It was my first time in a "real" recording studio, and I was impressed by the quality of the gear, the slick look and great acoustic sound of the physical space, the competence of the engineer, and the list of hit records he rattled off that had come out of there. Evidently one very successful late 70s-early 80s pop band—I'll call them The Vehicles—had a drummer who insisted on using his own crappy-sounding plexiglass drum set, and they literally spent three expensive weeks at Can Am trying to get a good sound out of them. Finally conceding defeat, he allowed them to be replaced by the studio's own Yamaha recording kit, and they had the sound in about a half an hour.

There were other Motown sessions. I remember one for a guy named John Hart that was nicely funky. Herschel Kennedy's record happened on Warner, with a band of heavy names that included his brother Will on drums. That was a fun session, and I laid a solo during the live tracking of the basic track with the band that got guys talking about me.

There were others as well. I have no idea how any of those projects fared in the world, which ones were actually released, or what. That's kind of how it works: you show up, you set up, you dial in the sound, you do the thing, then you pack up and you leave. Players don't usually contact producers or artists to ask how the project they played on is doing, and there's no entity tasked with updating the players: what we know about the status of something that we played on, once they've got our tracks in the can, is logistically irrelevant. And if it does go hit, we'll probably find out.

It's not a normal thing for someone as new to town as I was to break in to signed recording sessions like that. It was kind of a fluke that I had been introduced to two great players: A great bassist named David Coe and an incredibly talented keyboardist named Jimmy McKinney, who were good buddies. They partnered up on a lot of projects, bringing me in on whatever they could.

A couple of years later they invited me in on a great gig they had lined up doing the music for Bill Cosby's TV series, but I would've had to quit school. It was a tough decision, but I turned it down. Jimmy later went on to work with The Commodores, then was involved with the writing / arranging / production of a #1 hit for Billy Ocean. Maybe I should've taken them up on the TV gig; school would always be there, and opportunities like that are few and far between. We'll never know what that might've led to, but those early sessions weren't numerous, they mostly paid like crap, and besides: those early years in LA really were all about school. I was looking at the long game, laying the foundation for a lifetime. Regardless, the three of us naturally hit it off musically, and had great fun making noise.

* * *

After finishing the PREP program, I took a "filler year" driving truck all over the LA freeways to help my Dad refill the budgetary coffers, but first I took a one-week road gig playing the Stateline Casino in Wendover, Nevada...a wide spot on I-80 whose only two functions are as a gambling destination for Salt Lake City's weekend warriors, and a support mechanism for the land speed record hopefuls at the Wendover Salt Flats just outside of town.

Wendover at that time was a tiny, sleepy desert town displacing tumbleweeds, creosote bushes, and coyotes at the foot of the hills that rise up out of the salt flats. In front of the Stateline Casino there was a forty-foot-tall sheet metal cowboy waving with one arm, the mechanism squeaking and squealing through the night like foley from a bad horror flick. I have no idea if it's still there. Inside, the showroom was in an alcove opening off the main casino floor, and as strange as it sounds, the bands were forced to use the canopy Muzak speakers as the PA mains. If that wasn't surreal enough, nobody connected to any band was allowed to touch the mixing board, which was behind lock and key. The only personnel allowed to access it or run the sound were the security guards. Sometimes reality is stranger than fiction could ever be.

The schedule was Draconian: two bands split the night up, an A band and a B band, playing from 8:30 PM until 4:30 AM. The schedule was A-B-A-A-B-A-B-B. If you're a drummer or just know your rhythm, you'll recognize that as a paradiddle. So both bands had to hang out for most of that long night, and would have to set up and tear down repeatedly if they didn't work together and just share the gear using one of everything, which of course we did.

You haven't become a seasoned player until your performance has been shattered by a few unexpected things. At the Stateline, the showroom not being separated from the main floor by any wall, it was the jackpot bells and sirens.

(A pretty, soft keyboard intro leads into the first verse...a poised lead vocalist silently clears her throat and gently croons, "Desperado...")

BEEP!! BOOP!! BEEP!! BOOP!! SIRENS! BELLS! WHISTLES!

It helped break up the monotony and inserted comedy relief into proceedings, as Shakespeare might have done. Thus did lady luck bring culture to the driest reaches of the American southwest.

But the coolest thing was that the other band that week was The Sons of the Pioneers, the oldest and longest continually working band in literally all of showbiz. They've been on the Nevada circuit for so long, Roy Rogers left that band to become a film star. Assuming they're still at it, by now they've been playing joints of every type on the Nevada circuit, non-stop, for over a century. I can't even fathom the kinds of stories they must have. They keep passing it on to their sons, hence the name, I guess.

Naturally, we wound up jamming a lot throughout the nights, mixing and matching the lineups just to stay awake. An older clarinetist named Sonny was one of the founding members, and as I plugged in to play with him..."No shit, there I was playing with The Sons of the Pioneers"...I remember feeling like my guitar cable was a physical cord connecting me back through time to a very old legacy. They were fantastic musicians as well.

*　*　*

Budgetary coffers refilled, and having spent a year on a job that gave me a detailed working knowledge of the LA freeways that would serve me well, I at last found myself in the Composing Arranging Program (CAP) at Grove, learning how to write and arrange any style of music for any instrumentation. We had to have a chart on the stands every Thursday morning for a live band of anywhere from 17 to 40 pieces, depending on what style we were attacking that week.

Just to be clear, that means scoring an arrangement, then extracting and copying out every individual's part. Even just the "copying" is a big job, and being a copyist is an entire career path for some. I'm good at it because of who taught the copying class at Grove: Diz Mullins, who did the Tonight Show and the Oscars, among a lot else. What I learned from him about things like part layout and note spacing serves me well to this day, but I'm nowhere near patient enough to be someone else's copyist for a living.

As vital a skillset as copying is, it was a minor and peripheral thing compared to the learning of the actual musical processes: the harmony/theory, the composing, the arranging, how to manipulate the curve of development, the strengths, weaknesses and idiosyncrasies of the instrument families...and orchestration: the class I was in had Sammy Nestico himself at the chalk board right in front of us every week teaching orchestration! That was like being spoken directly to by a friggin' deity: "No shit, there I was, sitting in the front row while Sammy Nestico was at the chalkboard teaching us orchestration."

This was before any of this could be done with the aid of computers. It could take anywhere from 40 to 80 hours to do all that for one arrangement if you were fast, on top of the school's high-pressure, full-time curriculum. Songs were assigned on Fridays, playdowns were on the following Thursday, and every student got a different song to arrange every week. The motto was "You slept last year." That school did not fuck around.

The mission was to over-prepare us for a career in this incredibly exciting, competitive, horrible and beautiful industry. They succeeded. Having been trained at Grove carries a lot of weight in places where things matter.

The best illustration for how effectively the Grove school trained us is this: Years after I was done with school, a Naval Aviator was being interviewed for a documentary I was watching on TV about a massive military exercise outside Las Vegas he had participated in, called Red Flag. It encompassed every branch and discipline of the US military, as well as several allied countries. Thousands of missions were flown. A decorated fighter pilot, he said he had gone on to fly hundreds of actual missions, from the first Iraq war to Bosnia, and he never—NEVER, he emphasized—ran into a situation in actual combat that subjected him to anywhere near the pressures or challenges he had faced during Red Flag. When he said that, I literally jumped to my feet and hollered "YES!!" at the top of my lungs—

startling my dog, Boone—because that's exactly how I feel about the training I got at Grove.

* * *

Done with school, armed with just enough musical skills and know-how to blow everything up and lacking the experience not to, I launched myself happily at the world. For the first decade or so I went off in a direction that might be politely described as "sub-optimal", as you'll see, but those years were full of important experiences, lessons, wins, losses, struggles and extrications. What is life, if not a learning curve?

And I'm not suggesting that the shenaniganry of my youth continued, but during the year I spent driving truck, I discovered that a GMC dump truck with a 24-foot stake bed, having just been emptied and having such heavy duty suspension, handles a lot like a really big sports car. And that narrow, windy road hugging the steeps coming back down from the dump in the hills at the top of Figueroa had great S-curves and hairpins. That truck drifted like a dream, tires howling like a dying Orc in a Tolkien movie.

Chapter 7
The Wrong End of the Social Spectrum

LA, 1982: Smog-hued sunlight glints off tinfoil in the gutter, turning gum wrappers from silver to piss-yellow: a visual metaphor for most of the hit music of the time.

Against the din of jumbo jets, traffic and the glare of cement, no one seems to notice that rock and roll has all but died. Jazz radio playlists are discovering a cool new groove-oriented sound, destined unfortunately to become the emasculated, flacid bile we now call "smooth jazz", in a remarkable corporate-driven frenzy to lever perfectly good musicians into monetizing nursery rhymes. New Wave is the mainstream pop rage du jour, and will be for years.

Rock and Roll—real Rock and Roll, the actual dick-swingin' thing you'd hear in biker bars—has all but vanished from new releases, save for the efforts of a small handful of well-established artists like ZZ Top, Bryan Adams, Bob Seger, Van Halen, Spreengsteen and occasionally U2 and Billy Idol, who will provide most of the actual rock on the hit list for almost a decade to come. The vast majority of hit music sounds like it's missing a spine, wearing eyeliner and dressed up like a peacock. It's NOT the best decade to be a guitarist in a cover band.

Or in the studio, for that matter: On the sessions I played throughout the eighties and a good bit of the nineties, it was common for me to have to dummy down my chops and sound deliberately trashy, to match with the popular styles of the era. There were a couple of times I kept getting hounded to sound worse, until I just flipped the guitar over and played left handed. On a record. If that ever happens to you, I highly recommend you use a pseudonym. I can only hope those recordings never saw the light of day.

* * *

The edgy, scrabbling existence that one lives when starting out in the music business is as important to your training as formal studies. When you're broke, hungry and playing with any outfit that's hiring, you're not in the middle of your own little musical or social comfort zone. You're mixing and grooving hard with a lot of cultures you might otherwise remain alien to, which would be your loss. And you have to groove, play and perform like you grew up in those cultures, so you'll necessarily be learning things. Quickly.

In those emaciated and formative days following my parole from music school, there was immediate money to be made on the nightclub circuit. A nickel or less in my pocket and hope in my heart, young enough to welcome adventures that could have killed me, I first took a gig with a 9-piece Funk / R&B band playing around Watts and South Central LA., because after that much nose-to-score concentration and heightening of my technical command of music in school, I felt an urgent need to get back to my roots—"Back to Oakland"—and just play some good funk. It felt down-deep good, like liberation.

That paid almost nothing for 6 nights a week though, and one night I got the once-over by LAPD while loading out from a club because I "didn't match the 'hood". They weren't wrong, I guess...at 6'4" with long blonde hair and light European features, I stuck out from the crowd. But in all fairness, everyone in the band and the audiences really dug the way I grooved. Nonetheless, I needed to make a living and it was time to move on.

So I auditioned for and got a gig in one of the more successful 5-piece cover bands in SoCal, playing 5 and 6 nights a week on the "A Circuit", mostly around Orange County, booked solid six months ahead at all times. In the early and mid-eighties, SoCal had a thriving bar scene full of live music, and you could actually make a young person's decent living just playing nightclubs. It wouldn't buy you a house, but it would get you by.

I had to learn over 80 songs that first week to get myself current, which probably sounds insurmountable, but remember this was mostly 80s-era pop. The Top 40 of that decade was the most godawfully oversimplified flotsam ever to darken our airwaves. There were artists and songs that were exceptions of course, but they were just that: exceptions. Overall, in the 80s there was a lack of great melody writing, good chord changes, good grooves and important, cool guitar parts. And balls...who decided it was a good idea to chop the balls off of popular music in the 80s?

I also had to sing lead and backup, so my pipes started coming together, along with my repertoire of one-liners for my frontman mic patter: "This song is for the guy with toilet paper stuck on his shoe" always got a lot of people looking down. I eventually had dozens of 'em loaded into the breach, ready to go at all times. I was developing some entertainer / frontman chops, despite my druthers. It helped my employability.

Hating most of eighties pop (then as I do now), I told myself I'd just stomach the Top 40 scene for long enough to get on my feet, then pursue the more substantive things for which I'd been trained. Ah, the naivety of youth.

The work puzzle handled, it was time to score a new place to live. Given the choices of all of SoCal, my radiant display of poor judgement makes me wince to this day: I moved into what can only be described as Animal House. There was no college nearby; the fraternity was of a less academic sort. I'm including this story because those who are on a musical path are almost certain to spend some time at the wrong end of the social spectrum, surrounded by dubious characters and goings-on.

My experiences at that house left an indelible imprint on my past, present and future, the way the acrid, nostril-blistering stench from a cigarette butt in a beer-filled ashtray haunts a room for days. I actually remember the number of months I lived there—-it was 21.

Three-tenths of a mile downwind of the north runway at LAX, the house was in a neighborhood ideally situated to kill its occupants. If you looked on a map and understand local prevailing winds, you'd see that I breathed jet exhaust most of the time, probably shortening my life somewhat.

My housemates were an interesting spectrum of lawless misfits: An alcoholic 25-year-old paper boy loved only by his mom, who I almost killed at 4:30 one morning when I awoke to discover him drunkenly reeling and sliming spackle on my bedroom doorframe with his bare hand, where I had painstakingly spent hours with a straight edge and sanding block, doing such a fine job of fixing the damage done to the curved soffit by the cousin of another roommate who had kicked in my door a week before in a drunken attempt to witness, in closer detail, my progress with a female. All that poor slob could do was stand there at the foot of the bed with beer in hand, pitching left and right as if on a small boat in stormy seas, repeatedly drooling the word "abalooly." I remember wanting to kill him, too. It occurs to me in retrospect that for all the folly of living there, I must have been a very serious lad.

Then there was Chris R., actually a very reasonably-minded roady/mechanic from Philly, whose cousin committed the afore-mentioned trespass. Chris was really the only even-keeled one in the house...hell, probably within several square miles.

Then there was Krista, and finally there was the guy from whom we all sublet, rest his soul.

He had a masters in philosophy from USC, and so had naturally become a kick-boxer. He was a 5th-degree black belt, worked as a bouncer at a strip club not far away, liked to pretend he venerated Einstein, read self-help books on how to intimidate others and, despite trying so hard to be an asshole, actually had a heart of gold.

Women liked his Scottish good looks, he knew it and took all due advantage. He commonly brought home stripper friends the way kind-hearted restaurant employees bring home extra food for their roommates. His name was Paul B. and he went by Bucky, making him one of two friends I've had by that monicker who are now dead from too much heedless ignoring of the body's limits and needs (I'm not actually sure the other Bucky is dead, but based on his escapades while the two of us were roomies in Tahoe when I was 18, it's probably a safe bet).

The house next door was a cocaine supermarket, run by Bucky's best friend, a quasi-genius hailing from a noteworthy technical university who had discovered that he could make more money and have more fun hotwiring cable boxes and selling coke than teaching at Cal Tech or working at JPL. He proudly showed people how his education enabled him to freebase cocaine without using any nasty chemicals. His maid was an attractive, wayward 20-year old girl from down the street who he paid with coke, and who had an agreeable penchant for thigh-high fishnets, garter belts and pumps...and sneaking into my room in the middle of the night.

LAPD eventually carted the next door neighbor off, along with his sidekick roommate, who I had just seen the day before: He was standing atop the bar at a popular South Bay imbibery, pants down, farting to his utmost through his boxers and clearing the joint of clientele, all the while an expression of moronic bliss on his face.

Contrary to probability I've won my way to respectability over the years, so in an effort to maintain that image I should clarify that I'm not actually saying I was personally involved with those dubious behaviors; I'm simply illustrating the nature of where I lived, and saying that I'm not sure why I survived those 21 months. But I'm glad I did.

I mentioned Krista. Krista was an explosion captured in human form, a punked-out rush of impetus against the cosmos whose M.O. in life was to maintain a state of war with the world in general, her housemates in specific, and to be at odds with every aspect of existence. The girl made Wendy O'Williams seem like Marcia Brady. She had the rest of us—thugs, drunks, black belt bouncers and drug addicts, even musicians—cowering against the walls. We were at a loss as to how to deal with the tempest she presented.

One night, when living on the other side of the wall from her room (and her stereo) had driven me to homicidal extremes, I pounded on her door hell-bent on making an impression, hoping not to go to jail. I had forgotten that I was me though, and I found myself talking to her and her volcanic mind. Of course, I was discovering an individual. She turned out to be from Castro Valley, one of my home towns! Actually, now that I think about it, that explains a good deal.

Impaled on a knife stuck in her bedroom wall was a piece of scratch paper with this scrawled on it: "Only those who attempt the absurd ever achieve the impossible". The moment had calmed, as they tend to do when folks talk, and I asked her who the quote was from.

"Me", she said. I was rocked back on my heels.

The lesson? Don't underestimate people, it's been consistently proven to be a mistake. And to work in the music industry, you need to not just accept and embrace the myriad faults, blemishes and warts of humanity...you need to see the beauty in all of it.

And I didn't know it yet at the time—I lacked the wisdom you can only get from experience—but everybody is fighting their battles. Every one of us. Whatever it was that led Krista to be such a perpetual detonation, I'm sure it was horrifying. She probably deserves much respect for getting through it. I like to think that she's not only alive, but has doctored in child development and has a thriving psychiatric practice, a book on the way and will be interviewed on Kimmel soon. That's the way the pendulum tends to swing.

If I had to sum up those times in three words, I'd say "class five rapids". I'm glad to be writing this from smoother waters.

Chapter 8
The Lost Decade

Anything you do, if you do it for a living, can feel like work after awhile. Sam Clemens said it best: "Work consists of that which a body is obliged to do, whereas play consists of that which a body is not obliged to do."

And some things take less time to become work than others. By the end of the third week in that Top 40 band, I was getting tired of playing crappy eighties pop to drunk people in bars. But it was the job I had, the devil I knew. And at least the players were good. Just before landing that gig, I had gone for two or three weeks on a few well-rationed boxes of potato buds. I had a new respect for poverty.

Even though anything could happen to that band and gig at any time, it felt far more secure than other recent situations. This was when you could work five and six nights a week with the same band, basically meeting all your expenses, and it was nice to be a part of that. But it came with a heavy commitment.

If you're a member of a well-rehearsed, full-time working band that has slick vocal arrangements you're a part of, and bookings based on your being a member, everybody in that band is depending on you. That band's level of performance is how every member provides for their families. You don't get vacations, there are no "sick days", you can't sub out (get a temp replacement), in many cases not even for weddings or funerals.

To justify your leaving the team in the lurch—threatening not only a booking, but probably pissing off that agent, potentially costing hard-earned dates on the calendar—you damned well better be in the hospital, jail or the morgue.

As you'll see, I've been on stage playing with broken fingers, crushed ribs, a badly shattered heel and ankle, concussions, food poisoning, high fevers, diarrhea and laryngitis. Every musician I know has stories. It's not just some quaint little credo that "the show must go on". Your bandmates and their families gotta eat.

Personnel changes obviously have to happen though, whether someone is in the E.R. getting their head sewn back on, or a member is being permanently replaced. And that's a problem, because many club owners, hotels, booking agents and talent buyers require the lineup of musicians in the band to be the same as in the photo. To point out the obvious, this practice is idiotic. The entire entertainment industry operates according to aesthetics, and everybody uses badly out-of-date photos for promo. Actors, recording artists, public speakers, news anchors, attorneys, plumbers, authors—it's just the way things are done. Some band photos are well over a decade old, from back when the key members looked the part.

The bottom line, though, is that it really doesn't matter. I've consistently found that if the band sounds good and everyone's happy, then changes or not, the lineup doesn't matter. And if the band sounds bad and people are unhappy—changes or not—the lineup still doesn't matter. Basically, you will always sink or swim according to the actual quality of your performance. That's the only thing that matters.

There are indeed bands that'll put a hole in their calendar to accommodate a player's personal needs, if given enough notice and it's something undeniably legit, like a needed surgery, or your own wedding, or your kid's...but even that's not as common as you might think.

There's a chasm between the reality of a musician and someone from the "normal" sector, and it can be hard when two people in a relationship are from those two very different worlds, such as my wife and me. For me, the very concept of paid vacation days—not only being allowed to not go into work, but literally being PAID to not go into work—is completely alien. Ditto being paid to move, or a hiring bonus, or paid sick days, etc. Don't get me wrong, I think it's wonderful and actually makes sense, but for a musician to entertain such notions is, shall we say, unrealistic. I can just imagine it:

[The phone rings, I pick up]
"Hello?"
"Hi, is Byron there?"
"Speaking."
"Hi Byron, my name's Anthony DiFicustwit, I got your number from Biff Badaboom. I need a guitarist for a gig in Vegas on the 19th. Pays five hundred plus air and hotel. Are you available?"
"Maybe, what's your incentive package like? Do I get a signing bonus and paid vacation days? How about health coverage and a retirement portfol..."
[[click]]

Like I said, it's a whole different world out there. I know it exists, it's just not a part of a musician's reality.

* * *

Landing that solidly-booked gig and finally making a full-time living as a musician gave me a new appreciation for being versatile, but as a player I was more versatile than my guitar. That Ibanez Artist I mentioned had Gibson-style wiring. It was a great axe, but couldn't get anywhere near the number or nature of sounds that a Strat can, and which I needed for the gig. So I became a Strat man. Understanding the incredible machine that is a Strat is worthy of a few paragraphs:

The beauty of the Stratocaster platform, and the reason it's the most common design among solidbody electric guitars, is that it's a screw-together, modular system that can be made to be just about anything. Telecasters, too. Telecasters are inherently more stable and almost impossible to knock out of tune, because the neck routing has more body around it than a Strat, which has a deeper cutaway. So any time I'm headed out the door to play at a place that's a bit seedy and might erupt into a brawl, I reflexively grab the Tele. It's the experienced guitarist's weapon of choice in a bar fight. I wish I was kidding.

Either platform can have a whammy bar tremolo or "hard tail" bridge, a locking nut or an open one, any kind of wiring and sound you want (including Gibson style), any neck dimensions, any body wood, chambered or solid body, and any tuning machines.

If you're not into guitar and don't know what those words mean, don't sweat it, you get the idea: A Strat can be made into more things than any other platform. You can basically just choose your favorite of everything and either have a professional put it together, or just do it yourself. These are commonly known as "FrankenStrats" and "FrankenTeles".

I found that I'm a good enough guitar tech that doing my own work not only saves dough, it's also the best way to ensure that I get things set up exactly the way I really want as a player. More importantly, out on the road in the middle of nowhere, I would've been dead in the water on a thousand different occasions if I couldn't maintain my axes myself with the tools I carry. On bigger gigs when offered my own guitar tech, so far I've always said "no thanks". I'm peculiar that way. And when I actually am out of my depth as a guitar tech—which is often enough—I get more qualified hands and brains on it. I've always gone to John Carruthers, basically the finest repairman / luthier / builder / designer in the country.

I still have the original Strat that I bought back in '82...sort of. It started life as an Ibanez Strat knockoff called a "Roadstar", whose body, neck and fretboard were all a hideously ugly red. As of now, it's had six different necks (no idea how many fret jobs), three different bodies, several faceplates, six bridges and I have no idea how many pickups, nuts or sets of tuners and strap locks. It's my main workhorse, and there's not even one screw of the original guitar left. The last remaining part from the original guitar—one of the small wood screws holding on the faceplate, ceremoniously kept in its placement—got lost and went away a few years ago.

Its present manifestation is a freakishly perfect, magic guitar, unsurpassed for matching my personal tastes and needs, and for getting almost any sound imaginable. Along with the Guild D25 I got at age 12, it's the other guitar that I'll run through an inferno to save. It's been to and through several dozen countries with me, in both hemispheres, on every type of gig and session, has flown more miles than an Albatross, and is the single most recorded guitar I own. I've spent much time and money trying to get a ground-up custom build from John Carruthers to be as good as my FrankenStrat. Alas it's close—a great backup axe—but no cigar.

* * *

Apart from making me a Strat man where I really live, that first full-time gig also gave me important new understanding of what doesn't go into music if you want most people to relate to it. "Outside" means nothing without "inside". Learning that was a good thing for me, a needed thing, because since the age of thirteen I've loved the more outside stuff...progressive fusion, progressive rock, progressive jazz, and I guess what has to be called "progressive classical", in other words I'd always prefer Stravinsky over Beethoven or Bach. And lo and behold I've discovered, partly through my training and partly through experience and musical maturity, that it is exactly the more powerful, fundamental currents of simple music that provide the power under the hood driving things in the more sophisticated, progressive stuff. Good enough writers all know this.

I also gained other skills that might have eluded me without that particular gig, such as how to read a room, make a good setlist, get a good sound out of a space, and—how to put this—the unexpected ability to make it across a packed nightclub to the bathroom in a tight-fitting pair of white Levis, having just soiled my backside while singing a high note because I had recently eaten the wrong thing. Nobody ever knew. Be squeamish if you like, but you've gotta admit: that's proud.

I also discovered my love for the Eastern Sierras while in that band, when we got booked into the Whiskey Creek in Mammoth Lakes. I didn't know it at the time, but the area would become an important part of my existence. I still remember the moment, driving my '68 Mustang down what locals call "the grade", southbound on 395 just above Bishop, when I looked out at that heart-breakingly gorgeous view of Round Valley, Mt Tom and the Sabrina skyline, thinking to myself "Maybe someday".

* * *

Nightclubs can of course be dangerous. One Saturday we were playing a "KIIS FM Weekend Warmup" at a mega-club in City of Industry called Cattlemen's Wharf. It was an overly-publicized major event, featuring five-cent drafts and twenty-five cent wine (Tip: If you're going to play nightclubs, it's better to play places with expensive alcohol. Remember that).

Rick D., a famous DJ whose smile leered at SoCal motorists from billboards everywhere, was emceeing the melee and broadcasting his show from the stage during our breaks. The place was so far beyond capacity that nobody in the crowd could even move, let alone allow a musician to get to the bathroom to pee and back to the stage in a 20-minute break. That sometimes happened in the more popular rooms on the holiday weekends, but the density of this crowd was next-level.

The shindig came to an early end when a recently-bounced drunk returned to the front door and opened fire into the crowd, hitting the bouncer—a really cool guy who had become a buddy of mine—five times, and wounding several patrons. We couldn't hear anything from the stage and didn't know exactly what was going on, but we knew something was amiss from the jerky motions and panicked currents in the crowd. We stopped mid-song, helped clear the place with calm instructions on mic, then tore down and loaded out through a maze of police, paramedics and news crews. The bouncer lived, but that was it for the Cattlemen's Wharf. It never opened its doors again.

Chapter 9
It's Just a Scratch

If you want to remain employed, playing through injuries can be an important ability…all the more so if you're a tall person in a world built for smaller people, and have a level of coordination not quite in keeping with your size.

It was about this time that I got an afternoon recording session on Pausa Records at a studio on Sunset Bl, thanks to my keyboard buddy Jimmy McKinney. The artist was Jerry Bell, one of the vocalists from The Gap Band. I brought my Blonde 1961 Gibson L5 Archtop—an incredible guitar I bought from Norm's Rare Guitars for nineteen hundred and ten dollars during that "break year" driving truck, and probably the finest instrument I've ever played. Wherever it is, if it's still in good shape, it's worth around forty grand as of this writing, maybe fifty. That I ever sold it is among my biggest regrets, and not because of its monetary value.

After the session, I had barely enough time to hurry home, drop off the L5, grab my two solidbodies and lay rubber for the Top 40 gig in Orange County. Please believe me when I say that being late for a downbeat is never an option.

Arriving home with the L5, I had parked and was running while carrying its much wider guitar case in my right hand, charging into the narrow stairwell's opening in the cinderblocks leading up from the carport. At the moment I passed through the stairwell entry, I was taking a massive running launch to clear the first six steps, and heard a bright "snap", like a stick breaking in two. In my rush I topped out the stairs, ran another twenty five feet, did a 180 onto the next flight of stairs and ran halfway up those before it occurred to me:

"Snap"?

I stopped and looked down to see my left pinky hanging at a weird angle and missing a good deal of skin along the top. It hurt like hell to try to move it. My first reaction was emotional pain, not physical. I had been developing the strength, agility and independence of that specific digit since Allan Holdsworth had moved to town and become a buddy of mine. I had noticed that his left pinky behaved as strongly and dominantly on the fretboard as his other three fingers, and had made it a special project to develop the hell out of mine. My special baby had been coming along really nicely, and here I had left the poor thing behind at the corner of a cinderblock stairwell in Playa Del Rey. I was brokenhearted.

What followed was a wakeup call. I made the gig by downbeat, the pinky wrapped in a bloody paper towel. I limped painfully through the first set like that, then used the first break to tape the third and fourth digits together at what I hoped was about the correct angle, and bandage things a bit more realistically. And then I discovered something surprising: Pain notwithstanding, I could play that gig pretty easily with two fingers. "No shit, there I was, playing a full five sets to a packed nightclub with a full-on busted finger." Even the Van Halen solo in "Beat It" wasn't too far outside of what I could manage, if I borrowed the third digit for just a few notes, and that was the "shreddiest" part of the entire night. It hurt like hell and wasn't the most articulate delivery, but I could do it. Remember, this was eighties pop.

The next day, X-rays showed that I had badly broken the socket of the first knuckle (where the finger meets the hand) at the connection to its transverse metacarpal, one of the series of ligaments holding all your first knuckles together and in alignment. I could rotate the finger to an unlikely degree. The doc put it in a cast that went almost up to the elbow but didn't even go to the first knuckle, and failed miserably to immobilize the finger.

I went home, promptly chopped it off with my buck knife (the cast, not the finger), returned to the ER and sweet-talked a nurse out of some supplies that she snuck to me through the side door. Thus equipped, I fashioned one of those bendable, foam rubber-lined aluminum sheet metal splints to go up the back of the finger, continuing up the back of the hand and well past the wrist, form-fitted and taped in place at every joint. Now it was immobilized, and I could still play. Sort of.

I had been dimly aware that I wasn't realizing my potential on that gig, but this threw it in my face in no uncertain terms, and led to my having the first of many sit-down talks with myself about the path I was on. The break healed very gradually, and after about six months I could play without any tape on my hand. It took a year to get back to one hundred percent. Playing guitar full time for your dinner, it turns out, slows down that process somewhat.

The lesson here is this: whether you're a musician or not, don't underestimate what you're actually capable of. You'll never find the true limits of your abilities if you stay in your comfort zone and don't challenge yourself. You'll be surprised at what you can actually handle when the shit hits the fan and the chips are down, and probably not before. That said, ideally you'll stop short of breaking bones in order to find your limits.

***

You'll discover, on the musical road, that you can perform through any number of maladies. We all do. At one point I had been collecting foot injuries for some time: A chunk of driftwood about an eighth of an inch in diameter had been driven into the first socket of my right big toe from the side while jogging in wet sand and would take years to be fully absorbed by my body. A few months later I added an unrelated, small spiral fracture of the same toe's metatarsal (the bone going over the arch of the foot to the big toe), then finally a bad sprain to the left ankle. All of this cumulatively left me unable to ambulate, except for sideways to the right, with steps of about 6 inches. My long shuffle from the car into gigs had to look funny, especially if I had to park some distance away. It even made me chuckle, and I was in pain. I allowed an extra 15 minutes for this. It all eventually healed up to about 80 percent, but getting back to 100 percent took some special circumstances in Boise, some time later.

Meanwhile, after twenty eight months I left that band. Out of curiosity, I just now ran some numbers and the results are interesting: Using a conservative estimate of 5 nights a week, 5 sets per night (we played a lot of 6-nighters), we played 100 sets per month. I didn't know it at the time, but I sure felt it: I had just logged my first twenty-eight hundred sets of playing covers, probably more. This illustrates the experience and hours one amasses playing in nightclubs full-time. And I was just getting started.

Steadiness of income aside, I was keenly aware that Top 40 gigs are a professional dead end, and wanted nothing more than to escape that life so that I could get on to the bigger, more serious things.

Because of my background and my training, I was one of a very small percentage of the musical workforce able to compose and arrange anything needed, for any instrumentation up to and including full orchestra, with nothing but a score page in my lap and a good mechanical pencil. Yet here I was, spending some of the best years of my career playing cover tunes, many of which were downright nauseating, to drunk people in bars.

But developing inroads to better gigs and session work would require time, whereas having left that band, I was faced with immediate financial pressure. I had to take the first gig I could find, and that meant capitalizing on my being established among the denizens of the nightclub circuit, and a familiar face to the good agents.

This became a repeating logistic that kept me trapped in the SoCal cover band scene for years longer than I ever should have allowed.

Chapter 10
Allan

This book wouldn't be complete without addressing the single greatest guitarist of all time, and the biggest musical influence I'll ever have.

In the early 1980s, the highly-stratified hierarchy of Southern California guitarists was abruptly and violently flattened by a very humble, painstakingly polite, extremely sweet and soft-spoken British genius named Allan Holdsworth. Despite his genuine belief that he sucked, he was on a level so far above the entire community of guitarists that our unanimous reaction was one of stunned horror. Upon hearing him play, some of us reacted with the kind of manic, unhinged laughter you might hear from someone who had just been shown their own entrails but was intent on denying it. Others wore the calm, pallid face of those who accept doom, like a planet-killing meteor had been discovered and a swift death was imminent. All of us, from the top echelon of famous studio gods down to lowly music students, now occupied one and the same strata. It was surreal, it was wonderful, it was scary, and inspiring, and awful; it was blindingly brilliant, like staring at the sun. And we might as well laugh about it.

At no point was the effect he had on the scene in SoCal more powerfully driven home than after his first (now famous) show at the Roxy on Sunset. Pretty much every noteworthy guitarist in LA was there—200 or so of the best cats in the world, several of whom had been on the covers of the guitar mags more than once—waiting to see what all the hubbub was about. I was there with Pebber Brown, a blindingly good guitarist I met during my first year at Grove, one of my best buddies and probably the best woodshedding partner I've ever had.

Allan began to play, and immediately all the air was sucked out of the room. Nothing he did was in the slightest bit conventional...much of it wasn't even within the scope of what was considered possible. Our disbelief couldn't have been greater had he levitated off the stage, sprouted two extra heads and vomited fireballs. And he was just getting started. He went on from there, with the effect of a physics professor from the 24th century transported back in time to teach a class in the dark ages. By the end of the show, our collective game had been so effectively tossed out the window, we could see it glinting here and there as it tumbled down into the abyss in free fall, there to remain pathetically irrelevant for all time.

We were all brothers now, where just 90 minutes prior we had peopled all the various stations and elevations of musical society, from serf to royalty. We were unbathed beggars in His temple yard now, and we all knew it. The world of guitar would never be the same.

At the end of the show, he left the stage, the lights came on, and no one moved. No one said a word. I've never seen anything like it. We all just sat there, pasted into our seats, blinking around at each other in total, stunned silence, for what probably was a solid minute. Imagine it! All the lauded hierarchy of the SoCal guitar talent pool, having been steamrolled into one level plane and speechlessly regarding each other with thousand-yard stares, trying to process what the hell just happened, as the stagehands coiled cables.

The sense of stratification was suddenly gone. It remains one of the most powerful moments I've witnessed in this life, in all my travels and experience. At about the 30-second mark, a certain singer named Roth stood up to leave the room with his two supermodel escorts, as if to illustrate that too many elements of Hollywood are too predictable. The rest of us remained.

When movement and conversation began to return, I went upstairs to the greenroom to congratulate him on ending so many brilliant careers. He seemed a bit distraught and apologized for sucking so badly: "I just couldn't play a thing." This was to become a pattern.

I had first met and befriended Allan just a few hours prior to that. How that happened is this: He had been my biggest and most consuming guitaristic influence for years, though like almost every American guitarist, I had never seen him live. I knew that he was finally in town and would be playing the Roxy—had in fact been watching the date approach on the calendar for weeks—I lived about half an hour away, and knew when soundcheck was. So when he pulled into the parking lot and went to get out of his station wagon, I was there in the poor guy's face, introducing myself with hand outstretched before he could even stand up. He was too polite to tell me to get lost, so I attached myself to his ankle like a barnacle, and we became friends.

I wound up hanging out with Allan a good bit back in the IOU days and while he recorded his next album. I went over to his pad several times; he even came to a couple of my Orange County top40 gigs. There he'd sit, nursing his ever-present Coors, watching me suffer through that godawful 80s set list, so professionally embarrassed I could feel myself blushing onstage. But at no time did he ever give me the slightest hint of elitism or one-upmanship; not even a friendly chiding about the nature of the gig. He really didn't seem to understand who and what he was, or what he was accomplishing. And even if he did, I think he'd rather have died than be the slightest bit rude to any living being.

The memories I have from those times in Allan's life are many, and paint a picture of a soul too good and too artistically pure for the turd-infested waters of Hollywood; an inhumanly talented god, cast as an underdog into the ring with Warner, but who nonetheless somehow won his way to freedom, and was able to resume his pursuit of The Impossible. It's cool how he accomplished that, and it sheds a light on some of the more unsavory workings of the once-mighty record industry.

Allan had toured the U.S. with his "I.O.U." album, which he had recorded in England before crossing the pond. Upon arriving in L.A. at the culmination of the tour with that show at the Roxy where we met, he signed a multi-album deal with Warner Records. This connection was made thanks to Eddie Van Halen, who of course was a massive fan of Allan's. He was paired with a great producer, who was very hands-off regarding the day-to-day doings. But like anybody in Warner's halls of power, the producer's job was to produce money as much as it was to produce music.

Allan was booked into one of Warner's house studios on Melrose in Hollywood, called Music Grinder. It was a large place with a warehouse-sized main room for recording orchestral dates. I remember seeing the trio's tiny set up in the far corner of the cavernous space, a long way from the control booth. They used room mics for reverbs a good deal on that album. It's called "Road Games".

In a world where everyone records the basic tracks first, then overdubs the solos so that they can enjoy the luxury of multiple takes and stick with the winner, Allan chose to do his solos while recording the basics with the rhythm section. He would then overdub the basic chordal accompaniment. His reasoning was that the other rhythm section players could react to his ideas as he soloed, which of course they can't do if the solos are added later. He was right about that of course, but most of us mortals aren't good enough to work that way. He did it that way because he could—he was just that damned good. Being "of a certain age", I've had to work that way on countless occasions and actually had some good showings, because I had to. But given a choice, I prefer to overdub featured and chop-intensive things like guitar solos, so that I have the option of more than one take. Allan, on the other hand, preferred to play with live bullets at all times.

With Jeff Berlin on bass and Chad Wackerman on drums, his band was a trio of the most brilliant cats on the planet. But one of the best things about Allan's band was the incredibly fine pipes of his lead vocalist, Paul Williams. I don't mean the pop singer / actor. The Paul Williams who sang with Allan had pipes reminiscent of David Clayton-Thomas, of Blood Sweat and Tears. The man had a rich and robust vocal instrument that I'll never tire of hearing.

Having completed the album—an incredibly fine study of writing, arranging, performing and mixing—he ran the mixes by his producer, whereupon the other shoe dropped. The producer had a problem with Paul, probably in that he didn't look the part; there's no way that the issue was the sound of Paul's voice. Maybe in the producer's mind, he wanted something visually spectacular to help drive sales, like David Lee Roth did for Van Halen. I'll be the first to agree that Paul looked more like an Oxford math professor than a rock star, and as Zappa said, "People know good music when they see it." But goddammit, this is where Hollywood and I have always parted ways of thinking: I see the aesthetic visual as the single least relevant aspect of the presentation of music.

If you actually like music—if you even THINK you do—then fercryin'outloud, close your eyes when you listen and use your fucking ears. If you need spectacle, you're not a fan of music. You're a fan of spectacle. Go watch a fireworks show somewhere. And if you're given the honor of attaching your name to the work of a once-in-a-species talent like Allan, you don't make it all about the bottom line, and you sure as hell don't start trying to change things. Warner had a great stable of money-makers at the time, and the creative legitimacy of having Allan among their artists couldn't possibly be a bad thing. Sometimes the greedy pathos of Hollywood is stunning.

Whatever the reason, the producer didn't like Paul, and brought Allan's attention to a clause in the contract that enabled Warner to make personnel changes if desired. He told Allan to find a different singer to put on the album, or he'd either find one himself, or the album would be shelved and Allan would never be allowed to use the material for anything else. Believe it or not, this draconian bullshit was pretty standard with recording contracts.

It was also pretty standard practice for the record company to require you to turn over not only all mixes, but the multi-track masters as well. "Multi-track masters", at the time, were the big 2-inch, 24-track tape reels full of your individual tracks, which is what you record onto to begin with, before you "mix" all of that down into two tracks—a left track and a right track—for stereo consumption. The reason record companies liked to have those multi-track master reels was so that they could make further changes and remixes, replacing tracks and even personnel, ostensibly for different markets, but there are myriad stories of artists being taken advantage of, just because a record company had the logistical ability to do it.

I got a call from Allan one afternoon. He sounded really down.

"The producer's wanting to get rid of Paul's tracks and put someone else on."

"WHAT?!? Are you kidding?"

"It's a fucking nightmare. He told me if I don't put a different singer on it, he'll either choose one himself or shelve the album."

"Ohfercrissake..."

"Do you know of anyone who could do it?" He was obviously in over his head and desperate.

"Crap, lemme think on it...nobody's coming to mind right away."

For the life of me, I couldn't think of anyone with great enough pipes, who could sing such rhythmically and harmonically sophisticated stuff. I kept wracking my brain and coming up with nothing.

About a week later I got another call, late at night.

"I'm at my wit's end," he said, "this is a fucking nightmare. I can't sleep. I can't find anyone good, and now the producer's threatening to put Geddy Lee on it."

"Geddy Lee? No man, that can't happen. I mean, he's a great musician and singer, but that's not a good fit for your stuff...I can't hear that working."

He went on, "I've been going into nightclubs and asking singers in cover bands if they'd like to be on it, I've been asking strangers on the street...I'm just really desperate...and I'm having this other nightmare with immigration, trying to bring Claire over from England...I can't even sleep at night for worrying about all this. And I'm contracted to do more albums for Warner after this! I can't even think about it."

It was clear that he was beside himself and in some darkness. I felt bad that I couldn't think of anyone who could fill Paul's shoes in good form, but I couldn't. Then as now, I felt like I was failing him.

After another week or so went by, I called him to check in. He sounded cheerful and downright upbeat.

"So, I went up to San Fransisco to do another record with Tony Williams, and the bass player was Jack Bruce. I slapped my forehead! Of course, Jack! It's brilliant! Jack sings his ass off, he'll do a great job, so I'm happy...and he's famous, so the producer's happy."

"So it's all set?"

"Yes, it's all set."

"Well okay, then. That should be great, I can't wait to hear it!"

About a month later, I had decided that it would be an especially fun form of musical suicide to have Allan do some trade-offs with me on the solo section of one of my tunes, that I was about to do in the studio. I had been slowly saving money to buy one day in a 24-track room. The day before that session, Allan had me swing by Music Grinder to drop off a cassette demo so he could get an idea of what the tune was like. I entered into a scene I'll never forget.

Allan was sitting at the massive console, focused but relaxed, in stark contrast to the comportment of the engineer occupying the chair behind him.

"You're just in time. I'm De-Warnerizing the masters."

"De-Warnerizing?"

"I'm cleaning everything off the multitrack that I didn't use in the mixes."

It was then that I grasped what was going on. I suddenly understood why the engineer looked pallid, was visibly sweating and even shaking a bit, like he couldn't decide whether to puke, have a heart attack or bolt for the hills.

With tape recording, "cleaning" is done by recording silence over what's there, creating blank tape. This was before digital recording, so there was no "undo". What Allan was doing was cleaning the information off of every segment of every one of the 24 tracks that hadn't actually been used in the mixes, and he was doing this with one single run-through of each song, dropping tracks in and out of "record" at very specific moments, as the 2-inch 24-track tape went by the heads in real time. He was playing the console like a keyboard, creating a multitrack master whose actual information was a series of incipient strips, like a player piano scroll. He knew the track and the time in and out for every take that had been used for the mix, and he got rid of everything else—in one swipe, in real time, on a master that had cost more than a healthy down payment on a house. It was one of the ballsiest things I've ever seen anyone do.

I fully understood, though. On a human level, he was doing what was right and just. After what he had gone through in the making of that album, and with all the arbitrary detritus on those tracks from so many struggles over the steering wheel, it made a lot of sense.

The engineer looked at me wide-eyed from behind Allan's back, and silently shook his head in disbelief, the way one onlooker might look at another as they watch John Bachar or Alex Honnold free solo a tough climb hundreds of feet off deck.

The first song I heard go past the heads in this process was Tokyo Dreams. And that's how it happened that the first time I ever heard that incredible song was on a playback rig that cost as much as a house in those days. It was the finest and most incredible "first listen" I've ever experienced, before or since.

When all was said and done, the producer was very decent about things, recognizing that he and Allan might not be the greatest of working partners, and letting Allan out of the contract, as well as letting him keep the remainder of the budget, and releasing the album. I suspect that a certain guy named Eddie might have stepped in, but that's just conjecture.

The master stroke was this: The vocalist on the whole album was Jack Bruce... except for the title track "Road Games", sung by Paul Williams. And yes, Jack Bruce did indeed do a great job, as you'd expect.

Several months later, I heard Paul's wonderful pipes on "Road Games" through an open window of my apartment in Playa del Rey. It was being played on someone's stereo outside! This was freaky, because Allan was just as unknown outside of guitaristic circles as he was famous inside of it. That's still the case.

I stuck my head out the window to see a guy waxing his pickup truck below in the carport. It was playing on the car stereo with the doors open.

"Hey!" I called down, "You're a fan of Allan's I see!"
He looked up. "What?"
"You dig Allan Holdsworth!"
"Who?"
"That's Allan Holdsworth playing on your stereo!"
"Oh. Idunno who it is, it's just the radio." and he went back to his waxing.

Allan on the radio. Who'd'a thunk. I called him and told him.

The day I was in the studio with my guys doing my own stuff, Allan couldn't make it because he couldn't get his gear out of Music Grinder. So at the last minute I handed the chart to my good brother Claude Romig, a blistering alto sax player and my best buddy from the Grove days. He played Allan's part through the body of the song and we traded off on the solo section. It had weird time signature changes and weird chords, the chart was concert (meaning it was in the wrong key for Alto), and: Claude had neither seen nor heard it before. He was doing this cold, on-sight. And he absolutely slayed it.

Allan went on to record many more albums from the home studio he built with the remainder of the budget. And that's how he won his way to freedom. His family crossed the pond and joined him not long after.

The following illustrates what a wonderful person he was: I had fallen in love with one of his guitars while visiting his pad, so he traded axes with me for several weeks. It was a prototype White Charvel of his with a body made from an incredibly resonant Malaysian softwood called Jelutong, which he had been playing at his recent shows, and which had been on the cover of Guitar Player—and which said axe began my love affair with Jelutong. I gave him my 1961 Blonde L5 in return.

In relating my experiences with Allan, I'd be dishonoring the truth if I didn't mention that he's been a pivotal part of some very defining moments for me and my mental landscape.

When I was a young buck, barely old enough to get into bars and lacking in life experience, I believed that beating others at their game was what musical ability was all about. I was also dumb enough to believe that I hadn't heard anyone do anything on the guitar that I would never be able to do, if I dedicated my life to doing that one thing, and for long enough. Such were the things that I thought mattered at the time. Then I heard Allan, and I knew that no matter how hard and how long I tried, I would never be able to do that. Any of it. It would be like a dog chasing an airplane. It was shattering to me, since up to that point I had entertained delusions of grandeur, the like of which are only possible in the puffed up chests of sufficiently young men, who are sufficiently full of themselves.

Years went by, and as the post-Allanpocalypse guitar landscape in SoCal became the new normal, I became more and more consumed by his brilliance. Despite my having been educated as a composer / arranger / orchestrator of all styles and trained to have an abiding, open-minded love of good music from every century, decade, continent, culture and genre, nonetheless well over half the music I listened to was Allan. I started becoming dimly aware that I was losing sense of my own identity as a musician. This could not end well.

It was at about that time that I blundered across a line: On the Road Games album, Allan's entry into the solo on Tokyo Dreams is a blistering salvo I would never be able to play. But somehow it migrated from one part of my brain to another and got confused with my own licks, and I went to enter into a solo on a top 40 gig in a hotel lounge with said salvo. I got exactly three and a half notes into it, realized what I had done, abruptly hung my arms at my sides, looked at the ceiling and had a good laugh as my rig squealed with feedback. All good fun in the moment, as the businessmen and waitresses looked up from their martinis and scotch to see what had caused the Straticus Interruptus...but in the solitude of the drive home afterwards, I had to admit that a line had been crossed. I had a serious talk with myself, the upshot of which was that it was time for me to distance myself from Allan's influence and rediscover who the hell Byron was.

So I did. Other than going over to his pad to visit a couple of times several years later, I got away. It was a necessary move; I guess that at the time, his brilliance was too strong a drug for me to resist an untoward amount of influence.

A few years later, around 1990 or so, John Pena called me to his pad to do some guitar tracks for a project he was producing. This was very humbling for me, given the company he keeps. I asked him why he had called me instead of Luke or Landau. He said, "You're the best Byron Fry I know." This led to a longer conversation about musical identity, and it was finally, at long last, drilled through my thick fucking skull that everyone brings something unique to the table that is all their own, and that the point of your musical journey is to find and nurture that voice, and to become the best YOU that you can—who you truly, creatively, spiritually, musically, naturally and ultimately are. I owe my buddy John a great debt of gratitude for that. It set me free.

A few years ago, not too long before he left this Earth, I went and saw Allan for the first time in over 20 years. It was great to say hi and to be face-to-face with him after so long, if only for a few minutes in the crowded hubbub of the Baked Potato. It wasn't like I hadn't missed my old friend. Then I sat there with my lady, listening to him play and staring into that dark, familiar forest and the mental wilderness of lightning bolts that I had had such a cathartic time clawing my way out of—feeling the potent mixture of the coldness of an ancient inner battlefield and the warm, unabashed adulation of something impossibly beautiful, knowing that he is so much better than I, or anyone, could ever be. But unlike in my twenties or my thirties, now I was mature enough to be able to smile about it on the drive home, knowing that I'm the best Byron Fry there is, and feeling that on a good day, that's good enough.

Chapter 11
The Endless Highway

Harold Barney was a fantastic keyboardist I met at a rehearsal for a band that wasn't very good; it was the kind of band that'll rehearse forever and maybe never actually work. Watch out for those, they'll suck your blood. That is, unless it's really fun stuff to play, in which case it's acceptable because it's food for your soul.

Harold and I recognized each other's skills and had a merry little romp through Chick Corea's "Spain" in several keys and time signatures, while the rest of the band took a break. After we tore down and loaded out through the hot afternoon Burbank sunshine, we started talking in the parking lot.

He mentioned that he was involved in the production of an album for Syreeta (Stevie Wonder's wife) and invited me over to the studio, which was in her garage. We messed around with different sounds for pre-production (remember Linn Drums?), but that's as far as my involvement went for that particular album. These things can take years to reach fruition, and we were both too broke to hang around town waiting for a record company to actually pay somebody something that might trickle in our direction. So we opted to hit the road together in a variety band that Harold knew, playing Red Lion hotel lounges (no autographs, please), for what was supposed to be a three week gig. Cue the Gilligan's Island theme here: "A threee weeek tour…"

Months later, we were still on the road with that band when the wind blew us into Boise.

* * *

If you want an injured body part to really heal, sometimes the best medicine is to use that puppy as much as it can possibly stand.

My hometown buddy Kevin W.—he of the VW brakes in Palomares canyon, and little brother of Dave the manager—had been living in Boise for a number of years, and it was a great reunion. Avowed Frisbeeterians since adolescence and now in our mid-twenties, we made a point of spending about an hour every day running after frisbees, barefoot on the massive lawns in Boise's many parks. We called the game Take Off and Die Frisbee, the idea being that your opponent tossed the thing as hard as he could in a trajectory at least ninety degrees away from your position, and your job was to haul ass and catch it or die trying. It was actually a fairly athletic undertaking, and that many wind sprints, barefoot in the grass, was what finally healed my feet back to 100 percent. For the first couple of weeks they got a bit worse, then they started a trend of strengthening more and more, complaining less and less. By the end of that six-week booking in Boise, I had the feet of superman.

And I had seen the worst barroom brawls that I ever have, right there in the sleepy environs of the Boise Red Lion's lounge. All polished brass rails, felt walls, muted pastel colors, top-shelf booze and a soft-spoken, professional bar staff, the Misty's lounges at Red Lions were all identical. And though they all turned into a thumping meat rack for locals on the weekends, they looked like they had been designed by an interior decorator with a barbiturate problem and an agenda of lulling businessmen to sleep over their scotches. So it surprised me when, on two different occasions a week apart, the entire clientele of Misty's Lounge erupted into a no-holds-barred free-for-all, everybody in the club except the band and staff entangled in a gigantic dogpile that was taller than me, beating on each other with crazed murder in their eyes as if someone had injected aerosolized PCP into the air conditioning system: "No shit, there I was, plucking people out of a dogpile taller than my head." The only other brawl I saw at a gig that was anywhere near that scale was at a posh wedding at a millionaire's estate—groom's party vs bride's, if memory serves—and everybody wound up in the pool, laughing. I would've been laughing too, had my gear been set up a little farther from the pool.

***

That road just refused to end. The "three week tour" eventually turned into a solid year and a half of living out of a suitcase, blowing from band to band to band, on and on through myriad adventures and misadventures all over the western US, trying to get back to LA the entire time. An ex-girlfriend came back and left repeatedly; I'd find myself troubleshooting a band's vehicle in a blizzard at night with a pair of pliers, or lying in half-frozen slushy mud putting tire chains on the band's van because nobody else had any experience with it (or I was the only one dumb enough to admit that I did); happy hour patrons and waitresses would look askance at me, sitting at a cocktail table soldering a connection on a circuit board using a butter knife for a soldering iron that I had heated up in the sterno flame under the Hors d'oeuvres tray. I found myself staying in vermin-infested band houses that had been red-tagged, playing a five-star resort one week and an Arizona biker bar the next.

And there were plenty of fun times: There's a lake in a quarry just south of Ashland, Oregon with a fantastic high running takeoff over deep water. You have to sprint as fast as you can, weaving totally blind through head-high bushes, until the ground starts to drop a bit, whereupon you plant your good foot very squarely on a very particular flagstone, and jump as high and far as you can. As you clear the bushes in front of you, you still can't see the water. Then as you start to fall, the ground suddenly disappears and drops behind you—and you find yourself flying through space at least 60 feet off the water. It's one hell of a rush. There's a shallow rock shelf below that requires you to hit the water at least ten feet from the cliff base if you want to survive, and which kills a local or two every year; it's the reason you sprint on the takeoff. With the running start, you hit at about twenty feet out, but I don't recommend you trip on the approach.

Also at Ashland, on a different booking with a different band in a different season, I almost suicided myself on skis, thanks to a tree with a big broken branch sporting big sharp death spikes at the end, aimed right between my eyes as I came flying through the air directly at it after an unforeseen and out-of-control launch. I happened to be facing in the right direction to see it, and somehow flipped myself out of that trajectory. The result was a spectacular "yard sale" and an abiding sense of respect for narrow, steep terrain with lift towers and house-sized moguls in bad weather.

Good times and bad times aside, there was something more important eating at me. Every minute, I keenly felt the distance between the path that I was on and the one that I wanted to be on.

The silver lining in all of this was the company of musicians. This is a universal thing: In every band, even if it's an ad-hoc lineup thrown together for one night, we all relate, we're all of a type and intrinsically a team, we all understand each other's unspoken battles, losses, victories, family struggles, and the musical triumphs and defeats that nobody outside of music can comprehend. And we get all of this usually without even talking about it, because it's the life we all live. We all get it. It can only be called a kind of shared love.

So at least I wasn't lonely. At one point, I was in a band of incredibly talented people with a bandleader who was such a vile asshole, he literally took a piece of each player's gear and locked it in his cellar before hitting the road, to ensure we wouldn't walk off the gig due to his abuses.

At another point, I had to sub out one of the only decent gigs in The Bay for an emergency trip to Oregon to collect an ex of mine (yes, that one) from a bad situation with her abusive big brother, who belonged behind bars but wasn't. The weather turned in a historically big way as soon as I arrived in Portland, and we got iced in for five days—every road into and out of the city was closed. By the time we got back to The Bay, the bandleader had given my gig to the sub. Only by some silver-tongued coercion did I get him to agree to let me come and sit in, so that he could realistically do an A/B comparison of the players. I played Europa—what is it about that tune?—and everybody on stage and in the room was smiling. I was relieved to get the gig back, and the sub was even cool about it.

But the gigging scene in The Bay at that time was pretty emaciated. I was stuck in a cul-de sac and I knew what had to be done.

Chapter 12
Southbound Again

Compared to the SF Bay Area or any other big town—NYC, Chicago, Austin, Nashville, choose your poison—LA will always have much more musical commerce going on. The SF Bay Area has incredibly good culture and talent, which I love and which formed my musical foundation. LA, on the other hand, has the gigantic chugging machinery of the industry. In any one week during the eighties, there were as many recording sessions and live performances in LA and SoCal as would happen in The Bay in about a year. I was pretty much nobody in LA, but in The Bay I was treated like I was noteworthy, just for having done what sessions I had so far. In my mind, that only underscored my need to get back to LA.

After six months in The Bay it became clear that I'd never save the money I needed to move back in good form, so I finally just gave a three-week notice to the band I was currently in, and up and left. I drove south with two hundred dollars in my pocket, a '68 Ford Mustang with freshly rebuilt heads, my guitars and amp, some clothes and no gig lined up.

***

Lucky W., a good friend of mine from Grove, had agreed to let me crash on his living room floor in LA for three weeks. After that I'd have to go, or his marriage might suffer. It was a vital initial foothold, and I feel indebted to the man to this day.

Having finally won my way back to LA—the center of the musical universe, the shining Mecca where there's no limits to which you can rise—I might have gone into film or TV scoring, or record production, or even just applied myself more seriously as a studio guitarist. Alas, yet again I had to pull a miracle out of my ears immediately, and breaking into new circles would have taken too much time.

So the first thing I did, like moth to flame, was to look for cover band gigs in SoCal. They say that going back is just that, and this definitely felt like that. As Al Swearengen's character says in Deadwood, "Some people just can't go near a cliff without jumping off."

MCS (Musician's Contact Service) is a wonderful subscription networking platform for musicians looking for gigs and bands looking for musicians, and they actually do get some listings for major acts looking for talent. I had gotten almost every one of my gigs playing covers in SoCal from a listing I found there. It was always well worth the nominal fee, and still is.

There were three listings for full-time gigs that caught my eye: One for a full-time house band in Pomona (a "house" gig is where you play at one place for a long time—in big enough places or haughty enough circles, they might call it a residency), another listing for a full-time house band on a new upcoming cable TV show, and one for a classic rock band in the South Bay. I auditioned for all three. All three told me they had auditioned about 50 cats, and I got all three gigs. That is to say, the TV show suits hired three players, of which I was one, and I scored the other two gigs outright.

I'd love to believe that I'm just that good, but the actual reason I got all of those gigs is the mindset that Grove gave me. And okay, if I'm being honest, hunger was a factor too—don't underestimate hunger—but mostly, my training at Grove. And this bears a few words, because it's an extremely valuable lesson for anyone on this path:

I have no reason to believe I was a better player or a better singer. As I said, I'm not especially gifted. What sets me apart from the competition, besides the actual nuts-and-bolts understanding of things that I got from Grove, is the mindset of an arranger / producer. It makes you think in terms of what is needed from you (and every other musician present), viewed from the control booth, or the conductor's podium, or the MD's chair. You understand the function of every part you play or sing, so in a larger sense you get the reason you're being paid to be there. If someone with that perspective is auditioning against, like, some guitar player, dude...the more elevated perspective will always win.

Those who do the hiring have that perspective, and perceive that I'm one of their team, there to help them accomplish what they need to. I can't overstate the power of being a musician whose instrument is guitar, as opposed to just being a guitar player. Having that mindset and level of musical awareness has made all the difference in my career. So even if you just want to be an instrumentalist and never write a note, study composing and arranging. It's by far the single best thing I ever did for my chops and value as an instrumentalist.

Speaking of auditions, here are two more tips as long as we're on the subject. If you're not musical, you can apply these to job interviews. First off, competition is a numbers game, and the vast majority of competition just makes something good look better. So don't ever be afraid to put yourself out there. Secondly, you're always auditioning for each other. It's always a two-way street. Never forget that.

* * *

The gigging life continued to blow me around for awhile, but I could sense a change in the wind. My girlfriend and I moved from the West End to Universal

City, and immediately I noticed the difference: I couldn't even go out and grab a cup of coffee without bumping elbows with industry mover-shakers. There was a Wednesday night jam thing at the Beverly Garland Howard Johnson's Hotel, at Vineland and the 101, which was run by a great guitarist named Johnny Oliver, whose face you'd probably recognize. He was an actor and was in a lot of stuff, and was also a sidelining contractor. The jam tended to attract studio musicians, not the rock and blues crowd like most jam nights do. It was a great cadre of players to be around and play with. Johnny took a shine to my playing. As I walked in the door with my guitar in a case, I'd have to walk right by him on the little lounge stage. He had a good sense of humor, and started making a routine of standing up from his stool as soon as he saw me walk in, cutting me off and handing me his guitar on his way to the bar, without even making eye contact. It became a running joke. I'd be standing there with the band playing a song, a guitar case in one hand, his guitar in the other, not even able to wash my hands or pull out my axe.

This wasn't a venue, it was a hotel lounge, and the tables went right up to the stage. One night, there was a guy sitting at the first table directly in front of me, facing me from across the table, wearing a blue velour jumpsuit, gold chains around his neck, leaning back with his alligator cowboy boots up on the table, smoking a cigar and staring at my left hand on the fretboard. He just stared and stared at it as I played, and never looked away. He was intensely appraising my chops, and I had no idea why.

I knew he was somebody important—he was wearing the uniform and looked familiar—so I started experimenting with different things to try to get a reaction. I tried this lick...nothing. That lick...nothing. After a few more approaches, I threw in a Roy Buchanan quote. His eyebrows went up and he pulled the cigar out of his mouth.

"Gotcha!" I thought. I started channeling Roy, one of my earliest electric guitar influences. He started leaning in, boots on the floor. On the break, Johnny introduced me. "Byron, I'd like you to meet a good friend of mine. This is James Burton."

"Holy ever lovin' shit," I thought. I tried to be cool, but I doubt I pulled it off. This guy had been Elvis's guitarist! Back when Rock Guitar was first getting ejected from the volcano as molten lava, this man helped shape it into what it is. Talk about legacy! I shook his hand, we hit it off and started hanging out there every Wednesday.

One Wednesday night I brought a Les Paul to the hang to discover that Johnny hadn't brought an amp, so I had to plug directly into a cheap PA mixer. Please believe me when I tell you, there is no more pathetically limp noise in the musical world than a Les Paul plugged directly into a PA. There's no way to make that plinky-plink voice sound good. And if you're demoralized by the sound of your voice, it's tough to have inspired ideas.

James, as ever, was right there at that first table, cigar in hand, alligator boots on the table, calmly watching me flail and fail. On the break I sat down and introduced him to my new used guitar (I had just gotten it), and complained about not having an amp. As I handed him the guitar, still plugged in, he didn't even sit up straight or take his feet off the table.

"Well now, lemme see this hyar, Barn..." he said, and proceeded to rip the roof right off that goddamned joint in about 5 seconds. A blazing flurry of twangy double-stops, rowdy pull-offs, lightning-fast double hammer-ons, burning bends and hot licks came exploding out of that poor guitar in such a way that it really wouldn't have mattered what the hell it was plugged into. He non-chalantly handed it back to me, drawling "That's a nahss gee-tar, Barn. Nahss sound." My mouth hanging open, I stared down at my Les Paul, now sagging in my arms in a state of post-coital bliss and having a cigarette. It's one of the greatest lessons anyone ever taught me: You adapt to whatever sound you have, and do what you need to in order to make that work. I'll always owe James a debt of gratitude for that.

A couple of weeks later, James told me he wanted to put me on an album he was about to do with Eric Clapton and Jeff Beck. I tried to act cool: "No shit, there I was, talking to James Burton, and he told me he wanted to put me on an album with..."

That call never actually came, but that he would even say such a thing was an incredible honor.

Meantime, I was working in and out of town with a collection of bands. Show bands, blues bands, jazz bands, cover bands, rock bands...I felt sometimes like I had worked with every band, in every club, in the western United States.

* * *

Before I would make good my escape from the nightclub life, there would be other injuries...I drove my right temple into a 135-degree corner while tearing down after a gig in Santa Barbara, CA, the result being some extra-cranial blood vessels (under the skin but outside the skull) getting compromised and leaking the water component of my blood every time I got my blood pressure up, which happened every time a sang a high note. It took almost a year to heal those pipes and it required my actually quitting coffee, then as now my strongest and happiest addiction. I won't say that my friends and bandmates loved being around me during that time, but to be fair they were thinking about it all wrong. The remarkable thing is that I didn't become a violent sociopath, and they all survived.

On another occasion, I crushed the tips of my lower left three ribs into eleven fragments when the upper horn of my Strat's body was driven into them in a short fall from stage in Arizona during a guitar solo at a mega-club on the banks of the Colorado River called the Sundance Saloon. I was in front of about 2,000 drunken yahoos and yahooettes with the spotlight following me, and I just happened to land on my feet on the dance floor without missing a note.

To understand that setting, imagine the Colorado River about a hundred yards across, running deep and slow, and a daytime Fourth of July party scene on the river that was so densely packed, you could walk from the Arizona bank to the California bank on the boats without getting your feet wet. That had been the scene outside the Sundance earlier that day, and this was that evening. Generally speaking, drinking at a nightclub gig is cool, but being drunk enough that it affects your performance is unforgivable. So I'm not saying I was drunk...I'm simply stating for the record that there may or may not have been some alcohol compromising the individual who may or may not have been playing guitar, at a level which may or may not have contributed to a fall that may or may not have affected the show (and his ribs, though he wouldn't know the extent of that damage until ten weeks later when he finally went to a doctor).

Having landed on my feet on the dance floor in legitimate pain, still playing with the spotlight on me, the grimace on my face was mistaken for my getting really into the solo, and they all cheered. The following morning, waking up badly hungover in the comically dilapidated trailer that served as the band house, I spent ten full minutes trying to figure out how to get out of my top bunk without searing, crunching pain. If you've ever had broken ribs, you'll know that you can't breathe but you can't not breathe; you can't move but you can't not move, you can't laugh...it takes some getting used to.

As for getting out of that bunk, that entailed a sit up (completely out of the question), while rolling over to my left (even more out of the question), so I spent awhile imagining every possible scenario of spatial mechanics before conceding that exiting that bunk without bad pain was in fact impossible. So I just sucked it up and rolled out, directly over the crushed ribs. A few seconds later I was standing victoriously next to the bunks, waiting for the pain to subside and thinking "Okay. If I can do that, I can get through this."

Then I sneezed.

It was my first time experiencing a level ten on my personal pain scale. It's happened three more times since. Ten, for me, is when the pain is so intense that something in your brain shorts out and sends a blinding flash of light down your optic nerve, you almost pass out and are left nauseated, weak and shaking.

I quickly mastered the art of stifling sneezes.

Chapter 13
Give Me Space

Music is not something you do with just your body and your mind. It's not digging a ditch, driving a truck or working in a kitchen; it's not even like other creative things, like writing a book. Playing live, especially in a rhythm section, you feel the music as physically as the rocks under your feet when you're walking a trail, or the food you're chewing. It's somebody thumping you right in the chest, it's the wave you're surfing, the hill you're skiing, the rock you're climbing, the air you breathe, the lover you're entwined with in bed. It's a part of you, because you're a part of it. This is why it's important to avoid playing music that's ugly to you.

Many of the more pedantic pop hits I've had to play had all the inherent groove and pocket of noisy industrial machinery, mechanically clanking its way down a rut like a combine during harvest or a hydraulic pile driver on a construction site. There goes a perfectly capable rhythm section, imprisoned in a temporal quadrangle of repetition, marking measures of time as square footprints with all the creative nuance of bales of hay and steel girders, stretching out behind in a pattern that goes to the horizon.

You can damage yourself by playing enough of the wrong music. You know that song you really hate? Imagine having to actually play that every night. Burnout is a very real thing, and you have to be careful, because music can become to a musician what sex is probably like to a hooker. That's a very heavy price to pay, and all that it takes is accepting the wrong gig.

I spent my 30th summer in one of the most incredibly beautiful places I've ever seen, surrounded by some of the nicest people I'll ever know, playing the worst song list I ever have with the worst band I've ever played with, five sets a night, 6 nights a week. We were there for the 12 weeks of the salmon run.

Cordova Alaska is a fishing village of 1500 or so very sweet, hard working people, accessible only by air and water, and surrounded by thousands of square miles of heartbreakingly gorgeous virgin wilderness. I fell in love with the place immediately. I made some lasting friends and finally saw the northern lights, which had been an item on my wishlist for years. The whole village pitched in to buy me a bush plane ride for my birthday, so the band and I got a birds-eye view of the Alaskan wilderness and buzzed some glaciers. There was also an extremely cool gym I worked out in every day, and the best king salmon I'll ever eat—from the lure straight to the grill—as often as I liked. Bald eagles were everywhere I looked, and it's the most overtly green place I've ever seen. It rained almost every day, but that didn't dampen my love for the area's unspoiled beauty.

On the other hand, there was the gig. The drummer was a next-level alcoholic: if there were an olympic event for drinking he'd be on the podium for sure. He started on the Everclear (190 proof wood grain alcohol) at around one o'clock every afternoon, and by downbeat eight hours later, he was so tanked that any passing fisherman or his dog could have held a better beat. The keyboardist was a very intelligent guy and a dear friend of mine but, alas, lived in an alien universe where The Cars were the spearhead of musical innovation. Moreover, he provided keyboard bass for the band. There was a female singer who did her job well and brightened the stage and our lives, but the song list was a collection of all my worst nightmares from the 80s.

By the time I got back to L.A. I had been so musically beaten down, in such a sustained way and for so long, that all I could do was to put the guitar away and not think a single musical thought. I got a day job as a platemaker for a printing company and just waited. I knew I would re-emerge, but I had no idea how long it would take.

A week went by, then a month. Then another. Then, one day nine weeks after my return from Alaska, I was running a vacuum over the carpet at my pad, listening to Coltrane solo over something on the My Favorite Things album, and realized I was absent-mindedly taking a totally ripping solo over it in my imagination. I put down the vacuum, took out my Strat and was immediately playing the tastiest stuff that had come out of me in years, despite my chops being so rusty and weak. I was back!

The first audition I went on was a great match, with a 4-piece band of truly fantastic cats. Steve Stephens is one of the finest pocket drummers on the planet. He's worked in the Jackson camp, and when he lays down a groove you just have to smile. The bass player / bandleader Kurt also had superb pocket and was a sweet guy, Mark was a great keyboardist. All four of us sang. That band was a great liberating release and completed my healing, for which I'll always be indebted. We played covers, but the groove was so deep it never felt like covers, and the song list was cool stuff only. We worked 3 and 4 nighters, which was about as good as a cover band could do on the slowly dying SoCal nightclub circuit by that point.

I also got more focused on projects that would matter to me more, career-wise and musically. The first fusion band I put together was with Steve Stephens, the same drummer as the cover band, my good buddy Mike Acosta on saxes—to this day one of the most horrifyingly great sax players I've worked with—who went on to be the primary arranger of Brian Setzer's grammy-winning comeback album. We had Donny

Miller on bass, a true badass now living in upstate New York, and Scott Tibbs, one seriously incredible keyboardist, who was working toward a DM degree (musical doctorate) at UCLA, I have no idea why. A prolific writer then as now, Scott has the chops of doom, and you've heard his playing, writing and arranging on some award shows. We never took that band anywhere but a living room, but that was just fine with us. Some of the best and most important playing situations I've been in were never heard by anyone outside of the heavies I was playing with privately. We played charts by Mike, Scott and myself, along with the occasional jazz standard, which we always turned into its evil twin in one weird way or another.

About that time I also started getting more cool opportunities to play the kinds of gigs I'd always wanted to: Tim Bogert—he of Vanilla Fudge and the iconic trio Beck, Bogert and Appice—called me to play in his quasi-progressive rock trio. I felt duly honored, and I gotta say: he could lay down a stupendously massive foundation.

For me, playing in a rock trio of guitar, bass and drums had always been a matter of trying to play keyboard parts, string parts, horn parts and sometimes even backup vocal parts, all on guitar—as well as the actual guitar parts I'd be playing if all those other instruments were present. I always felt like things were naked unless I filled the space as much as I could. I'd drive home afterward feeling like I'd been playing first, second and third base, along with shortstop, catcher and left field. With Tim on bass, though, I was just surfing on an ocean of massive groove. It was wonderful. I could actually just be a guitarist, and nothing was lacking. Bass players who can play good rock trio bass are very rare.

I also played with Mark Craney and the Geniuses, which was a blast. I started by sitting in. Larry Wilkins, the guitarist, was a superb player (many years before this, he played that great solo on Surgarloaf's Green

Eyed Lady), and we discovered that we really dug playing together. He played an old Marshall Plexi half-stack with the "hall" missing from the nameplate, so it said "Mars", a clear indication of his character. At that time, I was playing a wonderful old Boogie amp, and on the front face of it I had put a large lapel pin that said "Give Me SPACE". So Larry and I were a good match.

It's rare for two guitarists to really mesh, for several reasons: For one, we don't play in sections like brass, woodwinds or strings, so we're not mentally wired for close formation flying like the Blue Angels, or for tag-teaming parts. We also don't typically have parts arranged for more than one of us, because there's typically just one of us in a band. And very few guitarists are arrangers, able to think in the right way to devise a part that compliments what another player is doing, so it's rare indeed to find two guitarists that work well together. Larry and I naturally just hit if off. After playing with The Geniuses a half dozen times, I was jokingly made an "Honorary Genius". Mick Mahon was on bass, a top feeder with a bio full of gigs with gods, as was Mark Craney, who had toured as drummer with Jethro Tull and Gino Vannelli. He had a dark, sardonic wit that worked well with my own. All three cats commanded huge respect in the local musical community.

There were others. Things were getting downright cool. I was the guitarist for The Bosnia Relief Concert, broadcast live from the Baked Potato, in a band put together by Tommy Eyre and Richie Hayward. In the early days of the internet, "Electronic Cafe" was an MTV special broadcast that attempted to have a band on the west cost jamming online with a band on the east coast. The band here was The Geniuses with me—Larry couldn't make it—with guest appearances by Graham Nash and Thomas Dolby. I was paying cooler stuff, in cooler company.

The tip here is this: Your musical animal—whether it's you or a loved one—needs to be nurtured, not tortured. Given the right kind of growth in the right situations, your beast can become a powerful force on which entire futures can be built. Subjected to the wrong work, in the wrong environment with the wrong people, it can be killed entirely.

Chapter 14
Doors Open

"Money doesn't make the world go 'round. Relationships do."

- A golden quote from Dick Grove that grows more golden every year.

Somewhere around 1990, I reconnected with my old songwriting partner, the incredible vocalist Terry Wood. I had lost contact with her while I was being blown all over the western U.S. in my little Homer's Odyssey. She had been hired into a recording session at Milagro Studios in Glendale, where my best friend Kevin W.—he of Palomares Canyon Brakes and Boise Frisbees—was now the house engineer, having moved to LA and gone through the Audio Engineering program at Grove.

After the session, Kevin came through my door raving: "Man, you wouldn't believe how good this singer was today! She blew my friggin' mind! She's worked with everybody, she's one of the top studio vocalists. I've never heard anybody that good, or worked with anyone that professional! She was amazing!"

"Sounds like someone I'd like to know. What's her name?"

"Terry Wood."

I laughed. "No way, Terry? Dude! She's a good friend of mine, and I lost contact with her! Yeah, she's a force of nature, as good as it gets. You've gotta put us back in touch!"

And so it came to be. She invited me to the house—a palatial testament to the blinding talent of two people, namely hers and that of her husband, John Pena. Terry introduced us, and that's how I met John.

You've heard them both on many, many things. If I were to paste their credits and discography here, it would require at least half a dozen pages. Suffice to say they're both basically at the top of the game.

John and I immediately hit it off, and he opened some pivotal doors for me. He's one of the greatest bass players alive, also a fantastic writer / arranger / producer, and also just a very cool human. We found that we worked well together.

He started having me provide guitars for some of the projects he was doing in his studio, then he and I retooled an instrumental fusion ditty of mine called "Salamander Breath", putting a jazzier, more Latin spin on it, turning up the heat a bit and renaming it "El Salamander Breath". We recorded a demo of our arrangement and presented it to Alex Acuna, along with the chart I wrote. John was in Alex's band, which was playing around the cool listening rooms. That led to my first time experiencing the giddying sensation of sitting in an audience while a piece I had a hand in writing was premiered by a band of world-class people. "No shit, there I was..." Alex's fusion project, "The Unknowns", was a lineup of unbelievably good dignitaries, all of whom had been (or would be) featured in the magazines for their respective instruments, i.e. Modern Drummer, Keyboardist, Guitar Player, Bass Player and the like.

John was on bass, Ramon Stagnaro on guitar, Pedro Eustache on flute, Otmaro Ruiz on keys, and Richie "Gajate" Garcia was on percussion. I've done other things with most of those people since, but none as many as Richie.

To illustrate what it means to be the percussionist in Alex Acuna's band, you should understand that at the time, Alex was himself probably the most famous percussionist in the world. He opted to play drums in his own fusion band, and chose Richie as his percussionist. Richie has worked with top feeder after top feeder, including another of the greatest drummers, Phil Collins. The thing I noticed about Richie's playing is that he transcends the myriad instruments he plays: He doesn't play percussion so much as he plays the song—he plays the arrangement. If you're a drummer or percussionist reading this, you might take a hint from that. Richie and I have gone on to make more noise—he had me play on one or two of his things, I've had him play on a ton of mine, and we've been hired on the same project on several occasions.

Upon being put back in touch with Terry and meeting John, I found myself abruptly boosted up several rungs of the ladder, into much heavier company.

John got me into Walfredo Reyes Jr.'s Latin Funk / Fusion band, called Wally World. We played The Spud (as local cats call The World Famous Baked Potato Jazz Club) and the other cool listening rooms along Ventura boulevard. I had never been in a rhythm section that good, and I'm not sure I have since. The brothers Wally and Danny Reyes are two of the heaviest drummer / percussionists in the world, and their father is Walfredo Senior.

The best way to illustrate the heaviness of Walfredo Sr. is for you to understand that Buddy Rich and Steve Gadd have both studied from him.

Wally Jr. is mostly known as a drummer, Danny mostly as a percussionist. I can't put all their credits in here, but just to give you an idea: Wally's been with Chicago for years. He was with Santana for years. When Traffic did a reunion tour and Ginger Baker couldn't make it, Wally was the drummer of choice. Danny's gigs are every bit that heavy, too. He's been with Earth, Wind & Fire and Chicago as well, and is now with Zac Brown. It seems like any time either guy is playing live, it's to sixty thousand people.

So playing with that band was, for me, both tall cotton and very deep pockets. I learned a lot. We had a great keyboardist named Harry Cohn, and the one time that John couldn't make a gig—it was a Unicef Benefit concert at The Palomino—the substitute bass player was Alphonso Johnson, of Weather Report. We took no prisoners.

These guys operated at such a lofty level that despite all of my experience and all of my chops, my focus most of the time was on not fucking things up, rather than on doing incredible things. Alas, Wally left town on a Santana tour and when he came back, his guitar player of choice was Frank Gambale. That's one of three times Frank has sort of replaced me on a project. Considering who he is, I'd be an idiot to resent it. In fact, I consider the connection an honor.

This was all happening as I continued to transition out of the nightclub cover band scene by fits and starts. Every bar I played reinforced my desire to win my way to better working environs. While loading out at the end of a 5-nighter in Whittier, I almost tripped over a guy lying unconscious on the bricks about 10 feet from the door with no one around, a puddle of dark, thick blood expanding around his head. His assailant was nowhere to be seen. He had a pulse and was breathing, but this looked bad; he needed immediate medical attention. I ran inside and yelled to the clubowner, drying glasses behind the bar and the only other guy in the room, "Call 911! There's a guy unconscious on your doorstep in a puddle of blood and he needs paramedics. And gimme a bar rag with some ice in it."

"I don't wanna call 911, the paperwork will take hours! And these rags cost 45 cents each, goddammit!"

Outweighing him by about a two-to-one ratio and a couple of decades younger, I was able to get that poor bar owner to see the error of his heartlessness pretty quickly, with no physical contact. I got the rag, got the ice and held pressure until medics arrived. I have no idea what became of the victim. But I drove home wanting, perhaps even more than ever, to never have to deal with another god-damned bastard clubowner like that guy again. "Enough of this", I thought. "I need a change." It was becoming an overly familiar mantra. And a change is what I got.

In a career of dealings with an industry whose value system favors visual spectacle over musical talent and worthiness, it made perfect sense to me that the most lucrative in-town gig I had gotten to date involved talent, but only as a prerequisite. What it really involved was lots of grease paint, latex movie makeup and tall platform boots.

Chapter 15
It's Not Easy Being Green

About the time that Disney "Imagineers" were in the news because their health was getting compromised from working with toxic substances in poor ventilation, and over at Universal, dancers in thick, heavy rat suits were passing out in the heat on the Fievel stage, I became a singing, dancing, guitar playing Frankenstein in a lineup of Hollywood monsters in the Beetlejuice Graveyard Review at the Universal Studios Tour theme park in Universal City. No autographs, please.

In certain circles it's no secret that most theme parks are not kind to performers, but people outside those circles aren't aware. So to shine a light down that hallway, I'll point out that theme parks tend to dominate the financial and political ponds they inhabit, and have ample resources and connections to quash most opposition in court. If a case is tight enough they'll still lose, but for the most part if you're a lowly performer and you've been screwed by the WeSaySo theme park's practices, you'll want to think hard before going up against that.

To their credit, they're pretty transparent about it. I remember the orientation at Universal Studios on day one, when the two friendly young people giving the presentation blatantly said, "Don't get hurt. Universal is not nice about it."

"Duh", I remember thinking to myself. I had heard stories. At the time I was a gym rat and very fit, so I didn't think much of it. I was an avid rock climber, fercrissake. How could I possibly get hurt doing a show on a stage?

I was one of three Frankensteins, and pretty much the beast of burden, doing the majority of the shows on the schedule. All told, I did roughly 450 shows over that summer. I was in great company. My immediate cast mates were legitimately talented, mostly singer / dancers hailing from Broadway, one of whom—Walter—was also a stunt man and went on to become The Black Power Ranger, complete with his own action figure. Best of all, Ellis Hall had a hand in developing the music, so it was slammin'. The choreographer had just won a Tony award for a Broadway show. Universal was doing a massive upgrade to the show, and spent lavishly on the new stage, props, computerized pyro and lighting, sound system, etc. We all got our own custom movie makeup, which in the case of Frankenstein, was much more excessive than any other character's.

One of the objectives of this book is to give the reader a feel for what it's like to work in the industry, complete with all of its wonderful warts, so here's a peak at the daily backstage ritual:

There was a specific sequence to getting into my Frank garb that was reminiscent of the scene in The Right Stuff when the techs are putting the astronauts into their space suits. First the pants. Then my feet went into high, heavy-duty canvas lace-up ankle braces with several metal stays sewn into them, then into inner boots that were pretty serious affairs, structurally...then all of that went into the outer boot: a massive, heavy suede affair that had long side zippers and went most of the way up to the knee, and which sat on 5-inch platforms. All told, they were heavier than ski boots and performed about the same, if ski boots were on 5-inch platforms. Franks had to dance most of the show in those things on an inclined "rake" feature of the stage, which was where most of the action happened.

Feet thus dealt with and not needing to be accessed until after the five-show shift, the upper body was next: First a wig cap, then the wireless mic and its wire frame, which worked by running around the back of my head and pinching in an irritating way at the sides over the ears. After that was the foam rubber "muscle pod" that went over my torso to ensure I'd be at risk for heat stroke, and which weighed a few pounds. Then a big black T-shirt went over all of that. Now it was time to get my head together.

The main part of that was a bulky latex flat-topped "Frank helmet", with the iconic high forehead and an integrated rock mullet wig that spilled down my back a couple of feet. It was custom molded for each Frankenstein, to integrate the guitarist's own face into Frankenstein's forehead and flat-topped skull, and covered the same parts of the head as a football helmet. It weighed two or three pounds, and got glued to my own forehead and face next to my eyes, across my brow and in front of my ears, every day, with spirit gum, which is a bit like rubber cement.

Once the upper body was all done and the Frank helmet was on, I had to be careful how I moved or the head could become detached. Next were the bolts at the side of the neck, which were simply spray-painted foam rubber, mounted on a C-shaped piece of coat hanger wire that went around the back of the neck. Then the grease paint. Lots of it, fifty shades of green...then black lipstick, crimson grease paint on the gash in the forehead...you get the idea.

After that, the wireless mic's transmitter went on the back of the belt, and the cable ran up my back to the mic's connector. Then, over the big black T-shirt and foam muscle pod went a massive, very heavy and very hot dark green blazer, festooned with spikes, belts, buckles and other "monster rock" regalia, then yet another heavy blazer over that, which was velcroed and got torn off in a "quick change" scene, along with another outer pair of velcroed pants.

I couldn't stretch between shows like everyone else, and that's what eventually led to my first spinal injury and surgery, where 75 percent of my L4/L5 disc was removed. I wasn't the only Frank to work that show who had spinal problems as a result. The choreography was fairly physical in nature, and basically custom-tailored to be destructive to Frank's lower spine. It wasn't because the choreographer had it in for guitarists, but because of all the stuff we had on. This is not to mention that guitarists don't typically have any background in dance to begin with—I sure as hell didn't—and for an entire shift of five shows over five hours, Franks were the only ones who couldn't get out of garb to stretch and cool down between shows. We couldn't do any moves an astronaut in a space suit couldn't do. Then we had to dance in platform ski boots on an incline, while fighting to remain conscious in the heat.

And it was dangerously hot. The stage floor was outside, facing south, with no shade structure over the front half, painted flat black, amidst acres of black tarmac in the summer heat of southern California. The microclimate on stage was what I can only call thermally hostile. It was almost never below 100 degrees, usually over 110, sometimes over 120. I would've been hot performing in a pair of boxers.

We had no backstage, they just parked a single-wide trailer behind the stage and called it good. And it challenges believability, but with all that free-wheeled spending on the show, somehow they couldn't afford an air conditioner for that trailer. I had to sneak across the tarmac to Fievel's backstage to cool off after a show.

There was one point in every show where I almost blacked out, as the whole cast was in a big line across the front of the stage during the end of a tune. I was holding the Bride of Frankenstein up off the stage in the crook of my right arm during the ending note, which was a long and sustained affair that climbed to a higher note just as I was running out of breath. I had to not only keep singing, but intensify my delivery to reach the top of my range. And almost every time we did that, despite my taking the most massive breath that I could beforehand, the world turned into a shrinking circle in front of my eyes. I'd fight to maintain consciousness for a few seconds longer, then just in time the song would end, I'd gasp a few breaths and the circle would grow larger, as the world came back and the crowd applauded. I never actually passed out, but it was almost always too close for comfort.

You might understandably be wondering by this point why anyone would put up with all this, and the answer is simple: It paid very well, for in-town work. But it exacted a heavy price.

I met kryptonite for the first time at 2:05 PM on Jun 2nd, 1992—about halfway through that summer of shows. I know that time because that's when the paperwork started. There was a particular move in the show's choreography that was especially hard on Frank's lumbar spine, and about the 200th or so time I did that move, I felt a sharp tearing sensation at the level of my beltline, followed by an equally sharp, localized burning.

I mentioned it to my cast-mates backstage after the show, and before I knew what was happening, management had made sure I saw the nurse, who gave me two Advils (which I likened to throwing a nerf ball at a freight train) and started the paperwork. Then I finished the shift and continued my schedule, limping along through the summer as best I could. They made me go through six months of every type of treatment short of surgery, including 36 chiropractic adjustments, before finally agreeing to give me an MRI. The results immediately green-lit surgery. The surgeon said the injury was the result of "sustained trauma", caused by the show's logistics.

The reason it took so long to get me into an MRI machine is that Universal Studios is "self-insured". In other words, they have so much money, they can keep a big enough pile of it in a kitty to dodge the legal requirement to carry insurance. This means they don't have to answer to anyone but themselves, so you just have to play their game—there's no process of appeal, like with American health insurance companies. They effectively own their own doctors too, until worker's comp law takes over and gives you the choice of anyone you like. Hopefully things have improved since then. The "company doc" they had me dealing with initially was a fine study of incompetence and subservience to his masters; the man would've been out of his depth working at a McDonald's. Fortunately, once the MRI results were in, I had my choice from the entire medical talent pool and did fastidious research. My spine surgeon was the top guy in all of SoCal.

Waking up after surgery, I experienced my second "ten" on the pain scale, as I clearly felt my body moving as two halves. The word for "spine" in the Japanese language translates loosely to "your center of life". Until you've had 70 to 75 percent of one of your lumbar discs removed, you really can't grasp the reality of that. A few hours after I woke up, the surgeon came in and told me how much they had had to remove. Then he said, "Okay, up on your feet. Let's go for a walk." It seemed like an absurd suggestion in the moment, but I'm glad he did. Some things are best handled sooner rather than later.

Universal set a defense lawyer of theirs on me who, according to my worker's comp attorney, had a state-wide reputation as a real pit bull. In one case that he handled for "a big studio tour theme park", where a performer had "literally been fired from a cannon and missed the net", he appealed it all the way to the state supreme court before taking no for an answer. He in turn sicked a P.I. on me who followed me around with a video camera for months...not because they were contesting whether I was injured, or how it happened—they weren't—but simply to get video footage of me that would indicate that my spine was all good to go post-op, to drive down the final settlement amount. Video cameras still bother the hairs on the back of my neck; not an ideal way to feel in this biz.

The surgeon offered to write up paperwork for a 15% disability, which I turned down. Ultimately, I figured the best compensation would be to just work my way past it. So I did.

With help from the spinal P.T. outfit that handled some of the biggest star athletes, I eventually rehabbed my spine back to the point where it has very little impact on my physical performance in everyday life. It was a matter of training my brain to use my core muscles as my new spine, which took a couple of years. I went on to climb my most difficult routes a few years later, not that climbing is harsh on the spine. It's actually pretty therapeutic, since you're not bending over and lifting things, or sitting for long periods, or dressed up like Frankenstein.

Perhaps the crowning chuckle is that California law required Universal to offer me "vocational rehabilitation", since I could no longer "wear platform boots and dance on an inclined rake". Such was bureaucracy's wording. And the requirements didn't stop there. Universal was required to offer me other jobs. One actually got my attention: It was made clear to me that if I wanted, I could become some kind of "entry-level management", which, it was made equally clear, would probably lead to being involved in production.

"Here it is." I thought to myself.

"Here's the breathless moment, the big hundred-foot-tall door cracking open to a cush gig in that big corporate studio world: MCA / Universal is lifting her skirts. I could wear a tie, become a cog in The Machine...probably wind up in some kind of theme park musical production department, speaking in company acronyms and making the right musical noises at the behest of the suits, working in a corporate studio environment for the rest of my professional life...make great dough fairly predictably, maybe even buy a house, have a retirement package and health coverage...it's all possible."

I had seen these people and worked around them all summer long. Nice folks, professional folks...religiously punctual and wearing just the right uniform of dockers and collar shirt, sleeves rolled up with a loose-fitting tie, creative enough to hang, riding that train down a professionally secure path while muttering under their breath about the cutthroat nature of office politics.

And for about thirty seconds, I was actually tempted. Then my head cleared and I knew none of that is who I really am, or why I was born a musician. I opted to keep my options open.

A little while later, one sunny afternoon in early May, the phone rang and underscored the wisdom of my choice.

Chapter 16
Wheels Up

Broken into musical consumer markets by language, planet Earth's Spanish-speaking population is by far the largest, encompassing the most countries. And Latinos are nothing if not wonderfully passionate about music. Michael Sembello, he who produced all the Flashdance hits back in the eighties (and a burning guitarist, by the way) recognized this and produced a tune in 1991 for an artist named Gerardo Mejia, better known as "Rico Suave", also the name of the tune. Remember it? In Southern California's market alone, that song went multi-platinum. Yes, that's as crazy as it sounds.

The Latino culture is not invisible to non-Latino Americans. It's everywhere in the states at all times, a massive component of who we are, predating all but the remnants of the Native American population. Yet most non-Latino Americans are radiantly ignorant of its nature.

Before we had smartphones to tell us who it is that's calling, what they've had for breakfast, how their marriage is doing and what mood they're in—so we can decide whether to interact as humans—we used to not actually know who was at the other end when the phone rang. Such was the case when I picked up the phone one fine spring day and said "Hello?"

"Hola, is this Byron, or is he there?" It was a crackly, long distance call. The voice had a thick Panamanian accent and sounded like its owner would be at home happily yelling over loud noises amid chaos between shots of tequila.

"Speaking."

"Hi Byron, my name's Manny. I got your number from Danny Reyes, he recommended you. You got a minute?"

"Oh, Danny! Cool! How is he? What can I do for you?"

"Danny's good, man. He says to tell you hi. Do you know who Emmanuel is?"

"Yeah, I've heard the name…" (I hadn't.)

"Is your passport current? And if it is, can you be on a plane in 72 hours?"

What followed was a rushed conversation filling in some details. I was basically hired over the phone for a major tour with one of the top acts in the largest market on Earth, in a conversation that lasted about three minutes. Manny was the road manager, Danny was down there on percussion, Emmanuel's guitarist had just been poached by Air Supply, who used the same management company south of the border, and it was common for players to be traded back and forth between the two camps. For some reason they had come up one guitarist short of a full stable.

My passport wasn't current, so that very afternoon I had to jump in the shower and get myself looking the part, then get a passport polaroid of me looking the part, then jump in my '67 Mustang and tear out over the Sepulveda pass to the big federal building in Westwood with my old passport, pay the extra charge for the expedited new passport (pretty sure they don't let you do that anymore), then fax a picture of my passport to Manny so he could green-light the plane tickets.

The next day I went on a manic spree buying clothes I thought were appropriate for the high-profile gig Manny described: "Emmanuel is basically the Latin version of Elton John, George Michael and Tom Jones all rolled into one. The chicks all go insane and throw their panties at him on stage. And this is a big comeback tour, so the promo is through the roof. It's all over the news in every Latin country." All of which turned out to be true, among a lot else, but what I didn't know was that the guys in the band dressed almost normally onstage...more like humans than peacocks. So I wasted all that dough pimping out my threads. Live and learn.

* * *

It might surprise you how tricky it is for a guitarist to travel with his or her signature voice, i.e. The Sound, though in this day of modeling technology it's easier than it used to be. A sax player or brass player travels with his or her horn, and that IS The Sound. Ditto violinists, and I've always envied flautists for how light they travel. Vocalists have The Sound right there with them when they wake up, notwithstanding the amphibian that might be croaking in their throats on early morning dates.

But if you play electric guitar, literally every piece of gear you use—which guitar, which pickups, which strings, which pedals, which amp, which speakers—is a big part of your voice, and changing just one of those things, or even just the order they're wired in, has a massive effect on that voice. And much of that kit is incompatible with "fly dates", in other words gigs that you fly to.

While the rest of the entourage skips happily onto the plane, the guitarist drags his tattered carcass and bloodshot eyes on board along with his guitar, having been up for several nights concocting a rig that might serve to overcome the inadequacies of the gear one encounters on a tour. He's had to repack his luggage during check-in because, even before 9/11, all the electronics raised suspicions. Then there was the inevitable gate attendant insisting that he check his uninsured, priceless and unique custom-built axe, thereby inviting its total destruction, on the premise that a guitar won't fit into the overhead bin when of course it will, the resulting fracas making children cry while their mothers covered their ears, escalating to a point just shy of SWAT dropping in through skylights, clouds of teargas, arrests and the evening news. Every experienced guitarist reading this is chuckling through gritted teeth.

It's becoming the norm now to use a software modeling device for fly dates, whose ones and zeroes come very close to duplicating all the nuances of any of the classic, high-dollar boutique hand-built tube amps of your choice, down to the type of speakers, cabinets, mics and their placement, the full array of effects pedals, where they go in the chain...all of it...arranged into banks of presets the player can program. I'll grant that it's easier to program if he or she is of the correct— how to say this—generation. Moreover, all of the guitarist's switching between sounds can now be done via midi or bluetooth, by the same master computer that's running the show's pyro, video and lighting. That is, if the player trusts robots a lot more than I do.

Physical amps are becoming a thing of the past on many tours, replaced by modelers that fit easily into overnight carry-on luggage...and now that there's a line of stage monitors designed specifically for guitarists using modelers, it's making more and more sense. Old-school barnstormer and tube amp snob that I am, I own three different modeling rigs myself. I even sometimes record with one of them. It's a brave new world. But at the time I got the call for the Emmanuel gig, all of that was still years away. And because of the short notice, I had zero time to put together a suitable pedal board for touring with backline amps.

"Backline" is industry jargon for whatever unknown, unpredictable amps (or other gear, such as drum sets) are provided. The smart mindset is to envision an amp that began life at the wrong end of retail's quality spectrum, was a problem child in school, fell off a delivery truck on the freeway, was picked up and glued back together, whose speaker cones were used by a cat as a scratching post, whose knobs are missing, whose power fuse is a wad of tinfoil, whose power circuit is built for the wrong continent, whose chassis is held together by duct tape and hope—basically, whose problems are so many and so unknown, you're lucky if just plugging into the thing doesn't kill you outright. Your best case scenario using a backline amp is that your sound won't be the greatest. It's folly to count on it actually being good.

If there was a silver lining to the short notice, it's that I had zero time to even think about assembling the right gear, which simplified the process. I just borrowed an old MXR Distortion Plus pedal from my good friend Mick O. and called it good. I figured there'd be enough support infrastructure on a major tour for me to put a suitable rig together down there. Ah, the optimism of youth.

Distortion pedals, you should understand, are designed to be used along with the warmth and richness of a tube amp. Vacuum tubes lend a beauty to guitar tone that can be gotten no other way. If you plug a distortion pedal into a solid state amp (i.e. no tubes)—or worse, directly into a P.A.—it'll have all the inviting richness and warmth of a mosquito in your ear, or a Skil saw on sheet metal. While that's an appropriate sound for some players, it doesn't work for me.

Upon arrival in Mexico City, where the organization was based most of the time, I met the crew and the band—a twelve-piece of amazing talent—then I was introduced to the backline I'd be using: a pair of Yamaha G100 solid state amps: the most remarkably cold, icy and sterile-sounding guitar amps probably ever built. They say the road to success is paved with bad backline. I can't disagree.

Because of last-minute cancellations, it turned out that the next show wasn't for another three weeks. They paid by the week, not the show, so I got paid to hang out at a 5-star hotel in Mexico City with some truly great players and learn the show, while also learning Espanol the best way: Living it.

Finally, I found myself playing that first show. The soundcheck had gone fine and I was glad to be doing the thing, earning the money I had already been paid. While we were playing one song, I noticed that all of my band mates were gradually cheating towards the back of the stage toward the amps and drum risers, crouching down, getting lower and lower. I thought it was a shtick, like when a cover band plays that old Motown tune "Shout" (get a little lower, now)...so I half-heartedly followed suit. I wasn't very far back or very low, but I had moved enough—barely—to not get my head blown off.

The pyro detonation was truly proud, and nobody had even told me about it: Five explosive squibs were stuffed with about a quarter stick of dynamite's worth of black powder—each—and set along the front of the stage at intervals of about ten feet, to be detonated simultaneously. I hadn't even noticed them. The concussion of the shock wave hit as if a mule kicked me in the chest. I was knocked back several feet, arms cartwheeling, gasping for breath, ears ringing, eyes wide. I'm glad I didn't have a headset mic on, or the crowd would've heard me reflexively holler "WHAT THE FUCK?!?" at the top of my lungs. I looked around to see if everyone was okay, then I was laughing, as was everyone else.

One of the many things I love about Latino culture is the "get it done" attitude, and how informal things are. So much can be done south of the border just by moxie and effort, and deciding to do it. Here in the States, everything is very controlled. In a lot of cases that's a good thing, because so many of my countrymen don't know any better than to step off the curb into traffic while staring at their phones. But in other cases it's just embarrassing. Do we really need to be told that the contents of a to-go coffee cup might be hot? On the Beetlejuice show at Universal, OSHA was a tangible presence at all times. We were carefully instructed about all pyro, and the show's blocking was carefully arranged so that nobody was close to any of it when it went off. And it was the smokey stuff, the sparkly stuff—not the blow-your-leg-off black powder. I'm glad for OSHA and all that safety, don't get me wrong, but in many areas American culture clearly takes things too far. We're becoming a society of pasty, pussified people who rely on somebody else filing off life's sharp corners, and padding them with foam rubber. South of the border it's refreshingly normal by comparison, and people are a little more engaged with the situations around them at any time.

Some of the stages we played were low enough that ladies would stand along the front of the stage with their chins directly on top of those squibs; they'd be transformed into puffs of red mist if the powder detonated at the wrong moment. Every show, the stage manager Rod Ossa—a good brother of mine to this day—would be out there with a few other stagehands, running back and forth frantically shooing people away from the stage just before detonation, then running out of harm's way at the last possible instant.

It was a time of playing things fast and loose, touring South America with a large and powerfully connected organization, in an entourage of incredible talent. We were at large, and living large.

When our tourbus rolled into Buenos Aires, there was a banner strung across the entire freeway that said "Bienvenidos Emmanuel" in four-foot tall letters. When we taxied up to the terminal in Lima, hundreds of screaming fans were out on the tarmac to welcome us, like we were the goddamned Beatles. Having been hurriedly escorted into the concourse by security guards, tired and bedraggled from a long flight and not knowing the language, I had a cute Latina news anchor and her camera crew in my face, interviewing me en Espanol as we walked up the concourse. Danny intercepted and saved my gringo butt before I could open my mouth and make an ass of myself.

There were crowds of autograph houndettes standing in vigils outside our hotels all over Argentina, invariably dressed in catholic high school uniforms, and who actually knew my name, which was freaky. Being a tall gringo with long blonde hair, I was instantly recognizable and couldn't walk down the street without creating a stir in some towns. I almost had a repeat of my experience in the third grade while trying to get back into the hotel in one Argentinian town...security guards had to break trail for me: "No shit, there I was, security guards rushing me through a crowd of autograph houndettes into my hotel."

Everywhere we went shows were sold out: Argentina, Uruguay, Peru, Mexico, even a show in Arizona, where the gringos never heard of Emmanuel.

We did five sold-out nights at Teatro Opera in Buenos Aires, one of which was a live international telecast on a TV show called Al Ritmo de la Noche. This was before online streaming, when broadcast TV was still king. Al Ritmo de la Noche was the nightly Latino music show, broadcast to planet Earth's entire Latino population. If you're old enough to remember Soul Train, Solid Gold and The Midnight Hour, imagine all of them rolled into one show. That was Al Ritmo de la Noche. And with all the hoopla surrounding Emmanuel's comeback tour, everyone watched it, in every Latin country. The viewership was truly massive, larger than the Superbowl.

At the appointed moment, we came running out on stage to the screams of a packed house, with massive TV cameras running around on stage, gigantic square lenses in our faces and up our wazoos. My Strat was plugged into that lonely, small-but-tiny MXR Distortion Plus. It was still my solitary pedal, looking as lonely and tiny on that stage as a kitten on a football field. It was plugged into the first of the two Yamaha G100s, which were slaved together. Tony Centron, a great drummer from NYC with great pocket, counted off the first tune, "Chica de Humo". As my pick hit the strings on the downbeat, the faces in front of me lit up like something flashed behind me, and they all gasped. Some pointed behind me. I had no sound—zero—so I turned around and saw one of the finest pyrotechnic displays I've ever beheld: Both amps had blown so spectacularly that they were shooting intense, focused jets of white sparks and white smoke six feet straight up, with flames around the edges. It looked like an effect, not even real, and it was so bright it was almost painful to look at. I immediately took my hands off the guitar and made a point not to touch anything metal, as the stage crew scurried around with fire extinguishers. Nobody was hurt and the band did the song, without my guitar part. We later figured out that the amps had been plugged into 220v power. They were built for 110. No one was hurt, and we had dodged a massive bullet.

But that left me playing live, in front of many millions of people, with nothing for it but to plug the distortion pedal directly into the PA via the stage drop. "No shit, there I was..." Kevin, the front of house soundman, put it through a fat-sounding outboard tube preamp, then attacked it with heavy EQ (tone controls), rolling off the nasty mosquito's treble, inflating the lower mids until it almost burst its belly, then he hosed it all down liberally with reverbs and delays (echoes). Within about 30 seconds of my new signal arriving at his booth, he had slathered enough lipstick on that pig to almost make it useable. I won't say it was pretty, but it worked. And the speed with which that crew got me back up and running was remarkable...I was ready by the second tune.

Kevin had been the house soundman at Madison Square Gardens, among much else over his distinguished career. A Vietnam Vet who had been blown up against a tree by a grenade and had a rod running down his entire spine, he talked a bit like

Wolfman Jack, but with the mannerisms and creative profanity of a sixties-era freak. He reminded me a lot of my Berkeley compatriots back in the day. He was very good at what he did, and very fast. I watched him soundcheck the drums at one venue: he dialed in the kick drum perfectly in about ten seconds. If you've ever been around that process, you know how incredible that is.

He joined the tour after I did, after we had become sort of a tribe. He was the alien newcomer, a full generation older than most of us. Who was this guy? The social environment of a band on tour is something you have to experience to understand. Everyone has to be "a great hang", in other words undeniably great at what they do, easy to get along with, have a great sense of humor (we're all comedians in any working environment, but especially on the road), take no shit but do it in the funniest, nicest and professional way possible, and more than anything, every individual has to be ON the team. Truth be told, we face serious challenges on tour. We have to have each other's backs out there.

We were all sitting on the bus facing forward when Kevin unceremoniously got on, and all conversation abruptly stopped. He froze at the front of the aisle, facing us all. There was an awkward moment of silence as he looked at us all, and we stared back at him.

Two seconds stretched to three. Suddenly he said, "Okay, so I was fuckin' this guy in the butt. But not like a fag...like a VIKING!!" We all cheered and laughed. He knew how to break the ice, and now we all knew he was crazy enough to be a perfect fit.

The creases in his face read like a map of the world. He was like having an old general on board, or maybe a pirate. Aside from his unceasing comedy and antics, he was possibly the most squared away guy we had with us...there was no situation we could face that he hadn't seen, probably many times. He put a rider in his contract that he had to travel with his own racks of outboard gear, and they were both gorgeous. A little bigger than mini-fridges, one had really nice sound processing gear, as you'd expect, and the other had double locking doors in the front that opened to reveal a stack of shelves and drawers, almost all of which contained tools and supplies to help keep the sound flowing on the road. But in one of the deeper drawers, there were fixtures to clamp in a fifth of booze, a martini shaker, two glasses and an ice tray. He stopped short of having the thing open robotically via hydraulics driven by remote-controlled servo units, but that would've been the obvious next version. The man did not fuck around.

I called Kevin the "Front of House Soundman", because as is usually the case, there were two mixing consoles and two engineers: One that ran the sound for the audience, called Front of House (FOH) and another one running the sound for the players onstage, i.e. the monitor console, or "Monitor World".

Mixing monitors is notoriously the most thankless job to have. This was long before the monitor engineer could run the board remotely via bluetooth on an iPad, so categorically speaking, he could never hear what he was doing. At all. To make things worse, many on-stage personnel in the industry failed to comprehend that simple fact (and still do), so monitor engineers were (and still are) the targets of much ire and verbal abuse from prima donnas, divas and dumbshits. One famous crooner beaned his monitor engineer with a gold-plated mic. It's no joke: Being a monitor engineer isn't for the faint of heart or the slow of reflexes.

Our monitor engineer was a wonderfully imperturbable guy named Ken, also a gringo, but who spoke Spanish fluently. He was a very cool, easy hang. Later on, when Kevin left the tour, Ken became FOH engineer. To the credit of our personnel, I never saw anyone giving Ken any attitude. Above a certain level of professionalism and experience, that stuff should go away. And as I said, nowadays the engineer can stand right next to you as the band is playing and dial in your monitor mix on a pad via bluetooth, as you both listen and talk.

Chewy was our lighting and pyro madman. A cousin of Emmanuel's from the scrappy streets of Spain, he was technically very adept, and also a prankster at heart. Legend has it that he broke in and rigged a hotel room to blow with multiple squibs of sparkly pyro when our M.D. opened his door in the Lima Hilton. One time in an airport gate seating area, he slowly crawled and squirmed like a snake, squeezing under the seat that one of our vocalists was occupying, and picked the wallet and passport out of her purse when it was right between her feet. Most of us could see him and acted natural. It was a good joke, but she freaked out almost to the point of tears.

On their tour that year, Genesis had just premiered Intellibeam Lighting (those high-tech computerized lights that move in X and Y axis, together or separately, following a director's programming), and our tour had 'em already, when almost nobody else did. Chewy already had great facility with programming them. He was brilliant for sure, but you had to keep an eye on the guy or you might get badly pranked. Like most of the entourage, I developed the habit of keeping him in front of me.

Rod Ossa was our stage manager, and the glue that held the logistics and technical end of things together. He did a LOT of troubleshooting and scrambling...we'd have been dead in the water without him for sure. He went on to become a good sound engineer / record producer. A native to NYC these days, he's gone on to work as FOH engineer for Sting and other dignitaries. We're still in close contact...I saw him just last year when he was running sound for a tour being put together here at Center Staging in Burbank.

There were some incredible musicians on that tour. Some were pretty interesting characters, many have gone on to great things.

Barry Danielian, on trumpet, went on to be lead trumpeter for Tower of Power—one of three trumpeter friends of mine who have had that gig—and is on tour with Bruce Springteen as I write this, playing to massive, packed arenas. Barry is a badass. He's a martial artist, as are his kids. Some guy made the mistake of trying to carjack Barry at gunpoint in NYC and paid for it dearly. I reunited with him for lunch when I was in Manhattan for a gig just a few years ago, and it was great to catch up. Like most great players he's a deep thinker and the proverbial "log in calm water" when chaos is happening. We all decided that he was the tour's unofficial but de facto M.D., despite one of the keyboardists having been appointed that monicker.

Bob Fransechini is one of the best sax players I've ever worked with—or even heard, for that matter. He's worked with the Mike Stern Band, Willie Colón, Dennis Chambers and the Victor Wooten Trio, among a lot else. He's a monster's monster.

Ozzy Melendez, trombone, has chops the like of which I haven't seen since touring with him, even though I've been working with the top feeders in the LA recording scene. He's worked with Aretha Franklin, Billy Joel, Blood, Sweat & Tears, Bruce Springsteen, Celine Dion, Diana Ross, Gloria Estefan, Jennifer Lopez, Marc Anthony…that's not the half of it, but I'm stopping there to save space. As I write this, he's on tour with Barry in The Boss's band.

Tony Centron has played drums & percussion with Dizzy Gillespie, Spyro Gyra, Ricky Martin and Joe Bonamassa. The man has very deep pocket.

Gene Perez is a great bass player, also renowned among East Coast players for great pocket. He's played with MAW, Willie Colon, Louie Vega, Bernie Williams & Elements of Life and NuyoricanSoul. I always felt a solid foundation and pocket from him.

You already know about Danny Reyes. As I write, he's played multiple arena gigs just this week with the

Zac Brown band, none of which looked to have less than sixty thousand people.

Hector Infanzon is one of the best keyboardists I've ever worked with. He's an orchestral composer / musical director of some renown, and his jazz projects have been very busy over the years, playing festivals all over the globe. When we had a short break in Mexico City, he had his quartet booked into a local jazz club and most of us went in support. I was surprised to discover that the man is a transcendent jazz pianist. You can't have any idea what someone can do from the parts they play on a big tour: things are too controlled, too pop, too scripted. You have to get them into a more organic, conversational situation. Hector blew our minds.

There was a Latina backup vocalist whose actual name I never did know—we all just called her "Guera" for her signature look: An amazing head of long, wavy bright blonde hair. She was gregarious and overtly friendly, even when she was putting someone in their place. She sort of took me under her wing when I first arrived, teaching me Spanish and showing me the ropes of getting around Mexico City.

There was another singer, another keyboardist and another percussionist, whose names I can't quite find in my attic.

Emmanuel was a cool guy to work with and for. He was a superstar I guess—he flew from show to show in his own jet—but he was just one of the guys at heart, despite his proud lineage of having been a famous bullfighter in Spain, like his dad. He was comfortable singing and talking to twenty thousand people in a stadium, and comfortable hanging out with the band backstage.

We almost all died several times one day up in the Andes, when the tourbus's uphill wheels repeatedly left the pavement as we went carefully creeping around reverse-camber hairpin turns in especially steep terrain. One driver was walking ahead, scoping the road and the wheels, giving hand signals to the driver. We were all crowding against the uphill side as ballast, but the uphill wheels were still leaving the pavement. I could see down into those chasms from the turns...hundreds of feet below every hairpin there was twisted metal carnage of large vehicles rusting into the landscape and disappearing below vines. Every time the bus slowly touched back down, we heaved a loud collective sigh of relief, then had our own little moments of private introspection. There were about half a dozen of those nerve-jangling turns.

The size of a tourbus, as you probably know, makes it incompatible for many situations. Major cities in Latin America tend to have lots of low power lines over the streets, even the major arteries. In several towns, we'd have to creep down the streets with one of the drivers walking ahead scoping things, then have to back out even more slowly.

In San Juan, Argentina, the World Rally circuit race was in town and every hotel was booked. We had no reservations because our schedule had changed. We had been on the bus for 24 hours (it didn't have bunks, since we were supposed to have hotels every night), and we spent another 4 hours looking for accommodations. I remember Manny yelling into lobby phones and pay phones in his thick Panamanian "Spanglish", trying to find something, anything, as we crept from hotel to hotel, constantly running afowl of the low power lines.

After hours of searching, we were finally saved when Manny found us a bordello. The ladies were cleared out before we arrived...I have no idea where they slept, or how much the organization had to pay, or to whom. I can only hope it was safe for the ladies. The Puticlub had a long corridor with a wall of unfinished plywood on one side, with doors sawed into it at regular intervals. Each door had two iron gate hinges on one side and a simple iron padlock hasp on the other, much like a low-budget Hollywood band rehearsal space.

Each "door" opened into a room, and each room had a theme. Mine had garish orange shag carpeting and a round bed that spun on a raised dais, beneath a mirror on the ceiling. Like most of us, I slept in my clothes on top of the bedspread.

In the morning, we met the family that ran the place. Not management per se, not pimps: these people were basically mom-and-pop hoteliers, with children, living in a surprisingly wholesome-looking wing of the building that was like a normal house. They cooked us all a magnificent breakfast. They were very nice, made us feel like honored guests, and that food was truly excellent.

I left there with the antique skeleton key that had opened the antique padlock to my room still in my pocket. Having realized it too late to return it, I hung it from the zipper handle of my leather jacket as a souvenir. I still have it.

* * *

Routing is a thing on a tour. Routing is code-speak for what your order of bookings does to travel logistics. If you're playing a series of shows heading up the East coast from Florida to New York, say, that's great routing, especially if they're in linear order. But if you've got one outlier show in the middle of that run that's west of the Mississippi, that's not good routing.

At roughly 300,000 square miles, the Argentine Pampas is the largest plain I've ever seen. Flat as a pool table, the major cities are arrayed around the Pampas in a vaguely oblong pattern. If your routing takes you in linear sequence around the oblong, travel times average four or five hours and you're golden. That had been our booking calendar, before the schedule got shuffled by flood-related cancellations. What we wound up with was more like a star pattern crossing the Pampas repeatedly, with average travel times of 24 hours. It didn't take many days of that before the driver of the equipment truck ran out of bennies, nodded off and drove into the drink of the flooded Pampas. He was fine, but I still have pictures of the scene we pulled up to an hour or so later in the tour bus: a semi trailer half-submerged and tilted at 45 degrees, with people fishing gear out from under the water. Fortunately, most of us had our instruments with us on the bus.

In Mar del Plata—four or five hours south of B.A. and the farthest South I've ever been—we played to a packed stadium of twenty thousand. When we left the hotel in the shuttle to the stadium, not one soul was on the streets—Argentina was playing Mexico in the Copa America Final, so everyone not at the stadium was watching the game. The town was completely, totally barren of any human presence out of doors. About three blocks into our drive, we suddenly heard the eerie sound of thousands of people screaming from indoors, then just as suddenly, every single door opened and thousands of people flooded the streets in manic celebration. We didn't have to ask who won, but it took awhile to creep through the crowd to the stadium.

There's a scene in Spinal Tap where the band gets lost in the catacombs below a stadium on the way to the stage as the crowd above is cheering for their arrival. It pains me to say it, but I lived that in Mar del Plata. We were all prepared and primed for the show and it was time, so the security guard came and collected us all from the dressing rooms to lead the way to the stage, as the crowd above chanted rhythmically. The entourage started heading down a long corridor that ended in the distance at a "T" intersection. After walking about twenty feet I realized I had forgotten something vital, ran back to my dressing room and got it, came back out and they had disappeared around the corner. Not knowing which way they had gone, I ran up to the intersection and looked: nothing in either direction. Shit. Thus began my panicked rat-in-a-maze quest for the way out..."No shit, there I was, lost in a maze below the stadium just like Spinal Tap..."

Then I heard the crowd erupt as the band ran on stage, then the first tune begin without me, and shit got real. The Spinal Tap scene was in my head, but my mantra was "Thisisn'tfuckingfunnyI'msofucked...thisisn'tfuckingfunnyI'msofucked...thisisn'tfuckingfunnyI'msofucked". I found my way up there before the end of the first tune, but was waved off and had to hide, then run on stage after the tune was done, so that it looked intentional. I didn't get fired or even in much trouble, but I felt terrible about it for a long time. I should probably be able to chuckle about it now, but the memory still stings.

There were a few experiences that really illuminated the things that I took for granted living in America: a badly overloaded 747 that I felt actually graze the fence at the end of the runway with its right rear landing gear during a takeoff that almost didn't happen; a carload of Gypsies that pulled the tourbus over in the middle of nowhere to try to rip us off—not a robbery, just a comedically bad attempt to read our palms with ham-handed efforts to lift wrist watches and wallets, which we found entertaining; seeing people living in low, round mud and thatch huts on the Pampas (though to be realistic, millions of Americans still live a lot like that, without running water, on reservations in the SouthWest); seeing the abject poverty afflicting hungry homeless families on the streets of many cities we played, as we traveled in our comfortable "rich people" bubble. America wasn't as bad then as it is now, and the contrast was more jarring. The U.S. is a lot more like a third-world country in many places now than it was during the nineties, of course. But to quote Gore Vidal, "at least we have the decency to deny it."

One kid, about 11 years old, was panhandling us as we hurried into an airport. We were running a bit late heading to a different country and didn't have time to change our currency at the Cambio booth, so we just gave what we had to the kid. It was pocket change to us, but assuming he survived the walk home, it probably fed his extended family for a year.

In Peru my work visa expired, and Manny had to take me to the captain of the local federales' office. Doing it the official, bureaucratic way was a non-starter, since it would have taken way too long, and besides: That's just not how things are done down yonder.

They chatted for a few minutes, as Manny and the captain politely discussed the pleasant afternoon weather and how the tour was going, then nonchalantly pivoted to the amount of the bribe required to get the magic rubber stamp out of the drawer. It would normally have been $200 USD, but because I was in the band it was twenty bucks, and the man got some choice tickets to our show. I happily paid the man and we were on our way.

I eventually bugged out of that tour over concerns regarding management. When I returned to the states, walking out of the Bradley terminal at LAX I had a strong sense that I had returned to the developed world from something more like the wild west. It bears mention that nowadays, when I return to US soil, it sometimes feels the other way around.

When I mention Emmanuel to non-Latino Americans, I still get blank stares. Down there we were truly big time, but inside America's borders it's like none of that even exists. What an insular country are we.

Chapter 17
Climbing

In order to be a good performing artist, you need a superhuman ability to focus, and you need to be able to relax so you can calmly walk the line of the positive amidst chaos. You also need to be very, very adaptable. Being up in your head doesn't help you think clearly, or troubleshoot a puzzle, or adapt to what's going on around you. So you need a hat trick that puts things in perspective and calms you.

For the most part, the secret weapon enabling me to be calm in situations that might panic other people is my experience as a rock climber. When things go badly wrong, I can compare that situation to some bad pickles I've been in. I'll use an example from this book: When those amps blew sky high on stage at Teatro Opera in front of millions of viewers, the first thing I reflexively did was to consciously compare that situation to a couple of times in the vertical domain when the odds of my surviving the next thirty seconds were not good. It dropped things right into perspective. I remember glancing down at that nice solid stage floor, and feeling all the security of having my feet firmly planted on a large horizontal plane.

And it doesn't have to be climbing—you've had your experiences with the pickle jar. We've all had iffy moments behind the wheel. Maybe you've been in a large earthquake or two, or been launched over a horse's head, or almost gotten squashed when you had to ride a bicycle partially under a cruising semi truck at the bottom of a steep hill when you were both doing 50, or almost gotten incinerated when your pickup truck got in a tangle with a petroleum hauler freshly loaded with 10,000 gallons of gas. Maybe you got stepped on by a large bear while lying in your sleeping bag. Maybe all of the above, as is the case with yours truly. Whatever your body of experience is, you've no doubt had close calls. Use those.

For me, though, it's climbing. And not just because it's a great means of comparing levels of actual danger: The thing I love most about climbing is the totality of focus. Nothing in my experience requires such focus—not getting giant air on skis, not making love, not playing over tough chord changes, not anything but managing my very effing physical survival itself. There have been moments behind the wheel of an out-of-control car, when I had to drive my ass off or certainly die, and some moments on skis like when I had to flip myself away from that death spike on that tree at Mt Ashland—those things required a total level of focus. But situations like that are unpredictable and, one might hope, few and far between.

Climbing is done systematically, by the numbers, and if you're climbing within one or two grades of your max ability level, on a sketchy highball boulder problem or leading a runout over a bad fall line, or with bad pro (all of that is just code-speak for "if you fail to cut these moves, you get hurt or worse"), I guarantee you're not thinking about your relationship or your bank account. The world literally disappears. It's a beautifully pure state of consciousness that I've been able to reliably attain only through climbing. You relax, you focus, you exhale and cut the moves, and nothing else exists. Things become so clear it seems like you can see molecules, and it's not just momentary: you sustain that state, because you have to. None of your problems or worries from the world outside of doing those moves can follow you. It's a wonderful purity of being.

My three life-changing injuries have each had their effects on my career, and I've managed to overcome pretty much all of the limitations they tried to impose on me. I'm including the stories behind them to illustrate what can be accomplished in music with a less-than-perfectly intact body. The lumbar spine injury at Universal was the first.

On November 23rd 1993, I got my tit in a ringer on a climb and met with Kryptonite for the second time. I had been trying to make a first ascent of a line at an area known to SoCal climbers as Indian Wells, and things didn't go my way. It was my own stupid fault, having let testosterone make decisions instead of my head. I found myself about 140 feet off deck, starting the third pitch, 25 feet out from the belay on a diagonal line with no gear in, the hoped-for line having petered out and become something like part of a giant vertical funnel. I had run out of holds and momentum, and was staying in place with body friction, tension and hope, spread-eagled against rock that was mostly glass-smooth. It was a 50-plus foot pendulum if I fell. And I hadn't realized it until I started feeling myself starting to slip, but the pendulum would probably saw the rope along some feldspar crystals I had just noticed, sending me to my demise on the pile of death-impaling boulders at the base. Climbing ropes don't snap under load, but they can easily cut under the right circumstance, and I had set things up perfectly for that to happen. Also, in my impetus-driven desire to ascend, I had overlooked the fuel gauge of my guns (biceps and forearms). They had almost nothing left, so I couldn't downclimb the sequence. I had to choose between the probability of falling if I tried to downclimb—resulting in probable death—or jumping down to the right in the direction of the belay, certainly breaking some bones, but not cutting the rope. I chose life. I impacted right at the feet of my climbing partner and belayer Gordon, who later said he had some nightmares afterwards.

Translated: I screwed up. Badly. I almost paid for it with my life and put my new girlfriend at risk for her safety (she was napping below, on the first belay ledge).

Instead of paying the price I (or we) might have, I got let off with a badly shattered right heel and ankle cartilage, fragmented fibula, a few other minor fractures in the joint and a big contusion on the back of my noggin.

After the fall, I was dangling in overhanging terrain about 25 feet below the belay ledge, but the holds were positive enough for me to swing in, reconnect and use my three good limbs to climb back up. Full of adrenaline, my guns were fine now. Once I had mantled onto the belay ledge, Gordon and I watched as my right ankle visibly inflated in real time, as if somebody was blowing up a balloon. "Well, that ain't good", I said.

I took my climbing shoe off while I still could. I was able to rappel off right to my car, which happened to be parked at the base of the route, and we were able to simply drive to the closest ER, about 90 minutes away in Lancaster.

It was the weekend, I was up in the area to do a gig in a very small scrub-desert town called California City, with a classic rock cover band of awesome LA players who were a lot of fun to play with. Gordon and I had agreed to meet in Indian Wells to make the most of things with an afternoon of climbing. The gig was at a bowling alley and paid fifty bucks. No autographs, please.

The X-ray tech in Lancaster said it looked like a bad dislocation. They put me in a half-cast to get me through the weekend and told me to be damned sure to report to County / USC hospital Monday morning. They gave me some painkillers, not that I was in that much pain yet. One odd thing about bad injuries is that for the first 12 to 24 hours, it's common for your endorphins to handle the pain. They're extremely good at that. The next day, well, that's a different story.

After the hospital in Lancaster, we doubled back to California City and I played the gig, sitting in a chair with my foot elevated. The band was 'Four out of Five

Dentists", a four-piece of really fine players and a rhythm guitarist / frontman / bandleader who had some of the best jokes I've ever stolen. He had the voice of an FM disc jockey. "Remember folks, usually you have to go to a bowling alley to get entertainment of this quality!" was one of his better lines. He actually said that that night, then went pie-eyed as he realized where he was. The musicians laughed, as the manager scowled. Everyone in the band had waist-length hair and made a point of dressing "hard rock" for gigs. For our "break" song (a short ditty a band plays as their break is being announced), we always stood with our legs majestically splayed, hung our heads and tossed our hair like we were Megadeath, while playing the cleanest, most lilty, jazziest and elegant sounding version of "Girl from Ipanema" possible. Alas, chair-bound as I was, I couldn't partake in that schtick.

 Purely by chance, my girlfriend and I had run into some good friends of ours at the hospital, Brian and Kathi D., who sometimes hired me to play in their band, which was also always a blast. They joined us for the gig. So it was a fun hang, despite circumstances. I had a feeling it would be my last time playing live for awhile. I was right.

 By Monday, the foot had swollen so badly it was a honeydew melon with toes. A CT scan at County/USC gave us the correct diagnosis: I had exploded the calcaneus (heel bone) left to right and drove it up three quarters of an inch into the cartilage between it and the weight-bearing surfaces above, shattering the cartilage. The fibula was in fragments at the bottom, the cuboid and talus might or might not be damaged and some other things were cracked, but they weren't really concerned with that. It was all about the heel and the joint cartilage. Surgery was scheduled for ten days later, since the foot was too swollen to operate on. They were talking about a likely fusion, which would hobble me to some degree for life. Ten days later the swelling hadn't gone down—it was still a honeydew melon with toes—but they had to go in anyway.

I remember waking up on the table in the middle of the procedure; there was some pounding going on that was moving my whole body (no feeling, though) and they were cranking Hendrix! The anesthesiologist noticed me lifting my head and trying to speak, and quickly reached for a knob, knocking me back out. I was trying to say, "Please let me stay awake! I wanna watch this!" Ah, well. Opportunities lost.

The surgical team, led by the best podiatric surgeon in SoCal, came and saw me after I woke up, big smiles on their faces. They showed me the new X-rays, sporting my new V-shaped plate and six long screws, and said they were really pleased that they were able to fish most of the bone fragments out of the joint, so I didn't have to have the joint fused! One doc pointed to the Xray and said, "See all those empty holes in the steel plate? That's where we couldn't screw into the calcaneus, because it would be like screwing into jello. You basically reduced it to powder."

I stayed in the ward for five more nights, laid way back with the foot way up and in traction, morphine pump going with the trigger in my hand, just riding that magic red button while cranking Brecker Brothers on my Walkman and practicing my knot craft with some 4-mil perlon.

I was pretty useless for the first couple of months, totally dependent on my girlfriend to take care of me. We had only just met a month or so before the accident, so it was a strain on both of us, but she showed up like a champ. On January 17, seven and a half weeks after the accident, when I was still unable to be upright more than a few seconds at a time, the Northridge quake hit and made things all the more complicated in our lives, especially hers.

I did let myself get talked into doing one nicely lucrative gig, for a high-dollar contractor who for some reason was fresh out of available guitarists. It was a fundraiser bash that winter in Aspen, attended by Michael Jordan, Ivana Trump and the like. The band was an 11 or 12 piece of fantastic cats from LA. I was up-front about my circumstances, explaining that I was still in the cast, taking painkillers, hadn't even had the stitches taken out yet, could barely get around on crutches and would need full logistical support. I still couldn't get my foot below my heart for more than a minute or two, let alone set up gear, so they arranged to have some guys in the band help me out. I did the gig with that gigantic, ugly cast on a chair in front of me. They draped it with the universal tool for hiding anything ugly on a stage: the almighty black tablecloth.

Rehab was a bell curve that lasted three years, the first few months of which I had to be in a wheelchair to go any place. Even knowing that it was temporary, being in a chair was a mindfuck. I've always had immense respect for anyone who lives in a chair, but since that experience, it has increased greatly. I asked the doc on one follow-up visit if I'd ever run again. He paused a beat and said, "Mr. Fry, I really can't overstate the severity of this injury. It would be wise to manage expectations".

By a year and a half later, I was doing wind sprints in wet sand. I limped like hell the next day, but goddammit I did it. It was along the shore of Horseshoe Lake in Mammoth on a gorgeous day, with that incredible view past the Mammoth Crest and Crystal Crag, up the ramparts and gorgeous snow-striped chutes of the Duck drainage. My baseball cap flew off my head I was running so fast, and I was crying and yelling with happiness as I ran. The lesson I learned, yet again, is this: Never underestimate the human body's ability to heal and overcome. That ankle isn't quite normal, and my right lower leg is three quarters of an inch shorter than my left, but I walk normally. I can tour, play shows, make flights on time and load gear just fine. I hiked Mt. Whitney some years later, putting in 20 or so miles on the last day while carrying

35 pounds. I typically hike a couple of miles a day. If there's an effect it has on me professionally, it's just that I've had to learn to use my left foot on the wah-wah. It remains a work in progress.

Now, if I need to put a dicey situation into perspective, I just transport myself to that glass-smooth scoop over all that exposure at Indian Wells, feel myself starting to slide, look down at those death-impaling boulders at the bottom and the line of crystals that want to saw the rope. Et voila, whatever situation I'm in isn't so bad.

We adapt, we overcome, we get past things. The body is an incredibly capable machine if you give it reason to be, as is the mind. Whether or not you're going to live a life in music, don't let the world around you dictate your expectations of yourself. And never take any shit from the status quo.

Chapter 18
Becoming

As I restrengthened my foot and body, I also started focusing more on getting a better grade of work in town. It started working. I know it sounds like some rainbow unicorn shit, but it's true: The energy you put out into the universe comes back. If you want a certain thing to happen and focus your energy in that direction, that's the direction you'll go. I started recording and arranging for TV and Film, and produced a couple of indies. John Pena called me to do all the guitars on saxophonist Corbett Wall's record on EMI, produced by John and David Garfield. We did all the guitars in a day. It's a great album.

My good brother Barry Coffing had his first number-one hit right around that time: "How do you Talk to an Angel" was a soft Pop/Rock ballad associated with a TV show called The Heights, and that instantly made him a lot busier and sought-after. He started using me a lot for guitars on everything from Disney sessions to broadcast TV things to records he was producing. His business partner Sam Wynans did a lot of similar work, and was also a great arranger / orchestrator. I played on some of Sam's productions too.

One day we did some adaptations for Disney that were a really cool exercise: Duplicate an already existing production. These have been used in TV and Film for decades. You've heard many of them, and probably never knew that they weren't the original production and artist. Such is the magic talent pool and bag of tricks in LA: We can be really devious bastards when we need to be.

The reason for duplicating a production in the studio, as always, is money. The cost of the license to use a hit song in a TV show or film—in other words, the writing and the arrangement—is typically half the cost of adding the license to use the actual master recording of that song, and that difference is usually more than what it costs to just hire some good cats to duplicate the thing.

And it's an interesting process: You have the original to refer to, so all you have to do is get every instrument to sound exactly that way, and get every musician to play exactly those parts. You have a crystal clear idea of the goal, which makes it something like paint-by-numbers; very unlike the usual creative process. We turned "Walk This Way" by Aerosmith into "Womp This Way"...evidently Disney was launching something that went by the monicker "Womp"...and the Aerosmith thing was pretty easy to duplicate. But then we did "We Will Rock You" by Queen (We Will Womp You), and therein, to quote The Bard, lies the rub.

The only way to sound like Brian May is to be Brian May. Those guitars of his are now available as a retail item, but back then only his originals existed, and they were hand-built by him, with a lot of iconically unique wiring and other design features. His brilliant use of Vox AC30 amps, and the tone he gets out of them, is of course the stuff of legend. Not only is my name not Brian May, I didn't have his axe and I didn't have an AC30. I had a Strat and a Boogie. As the pow'rs that be are my witness, I did my absolute best to get my rig to sound like Sir Brian's. Barry and Sam were both happy, and I never heard the final mixes—which can change a LOT of things—but honestly, my tracks themselves were a far cry from sounding like the real thing.

Those versions were for a private Disney corporate launch party and they never saw the light of day, so we just enjoyed a fun hang in a good studio and getting paid to do it. As is commonly the case, the top-dog players on that were amazing company.

* * *

"TV Mixes" are what we call a mix of a production with its melody track removed. This is what you hear when a star appears on Oprah or some such, and sings their latest hit live, but over recorded tracks instead of a live band. It's fairly standard procedure to include TV mixes when producing someone.

Barry had some orphaned TV mixes from a well-funded project he had produced, whose deal had gone south. They were bound for the dust pile, so late one night he had me come over to the studio and wildcat some improvised guitar melodies over them. These were mostly very lush Pop / R&B ballads, beautifully arranged, with live orchestra and an eyebrow-raising list of top cats playing featured parts. Very expensive stuff. With a band that size, recorded and mixed that nicely, and with such top-shelf cats involved, the orphans I was playing over had to have had a budget of around a hundred grand, in nineties money.

We went from song to song to song, no charts, no listening to a song first, just a single pass in "go for it" mode. The first time I heard each one of those songs was also my only pass recording melody over it. It was very "Zen". I have no idea what Barry did with those, if anything, but it was a fun way to pass an evening if nothing else.

Any call from Barry is likely to be a good one to get. He and Sam were running a pretty busy production schedule for quite a while, and would have me over to do a checkerboard of guitar tracks on several different projects in one session, to fill things in a bit. Power chords and nosedives for the ending of "Million Dollar Pyramid", followed by some things for Ruth McCartney, then a solo on this other thing over here, then a quick slide guitar hit on that other thing over there. From the same chair in the same session I'd make noise on a whole list of things: Hang Time, Tazzercise, The Best Things about Christmas...I'd drive away after an hour or so, having touched up a lot of productions, unassociated with each other except for having been built by the same production team.

Even before the internet, it was a common thing not to be in the same room at the same time as the people I was making the music with. Some of the names on my discography are people I never met: Michael MacDonald, Tiffany, Roz Streisand and Kidd Glove are just a few of the many people with whom I appear on recordings, but have never met. Nowadays, recording separately is how the vast majority of music gets done, because once the internet and home studios happened, everybody started recording their tracks at home. People who lived two miles apart would record separately, and not only for convenience: a home studio tends to be optimized for the specific needs of that person and his or her instruments. Mine is best suited for recording guitars and other fretted instruments, though I also do horn and vocal dates here. A horn player will have different mics and preamps that are good matches for horns, a drummer's rig will be optimized for that, and so on. If you hire me to play on your project, you'll want me to do it at home, surrounded by all of my gear and tools, where I can take my time dialing in sounds, ideas and performances to a degree that can only happen in the comfort of home.

With that said, there are a lot of things that are best done with everyone in the same place at the same time. Most things, in fact. We just don't live in a world where that's very common anymore. Back in the nineties, if you needed to record a TV theme song, say, you took proceedings into a studio geared for ensembles large enough for your needs, and cut it in one session.

The phone rang at almost 11:30 one night in the mid-nineties. I picked up and it was Barry:

"Yo, Byron! Sorry for calling so late. Please tell me you're available for an AM hit tomorrow in Burbank. John Blaylock and I just found out that a ditty we pitched to the suits at CBS for the theme song for The New Newlywed Game got accepted!"

"Dude!! Congrats! Holy shit, that's great!!"

"Yeah...but the thing is, they need it by end of day tomorrow."

"They need it PRODUCED by then?"

"Eee-yep."

"Wow. Yeah, I can be there. That's short notice, even for TV, but how else would it be, right?"

"Tell me about it."

"Do you have all the players?"

"I'm thinking the usual guys from the "abuse" list— Marc Huganberger on keys, Osama Afifi on bass, Carlos Hatem on percussion, Carl Lott on drums, you on guitar, and some horns."

This was, for the most part, our lineup from a very cool "club band on steroids" that Barry put together for a very cool house gig at Luna Park in West Hollywood, one of LA's premier trendy rooms at the time. We had thrown down every Wednesday night with a really cool song list, and had a blast doing it.

"So basically it's the guys", I said. "Cool."

Then there was a pause, and he said "Y'know, I'm just thinkin'..."

"Ohgawd, don't do that..."

"Well, with the horns coming, I'm wondering if we shouldn't have some charts of some kind, or something."

It was only then that I realized his situation, and the point of development this thing was actually in.

"Holy shit Bee, you don't have an arrangement and charts?"

"Uh...nope. The chords are super simple though..."

"That doesn't matter," I said emphatically, "horns can't do anything together without being arranged...you need charts, man!"

"Well, do you think you could knock something together? It doesn't have to be too involved..."

Barry is a songwriter—an extremely good one, also an extremely good producer. And like most great songwriters, he's not a super technical sort of guy musically, which is precisely why he has number one hits and makes so much more money than I do. Nobody who has ever scored and orchestrated something, then extracted, laid out and copied the individual parts—however simple—would ever say it's not involved. Barry is my brother, we have a lot of fun working together, and he needed some help.

"What's the call time?"

"9:30 tomorrow morning."

"That's ten hours, less loading and drive time..." my Grove training kicked in. "Yeah, I'll handle it. As we used to say in school, 'I slept last year'. You'll have to toss me some extra dough."

"No prob. And there's more...you're especially gonna love this..."

"Hit me, Baby."

"We need a 90-second version, a 60-second version and a 30-second version of the theme s..."

"Are you fucking kidding me?" My heart started to race a bit. I started feeling a bit clammy and queasy.

"...as well as bumpers that are 18 seconds, 15 seconds, 12 seconds, 10 seconds, several each of 6 second, 5 second, 4 second and 3 second, and I shit you not, we need a one-second bumper." To clarify, a "bumper" is that short cue of music you hear between scenes, or when a show comes back from commercial.

I let several beats go by as I took a slow, deep breath and waited for the room to stop spinning. Then I heard my disembodied voice calmly say, "Okay, then. How does it go?"

It was an up-tempo Jump-Swing Boogie, which he said needed to sound sort of Stray Cats-like. He played me a cassette tape of it over the phone, phrase-by-phrase, while I transcribed. Then I got to work. I didn't even use a score, I just went direct to individual parts, which saved time, and I did a master rhythm chart (one chart that everyone in the rhythm section used), for the simple reason that there was no time to do otherwise.

Thanks to Grove, I pulled it off. I had to triage what I could and couldn't do with the time I had. As much as possible, I planned to use every chord, phrase and note I wrote in several ways, on several things. I didn't write more than one or two of those bumpers, for instance—for the most part, we just cannibalized phrases from the main arrangement that had the right length, rehearsed the band a couple of times through to sanitize its presentation, recorded it, then went fishing for the next phrase to cannibalize. Barry and I also did some adaptations of the arrangement's "roadmap" on the fly during the session, to get the different lengths of theme song needed. I think I remember doing a 30-second chart and a 60-second chart, but I'm not sure. The 90-second (closing credits theme) just had an extended boogie-woogie piano solo at the end by Marc...as always, he absolutely slayed. You just do what you can, with whatever you've got. There's almost always a way to make things work.

There were a lot of other things I did with Barry in the nineties; other films, other records. Then as now, it was always a busy time in his world. It seemed like every movie or TV show that came out of this town had a song of his on board.

One of the greatest solids he did for me was to let me use his studio to mix an album of mine while he was out of town—he had a much better mixing environment and rig than me. Alas, my timing was comedically bad: I finished it right about the same time that the digital apocalypse was really ramping up and major labels were tumbling into the abyss. But I haven't forgotten that favor. And I was able to shop the album to a few labels before things entered free-fall.

* * *

If you haven't figured it out yet, I really never cared for the classic business model of record labels. The record industry was founded, primarily, as a money laundering mechanism for the mob, which explains why nepotism is rampant, musical creatives are scoffed at and the money flows uphill at all times. The success stories you hear—the artists you know about, in other words—are the exceptions. On average, for every album that got released, nineteen others would be shelved. The one successfully released and promoted album in twenty would more than reimburse the recording budgets of the others, while in many cases, due to technicalities in contract language that no musician could be expected to understand, the hapless artists whose records were shelved were sometimes required to reimburse their recording budgets, having already spent said budget making the album they had been contracted to make with that budget. The riders in the contracts that could enable record companies to do this were usually erroneously stated and hard to shoot down in court, especially in a town where the companies held so much influence. The legal world has zero clue whatsoever about music, so the company could make up any far-flung musical premise they wanted and present it as a breach of contract, and any attorney defending an artist would be hard-pressed to convey any understanding to the court as to why the company was full of it. 'Twas ever thus.

And the A&R (artists and repertoire) executives were sometimes cool and qualified, but most tended to be crass, abrasive, overtly hostile to prospective signees, and radiantly ignorant about music.

It was the world we lived in though, and I needed to get this album out there. What I needed was called a

P and D deal (pressing and distribution), so hunting I went. Any A&R person had a backlog of a couple of thousand demos or albums to listen to, so mailing it in and waiting for a reply was a fool's errand. You had to sit down face-to-face, or it was guaranteed that nothing would happen. But A&R execs didn't do face-to-face appointments, so one had to be inventive.

Those companies were nothing if not competitive, so I used that. My approach was to tell the secretary or gatekeeper of company A to tell their boss that their competition at company B liked my album, but I wanted to give company A a chance to counter-bid before I signed with company B. It worked like a charm: I got several appointments. Sony actually nibbled at the bait—their A&R guy was actually a qualified professional—but I didn't like the terms.

The most memorable appointment I had was with an A&R person at Geffen named Blaark Signor (not the real name). On the appointed day, I drove to downtown Hollywood, emptied my wallet slaying the parking dragon, navigated a sidewalk crowded with tourists, goth-rockers, junkies and dog shit until I was standing in front of Geffen, looking up at its imposing, glassy edifice. I walked through the front doors, took the elevator up and located the office; the receptionist waved me by. I walked through the massive double inner doors into a large, quiet office with a nice view of the Hollywood Hills, sparsely furnished with a couple of chairs, a massive desk piled high with cassette tapes, and the obligatory gold records on the wall. Behind the desk, in a huge leather executive's chair, was a 14-year-old girl.

"Hi" I said, "I'm here to meet Blaark Signor. Any idea when he'll be back?"

"I'm Blaark", she said, a bit apprehensively, almost apologetically.

[I took an imperceptible beat, one eyebrow reflexively raised] "Oh. I see. Please pardon me...you're a bit young to be doing this, aren't you?"

"I mean...I guess so..."

"If you don't mind my asking, how old are you?"

"I'm fourteen."

This poor girl's expression and comportment, throughout the entire meeting, clearly said "Please don't be mad, I know this is ridiculous, I don't belong here, I'm way out of my depth and I have no idea what I'm doing."

"My uncle gave me this job" she continued, "and told me to find music that goes... 'up'". When she said the word "up", she made a shrugging gesture, palms toward the ceiling.

"'Up'?"

"Yes, he just said to find music that goes...'up'." Again, that shrugging gesture.

"You mean, like it crescendos and builds? Or that it climbs in range or melodic contour, or that it modulates key?"

"Umm...Idunno...I guess...maybe...he just said to find music that goes... 'up'". Yet again, that shrugging gesture.

"Well, every song on this album does all of those things, that's pretty standard procedure in making music. Tell me, do you play an instrument?"

"No..."

"Do you sing?"

"No..."

"Do you have any musical training of any kind whatsoever?"

"Um, no...all I know is that my uncle said to find music that goes..."

We both said it: "Up".

Another beat or two went by as we looked at each other and I pondered the possibility that this was a hoax and I was on "Candid Camera". I looked around the room and saw no holes in the walls that would hide any lenses, and that appointment had been difficult to make. I decided it wasn't a hoax.

She had me add my cassette to the gigantic stacks on her desk, and I left. I drove away pissed at the waste of time and effort, but also laughing, because: Hollywood. Whatcha gonna do. To this day, I wish I had been able to video tape the whole thing. I never got that album out into the world, outside of family and friends.

Chapter 19
Playing In, Playing Out

Among grownup professionals around that time, I started booking my own fusion projects into the good listening rooms along Ventura Boulevard. Seeing my name on The Baked Potato's marquis was both humbling and validating. I called my fusion lineups various things, the invention of good names not being a strength of mine: "Fried Guise", "Plus Eleven", "Byron Fry and Friends"—it was almost always a different name. We did some good throwing down, taking serious liberties reinventing Jazz standards in ways that were sufficiently unhinged to qualify for The Noiseletting. Jazz Standards are now being called The Great American Songbook, and I like that. "Standards" always struck me as a glib and dismissive monicker for what comprises much of the finest writing of the last century. Not that that protected these iconic pieces from our chainsaws: we turned them into any combination of genres we dug: R&B, funk, rock, Latin, fusion, math prog...nothing was safe from our mills and welders. That's still the policy hereabouts.

I conscripted various luminaries into my dubious enterprise: Morrie Louden on bass—an inhumanly talented cat, who has since moved to the other coast—also Larry Antonino on bass, just as incredible and a true pocketmeister, as was Larry Seymour. Drummers ranged from Dan Potruch to David Anderson to Steve Stephens to Ronnie Ciago to Pat Bautz. Keyboards were either Bob Luna or Marc Huganberger. I sometimes had a sax player, usually Mike Acosta, sometimes Steve Grove, and for a brief interval there was a somewhat lighter version of this called "Copper Lode", with Janelle Sadler on vocals and Pat Bautz on drums. It felt great to be putting some good projects out and about, and to be making good noises with such blindingly good players. It was the kind of thing that can be thrown together, as we say, "Only in L.A."

As I've said, LA has the best musical talent pool on Earth, gathered here from all compass points of the planet in service of its almighty industry. At the behest of some corporate brass or other, these players make their living by applying otherworldy talent to the creation of just the right noises to drive the sales of everything from retail products to Films and TV shows to concert tickets to records and many other things.

But these players—these gods—have voices that you've never really heard, and if you ever hear them seriously flex their muscles, you'd better have your seatbelt fastened. And you have to know where to go. It's sort of like the smaller the joint, the more incredibly the players can cut loose. Certain little cafes, cuban restaurants, corner bars, even some of the smaller listening venues, are known and beloved among musicians as outlets for The Noiseletting—the unleashing of the creative voice—like so many flowers growing up and blossoming through cracks in the industry's grimy and bustling sidewalk, surrounded by soot, gum and cigarette butts. The musical events that are the most important to musicians around here happen in little hidey-holes. Hands down, the coolest, most enjoyable and most important gigs I've ever done have been in small listening rooms. In fact, some of the heaviest playing experiences I've had, and with some of the heaviest and most important company I've played with, took place in living rooms.

* * *

Also during the nineties, I got pretty busy doing "casuals" on the weekends. "Casual" is code-speak for the unlikely reality of highly overqualified players, fresh from recording sessions or in town from world tours, playing a doinky songlist at a stranger's wedding, bar mitzvah or office party, while sweating in a tux.

I could put on my tux and make as much for one night as I used to make in a whole week of playing the nightclub circuit. Bands were pieced together weekly by a few different competing contracting offices, each of whom had their stable of talent and liked to think there was no overlap of personnel. Let's just say that that worked on a "don't ask, don't tell" basis.

All the players in these stables basically know all the same songs and arrangements ("the book", we call it) so, even though these lineups changed from week to week, it always sounded pretty polished despite the fact that most offices rarely rehearsed their talent. The players tended to be pretty top-shelf. People who were out touring with the Eagles or Elton John one week would be playing a wedding or corporate party in Bel Air or Laguna the next, if they had nothing else going on. I was always in proud company on casuals. Although the song list always had some dorky things and we were dressed like waiters, the pocket always grooved hard, because the cats were so good. That's how that works, you see: I like playing just about anything if the players are good, and nothing if they aren't.

All the contracting offices have identical business models: They charge the client at least double the amount per musician that they pay the musicians. They get clients through wedding planners, photographers and hotel food and beverage directors, with whom they curate their relationships carefully, and whom they incentivize creatively.

These offices make great bank and have opulent headquarters in places like Beverly Hills, where fetching and well-dressed office girls serve prospective clients champagne and strawberries, while showing them expensively produced highlight reels of the bands doing their magic.

The gig stories from casuals are myriad. I mentioned the brawl that broke out at one wedding, winding up in the pool with everyone laughing. Toward the end of every casual, people are more inebriated than they would be at a bar, maybe because these are all special events in these people's personal lives, so they get more into the spirit of things and toss back more alcohol. Whatever the reason, the last hour or two tend to be messy.

And the decor can be over the top. Somewhere in the mid-to-late nineties, I played the bar mitzvah of the son of the president of Sony records. Each table's centerpiece cost twenty-five hundred dollars. Some wedding planners really feel they need to prove something, to do something more outlandish than the competition. Mother of Bride can easily be made to buy into that, so it becomes a sort of Smiths-and-Jones brinkmanship. And they make some dumb choices.

At one wedding I played in Beverly Hills at a hotel ballroom, the bride and groom's table was up on stage in front of the band, along with several other tables—which was a bit weird—and there were candles with open flames everywhere. Real ones. Now, call me paranoid, but so many real flames in a setting full of drunk people in close proximity to each other's elbows and scotches is not a winning idea.

The photographer, a nice lady with lots of hair and hairspray in her 'do to keep it out of the way (you probably know where this is going) was leaning way over a table from the side, less than ten feet in front of me, to get a closeup of the wedding couple. Her head was getting closer and closer to a candle. We were playing, there were two tables between her and me, and being tethered to my amp by my guitar cable, I couldn't get to her in time. I was yelling "WATCH OUT! YOUR HAIR IS RIGHT ON TOP OF THAT CANDLE!! HEY!! WATCH IT!!"...but she couldn't hear me, because I didn't have a mic. She bent over that table one more inch to get just the right angle, and poof! Up went her hair. For a few seconds she didn't know it, and I kept hollering at the top of my lungs as the flames grew. Finally she realized what was happening and bolted off through the crowd, blindly bumping into people and screaming. She covered ground at a rate that would make a coyote proud, zig-zagging her way toward the exit at the back of the room, looking like a runner carrying the Olympic torch. I saw her on the next break, sitting very still on a bench outside, sporting an exciting new trailblazing 'do and a thousand-yard stare. Physically at least, she was fine.

Some of the clients were powerful entertainment industry entities, and it was fairly common to share the stage with some iconic talent. There was a lot of this, but I don't remember most of the names. Basically I went, set up and did the thing, tore down and went home, once or twice a week for about a decade.

One of the more memorable casuals was on the Paramount lot in Hollywood: It was a wrap party for a film Steven Spielberg had just finished shooting. The Temptations fronted the band for a set, choreography and all, so that was cool. And Spielberg stood next to me and used my mic to talk to the crew and cast, which was also cool. I have no idea what film it was, or who was in it. The more noteworthy thing about that gig, to me, was playing with a drummer I had never met, namely M.B. Gordy. He was on break from touring with the Doobie Brothers and, besides being a fantastic drummer, was a really fun guy to groove with. He's a good hang too, and we've done several other things since.

Nowadays, those contracting offices no longer mix and match players, preferring to have established lineups that can be made to be musically tighter and more coherently marketed. This makes these offices basically booking agencies for high-dollar gigs, spelled: "events".

Chapter 20
Acting is Hard

"No shit, there I was, chatting with Heather Locklear as we had our makeup done." I hadn't expected such a big star to be so friendly, down-to-earth and engaging in conversation. Or such a comfortable hang, for that matter. Not being one to follow celebrity gossip, I hadn't known she was married to a guitar player.

An avowed functionalist at heart, I never bought into the relevance of aesthetics until one day in the nineties when James Hurley—one of my best brothers, a blindingly good guitarist, a mechanical genius and one of the smartest guys I know—said to me "But Byron, form is a part of your function." James speaks like he's part Carl Sagan, part Rod Serling, and has an annoying inability to be wrong. It's hard not to give weight to what he says. Churchill once said that "Speaking with Franklin Delano Roosevelt is like opening a fine bottle of wine." That's exactly how I feel about talking with James, even if our conversations do take place at the other end of the social spectrum.

Having thus had my head removed from my ass, I refinished my Strat so it looked less ghetto, and started wearing better clothes to gigs. Hey presto: My phone started ringing more.

One of the calls I got not long after was from Christine Day, a friend of mine as well as a vocalist and music contractor I had worked for off and on, who books musicians onto films and TV shows, in front of the camera. This is more or less a musician's equivalent of being an extra, but it pays better because there's actual musical skill involved. It's called sidelining, and I've done a good deal of it over the years. You may remember Johnny Oliver, who introduced me to James Burton. He booked me on my first several sidelining gigs, and had been Christine's big brother. Christine took over the business after Johnny passed away unexpectedly.

I played Meatloaf's lead guitarist in Bat Out of Hell, which was a good week or so of shooting, in a few different locations. I was a German techno-punk keyboardist with a massive head of ratted hair in an episode of The Buddy Faro Show. That was sort of a featured role with a name but no lines, filmed over several days in several locations including—much to my girlfriend's ire—the famous jacuzzi in the Grotto at the Playboy Mansion, with a few bikini-clad bunnies. I was a guitarist in the background of The Elizabeth Taylor Story, as well as on an episode of California Dreams—coincidentally about the same time had recorded some guitar tracks for that show. I was in several episodes of the cult-classic series Kindred, as a guitarist in a band fronted by one of the main characters, and I was in Firefly as a farmer on an outlying planet who played a Pipa (a Japanese fretted instrument). They gave me an Amish-style beard for that one. I have the production polaroid of my getup: the Amish beard made me look a bit like Charlton Heston.

A Film or TV shoot is a massive affair, employing dozens of people for a small one, hundreds for larger scenes. Every minute is very expensive, it's a highly fluid environment with many different technology platforms that have to work flawlessly, and things go sideways all the time, so shooting schedules get shuffled. For this reason, they tend to want everyone on the set they could possibly have use for. The budgets reflect this.

They might keep you waiting for sixteen hours and not actually get to your scene at all, or you might be in and out in just a few hours. It's always a cosmic roll of the dice with that many unpredictable factors. Past eight hours, your pay goes to time and a half, and past twelve hours is what we call "golden hours". It adds up. Also, you get royalties. I've picked up several thousand dollars in the mailbox over the years for the work I've done on camera—always a pleasant surprise. So the pay is good, and it's a fun hang.

Depending on circumstances, you might actually be playing live, but almost always you're finger-syncing or lip-syncing to tracks that are playing in your spy-like hidden wireless earbuds, so that the set can be silent while they shoot dialogue. Music, crowd noise, foley and all that are added in post. The finger-syncing is where the skill comes in. You'd be surprised how hard it is to finger-sync another player's tracks convincingly.

You might be in the foreground, or background, or wind up on the editing room floor, you'll never know until it's been aired or premiered. You just show up ready to do the thing, and you never know—you might have a fairly high-profile shot, interacting with principal actors, as happened with me on Melrose Place. I have very little training (or talent, we can assume) as an actor. I was blindsided by it.

In the storyline, Eve (played by Rena Sofer) is a singer who is performing with a new band of unruly rocker-types. I played the most unruly one—you guessed it, the guitarist—standing next to her on stage, finger-syncing along with the rest of the band as Rena lip-synced the song. No prob so far.

Then suddenly, the director started yelling, "Okay, guitarist, I need you to hump-dance her!"

"What the hell?" I thought.

"Get up against her! Get rude and lewd! Hump her leg! Run your tongue up and down her neck!!"

I tried, but it felt so wrong I just couldn't get my body to obey my brain. My big Brother Randy once went skydiving for his birthday, and described jumping out of the plane as being "counterintuitive on a cellular level". This was like that. I had been chatting a bit with Rena on set during the long wait...she was just really cool and nice, a sweet girl from farm country somewhere in the midwest if memory serves, not at all a plastic Hollywood type. She was a really comfortable hang. And here I was basically being asked to sexually assault this nice girl on stage. We had to do four takes because of me, each time with more of the crew cheering me on, because I couldn't bring myself to be that guy. Finally, she turned to me between takes, looked me square in the eyes and said "It's alright, just do it! You're not gonna break me, and we need to get this done." So I did. It felt like dumping a truckload of crude oil on a beautiful virgin wilderness, but I did it. She acted her part of being disgusted and violated, then storming off stage in the middle of the song.

My girlfriend at the time was an actress, so I expected her to understand when we watched the episode air a few weeks later. Alas, after seeing a closeup of me slathering my tongue up and down Rena's neck...no.

* * *

Speaking of actresses, right around that time I had the honor of playing a show with Maureen McCormick, best known for her iconic role in the seventies as Marcia Brady. Barry Coffing was M.D., the show was at Indianapolis's ice hockey stadium after a game. Barry, most of that band and I had just spent a couple of weeks in daily film score recording sessions at Barry's pad for an indie film called "West from South goes North". I was on guitar, we were using a Ry Cooder vibe, so I was playing a lot of slide. Also, to add dimension, Barry brought in Steve Hill as a utility man. "Utility man" is code-speak for a multi-instrumentalist with blazing enough chops on several instruments to be professionally useful on all of them. Steve played the hell out of guitar, pedal steel, fiddle, dobro, mandolin, banjo, harmonica...and for all I know keyboards, tuba, ocarina, slide whistle and nose flute. Suffice to say that utility players piss off the rest of us mortals.

It was a good thing Steve was there too, because on a break day about halfway through the scoring sessions, I was hiking out of Devil's Punchbowl with some friends after a great day of climbing, descending a slab of sandstone, when I slipped on some gravel and went down hard on my butt, slapping the ground next to me just as hard with my left hand, palm down, to arrest my fall. Alas, dirt is not what my hand encountered.

There, growing out of the sandstone in an impossibly dry and wind-blown placement, was a scrappy little old yucca that was less than ten inches tall but must have been ancient. Its spikes were steel-hard. I looked down at my hand, fully expecting to see the spikes sticking out the back, but none were. So, no total impalements, but my hand was still stuck on that thing like a slice of cheese slammed onto a pin cushion. I took a breath and yanked my hand up off of it. There were about a dozen spikes stuck deeply in it, one of which went in almost an inch, just left of the base of my second finger, grazing the nerve. As I slowly pulled it out, it just kept coming. It was clear that it had almost come out the back.

Yucca is mildly poisonous. It won't kill you unless you're allergic, but it'll have some effect or other. My hand got swollen to the point that I just played slide fills on the film score from that point on, using a glass-smooth white ceramic coffee mug as a slide, because my hand was shaped a bit like a catcher's mitt and I couldn't use a regular slide. The swelling started going down after a few days, but it was kind of funny using a coffee mug held in a catcher's mitt as a means of playing guitar. As always, we use what we've got on hand.

By the time we did the rehearsal for Maureen's show, my left hand was starting to look like a hand again. Off we flew to Indy, where we did the show on the ice right after the game. The crowd stayed. In case you're wondering, here's how that works:

One single big, burly carpet, roughly 30 feet on a side, gets parked on the ice. The band sets up, the stage drop (i.e. the snake of audio cables to the house P.A.) lives on it, everything is set up like it's a normal stage—drums, amps, mics, monitors, the whole shebang—all on the carpet. After sound check, about a dozen big guys carefully drag it off the ice into the area behind one of the goals. Then after the game, they just drag it back onto the ice and you're ready to go. Steve and I let our instruments get accustomed to the temperature during the game, so they'd be stable in the show. It worked! So did my hand by the way, temperature notwithstanding. Steve and I had some head-cutting trade-offs in the solo sections, and despite recent yucca impalements, I was able to pretty much keep up. My left middle finger never healed past ninety percent of its original strength, though. It's something I would never notice playing guitar, but it would make a difference on the more difficult climbs.

On the way from the stadium to the hotel in a pearl-white Mercedes stretch limo, Maureen had us stop at a liquor store so she could buy beer and booze for the band and the crew. She was a pretty cool jewel...friendly, comfortable, smart and at ease.

At the end of the night, after the band and crew party in the lobby wound down, she and I wound up alone and lying head-to-head on our bellies in the hotel hallway, faces less than two feet apart, quietly talking about nothing in particular as we sipped Herradura..."No shit, there I was lying head-to-head with Maureen McCormick..." Then we headed off to our respective rooms.

It wasn't like you're probably thinking, I was happily spoken for at the time, as I imagine she was too. But I'd be lying if I said a part of me hasn't always wondered.

Chapter 21
Music is Harder

It's a familiar notion that there is someone in charge, that there is a "they": some invisible organization of string-pullers and deciders, controlling the trajectory of humankind. Maybe they are some dark government entity, maybe deities, or maybe they wear lab coats and play with beakers and cackle evil laughter as they joke about not designing the better mousetrap or how to make more traffic lights turn red in front of you.

But of course no one is in charge and nothing is under control, so we can relax and let all that go. Our great civilization is guided purely by chance. If you feel a need to give it a cosmic leader with an identity, I suggest a drunken, headless giant stumbling around in the dark, stubbing his toe and hopping sideways off a cliff.

Society arrives at its social norms in ways that are just as haphazard and random as those norms themselves. Sometimes someone powerful with an agenda grants a premise and imposes it on the world around them, or sometimes it's an idea too good not to take hold, like the wheel, or democracy. And if the new thing gets upheld in a challenge, it gets added to the marble edifice of precedent. If it gets accepted outright, it's backed by the most irresistible tide of all: Social consensus.

Either way, we arrive at the new accepted way of doing things by a process more brainless and uncontrolled than most people care to believe. No entity or process is in place to determine which new ideas are good and which should be drowned at birth.

In no area of human endeavor is there a more dire need of control and oversight than new tech. Our technological advancement is outpacing our control of it like an F18 Hornet taking off with full afterburners outpaces a bicycle. New tech gets quickly adopted and put into use by society in ways that violate ethics and moral code, via the gloriously heedless convenience that is social consensus: "Everybody does it."

Crowds operate at the level of the lowest common denominator, as we've seen, and enthusiastic adoption of new tech, and making it a new norm, is in itself a new norm. There's your schematic for disaster. If there were a place to write a eulogy for a species or a planet, I'd suggest mentioning that in ours.

In the mid-to-late 90s when music became digitized and mp3 encoding tech made it possible to duplicate and share, suddenly endless copies could be made for free. And just like that, we saw the demise of the mighty record industry in the digital apocalypse, because technology enabled the herd to embrace a consensus so astounding, it's hard to even believe it could happen:

It's okay to steal from musicians.

The rationale is so lazy it doesn't even pretend to address propriety: A simple shrug and the nonchalant rubber stamp excuse: "Everybody does it."

Since music files could now be easily ripped and traded, society collectively started e-shoplifting music, taking money out of the mouths of hard-working, struggling artists. I wish I could put a phonier, happier face on it, but that's the nuts-and-bolts truth of the matter.

In the musical community, it was like the San Andreas fault finally cut loose and dumped California into the sea. Regardless of what sector a musician primarily worked in—the studio scene, nightclubs, casuals, tours, or actually being in a signed band—even teaching—it was a massive hit, because so many major labels toppled over into the dust that it sent waves of attrition out into every other sector...and it had already been the most competitive industry on Earth. In the worst year—'97 or '98—sixteen hundred signed recording acts hit the streets, because their record companies suddenly no longer existed. That is a LOT of mouths that were suddenly hungry and looking for work.

It took years for the new normal to get established, as a panicked musical workforce tried many ways that didn't work. There are several viable approaches to a life in music now, and I sometimes give clinics at music departments regarding what they are. I run them down for you in this book, but I'll say this much now: None of them involve a record company or dependance on the legalized mathematical insult known as streaming royalties.

I felt the hunger, too...'97 and '98 were probably my two darkest years. I went through a rough patch financially that would take awhile to dig out of, as well as a very tough breakup. I reached what I promised myself will be the lowest moment of my life.

But the universe likes to stir the stew, and with its penchant for reciprocity and wild swings of the pendulum, it brought me up out of those depths with the deepest beauty and greatest joy I've ever known. As Sam Clemens once quipped, "Familiarity breeds contempt. And children."

* * *

One quiet and sunny afternoon I was sitting alone on the couch in my living room, opening the mail. I opened one envelope and abruptly discovered that I had a daughter, who was about to turn ten years old.

Without too much of a digression, I'll just say that the picture that found its way to me was nothing more or less than a picture of myself, aged nine years, had I been female. I was looking into a mirror; there could be zero doubt of lineage. Looking into that face, and those eyes, was the most intense experience of my entire existence, and the most life-changing. Time stood still, life stood breathless and I heard deafening silence as my blood roared in my ears like Yosemite Falls, and the universe did a 180 on a dime.

Five minutes earlier I had been broke and emotionally wrecked, spiraling down into darkness with no path forward to offer light at the end of the tunnel. Then she happened, and suddenly I found myself taking an inventory: I had friends who loved me, advised me and who had my back, I had my skills, my tools, my reputation and business contacts, a roof over my head, telecommunications and a '67 Mustang that turned heads.

If you've learned anything from this book, it's that music is a tough career for someone who wants a family. And make no mistake: it is. But what I discovered, having become this strange new "Dad" guy, is that my future no longer belonged to me, nor did my decisions...hell, my body didn't even belong to me. It all belonged to the next generation.

This had a powerful effect on my professional choices, and the results were immediate. Other than having quit smoking pot, I wasn't consciously going about things differently than I ever had, but I was aware of being different. I shook the ground when I walked. And I found that decisions that might have been tough for me to make before were very simple now, because I had a Daughter filter to run them through. If you're a parent, you know that of which I speak. It's a very simple, binary system:

Q: is it good for the kid?

A: enter Y or N at this time.

When I was a scrappy, scrabbling musician, blowing around on the wind through the western US with my fellow mangy partying coyotes, bouncing from town to town like a pogo stick, life and society seemed to disapprove of me for reasons I never understood. But when I arrived at fatherhood, I was gratified to notice that the world had come around and started behaving itself.

My daughter is the best thing that ever happened to me, and she'll tell you that I'm the best thing that ever happened to her. We love each other madly. And without being the man who I became in order to be her Dad, I'd never have won the love and the hand of my wife.

What an incredible thing is life.

* * *

Also in the late nineties, I got a call from a film composer named Richard Kozinski—I was recommended to him by a good brother of mine, the great drummer Gary Ponder. Gary is one of LA's many inhuman talents.

Koz needed guitars on a one-hour Fox TV special ("one hour" in broadcast TV at the time actually being 42 minutes, to allow for commercials). His studio was one of many in an office building on Ventura Boulevard in Universal City called "The Centrum". It's an odd looking building viewed from the side. Five or six stories tall, the front wall is mirrored glass and leans out over the sidewalk by 15 or 20 degrees. If you walk under it and look up, you expect it to fall on you. There was a trendy restaurant on the bottom floor called L'Express, whose second floor became a listening room for about a year—I booked my band Copper Lode in there a couple of times.

The upper floors are mostly recording and music production studios, owned by TV and film score production companies, jingle companies and music libraries. There's always a lot of commerce and business going on. It's not the environment where you'd expect to see studios—the walls aren't very thick or soundproofed, the doors are just normal office doors. Koz's studio was an office maybe fourteen feet by eighteen, and the walls between it and the offices on either side didn't even go all the way to the back wall, so there was a common airspace and everybody could hear everybody. But everybody somehow made it work.

There's an image in the collective's mind of what a recording studio looks like, and this is a good place for me to point out that for the most part it's bullshit. Statistically at least, the vast majority of studios aren't pretty, they're a utilitarian working environment. There are pretty ones, sure...lots of them. You see them in the studio porn featured on the cover of Mix Magazine. But those studios are for hire, which is a different business model, requiring slick looks, great gear that functions, sanitary wire management and the like. They don't represent the vast majority of professional recording environments, which nowadays are owned by the people or production companies who use them, as opposed to renting them out to others. This latter type doesn't typically sport a great amount of awe-inspiring equipment or cosmetic vanity. There's work to be done.

Most working-Joe studios are uglier than your dentist's office. A lot of that nice sounding music you love comes out of beat-up wheezy gear, kept operable by colorful language and the occasional swat or shake, sitting on ratty carpet or linoleum under cheap lighting, a short-circuiting cable-end held in place at a strategic angle by duct tape or a tactically placed coffee mug, while a mixing console rocks on three feet and has all the integrity of a Boeing B-17 returning to base on one engine, trailing smoke with half its tail shot off. Players try to find one pair of functioning headphones, as traffic noisily trundles by outside. There are a hundred cables running everywhere, the bathroom may have no hot water, paper towels or hand soap. And when a buzz inevitably crops up, identifying the source can take hours. It's not uncommon to spend more time getting things to sound right and to behave, chasing down demons, gremlins, buzzes and pops, than actually recording.

I know a lot of musicians and several engineers who will swear to you that Milagro Studios in Glendale was haunted by the ghost of Karen Carpenter (they recorded all their hits there). Milagro is gone now, but it was one of the pretty studios, in business as a recording environment for hire, and with a very impressive discography. But its random buzzes and pops had people offering premises that exceeded the boundaries of respectable logic. I did several sessions at Milagro, and never noticed gremlins there that were any worse or better than anywhere else. I'm probably going to get taken to task for saying that, but there it is.

Suffice to say that a well-functioning studio is a wonderful thing to find. Venues, too: you'd be surprised how many theaters have badly sub-par wiring and power supplies, guaranteeing that you'll spend most of soundcheck and at least some of the show dealing with "tech diff".

Any experienced musician will tell you the following axiom: the scale, stature and importance of a gig or recording session runs in direct and inverse proportion to the quality of the gear involved. It's like a cosmic Murphy's Law that runs the behavior of musical gear. I can't buy the notion of Karen Carpenter's Ghost, but I'll testify to the reality of Murphy's Law any day.

* * *

Koz and I hit it off, and he dug the guitar and bass parts I came up with. He started giving me quasi-regular work and, being a very busy guy, started using me as a ghost writer as well. Ghosting is how people break into film scoring. I've done a lot of it. The way it commonly works is that a prominent composer will land a big job, and employ a team of people to get it done. We don't always get on-screen credit, but we always welcome the work. Our names are usually on the cue sheets, so we do get royalties, and some insiders will know who we are. But the world, or sites like IMDB, won't have a clue.

Over the next few years, Koz and I scored a lot of things. I think we scored about 16 or 17 hours of footage. We did a bunch of one-hour specials that aired on FOX:

The Dark Side of Figure Skating, parts I, II and III—the gig was to create action and suspense scores to accompany footage of figure skaters, crooked judges and talking heads, which was an interesting dichotomy. We pulled it off evidently, because work from that same production company kept coming:

"World's Greatest Animal Rescues", parts I and II, which was legitimately suspenseful footage; and "World's Greatest World-Record Breaking Stunts", parts I, II and III—also pretty hair-raising footage. We also did a couple of movies, and a TV series for Discovery of ten one-hour (42 minute) episodes.

Lest you think things make more sense in the larger, more syndicated or published projects, I should remove the wool from your eyes. As a general rule, the tastier the pie, the more the work gets passed around the inner circle. On the Discovery series, the music supervisor was a producer's wife who, aside from being innocent of any musical understanding, didn't comprehend the function of a score. In fact, I suspect she didn't care for music much at all...or her job, or the show.

Koz sent her a VCR of an episode for her to okay the score, and she griped that "The music made things too interesting and kept drawing me into the show, when I was trying to do my housework!" She was seriously complaining, not being funny, and wanted us to change the score to make the show less interesting. You can't make this stuff up.

On another occasion, Koz told me on the phone that a client wanted a cue with samples (samples are short snippets of digital recordings) of farting hampsters for the melody, and I was so accustomed to the absurdities that came out of the mouths of clients that I didn't even blink...I just started brainstorming out loud about ways of making something like that happen technically. It turned out that Koz was pranking me, and we had a good laugh...but the things that clients say are so far-fetched, I just dug right into the idea.

On some of those projects, I wound up doing the majority of the score. Koz told me that at the end of it, about 70% of the Discovery series cues were mine. Koz always paid me fairly and I've made some half-decent royalties. Nothing that would buy a house or put a kid through college, but more than nothing.

* * *

Most great drummers I know are hyperactive, but my good brother Gary Ponder—with whom I've made a lot of great music and who introduced me to Koz—is an electron wearing a human suit. He talks at about 220 words per minute, in a steady stream of rapid-fire hilarious antics and jokes, one after another, all the while either fidgeting or drumming on something. One day in the late nineties, Gary and I were on the phone, and as always I could hear him practicing his rudiments on his practice pad. He had a whole drum kit of practice pads, plus the ever-present one that he strapped to his knee, so that he could sit anywhere and do a bunch of dizzyingly fast stick work to a metronome. Such was the noise in the background as we spoke. His stick work was amazing, I could hear it clearly: Flamadiddles, paradiddles, 16ths and 16th triplets, 32nd notes and triplets, rolls and every type of pattern and polyrhythm, all at a super high tempo, perfectly and articulately executed, and all the while telling jokes and stories in his rapid-fire mode of speech. This went on for about ten minutes as we talked, the stick work never pausing or faltering. Then it stopped abruptly, as something faltered that I couldn't detect, and he said "Shit!"

"What?" I said.

"I'll never get my fuckin' feet together."

All that time, he had actually been sitting at his practice pad kit, no sticks, and I had been listening to his feet on his kick drum pedals. Such is the amazing level of talent here in Los Angeles. I've never gotten used to it, and I hope I never do.

Chapter 22
The Fittest Band

Not every gig's value is measured in how good it looks in your bio, how much of a musical achievement it is to have the gig, or how hip the book is. One of the most enjoyable gigs I ever had started in '96, playing on and off with a classic and southern rock cover band called Dakota. The reason it rates so highly with me is the bandleader, Bill Rotella.

For the most part, bandleaders manage the players. Some are asinine insect authorities, some are nice people and comfortable leaders, but either way the job they do is to manage the players. Bill wasn't like that. He was an advocate for the players, everywhere we went. He made sure we got every perk and comp possible, almost always including a gym membership nearby, because Dakota was a very fit band. We were a five-piece—drums, percussion, bass, lead guitar and rhythm guitar, nearly all of whom sang lead and backup—and people used to comment that we looked like Chip and Dales guys, except for the hair. No, we didn't dress that way. The muscly look was indeed good for marketing, though. Dakota had corporate sponsorship, and some booking relationships in Scandinavia, which is how I got to go play Helsinki for a few weeks. It was an absolute blast.

Finns are the most well-educated population on the planet, and it's evident in every aspect of culture. They're generally good at everything they do, and there's very little crime. And since this was more than a decade before I met my wife, I'll risk saying this: We were a roving pack of girl watchers, in an extremely target-rich environment. It seemed like every other girl on the streets of Helsinki was a super model. Ditto Tallinn, capital of Estonia and a 90-minute ferry ride from Helsinki. Thus did we get to tag Russian soil for a day.

At that time in my personal life, getting out and about with a band of brothers was precisely what I needed, and it was good for the soul. The gym that Bill scored us membership to in Helsinki was a three-story megaplex called Alexium, with only the best equipment, and a decorative sheet of water falling down a giant 3-story high pane of glass into the lobby. It was the swankiest joint I've ever graced with my grunts and sweat. I was there every day.

And the gig was simply fun. The guys covered their sectors without having to be policed—Bill's leadership just brought that out—and we had good vocal harmonies. Though I guess I'm really a jazzer at heart with a rep for funk / fusion stuff, I've always loved playing classic rock. It connects me to my first band back in Berkeley, and ten-year-old Byron's experiential roots...but it's also just freaking fun to play. All of the different music that I've been involved with stylistically, from the simple to the really sophisticated, and all of the things I've learned, in school and since, have only made me appreciate great classic rock all the more. I've never tired of it, and probably never will. Jazzer though I am, I will never for the life of me understand jazz snobs, known in some circles as jazzholes.

Dakota's song list was wonderful, too. Grand Funk, Traffic, Almond Brothers, Free, Bad Company...not so much the "trade route" tunes like ZZ Top or Seger that most classic rock bands overemphasize, and that I actually had gotten a little sick of playing. The song list was enjoyable, the genre simple, the band solid, and I had ample opportunity to stretch out in the solos. That made for a really fun time.

I don't know how it started...maybe I told Bill about playing slide with that coffee mug on that film with Barry...but he started doing a shtick where he'd have people send up unlikely objects for me to play slide with. It started out as you'd expect, with beer bottles, shot glasses and the like. All well and good. Then over time, things got more challenging. A lady sent up her purse...I just used a metal part of a buckle. Then a leather jacket...I think I used the zipper handle. Then one night a guy sent up his leather work boot. The thing looked like he made his living wallowing in mud or maybe pouring cement, or maybe he was a farmer. Whatever it was caked with, it wasn't what you want on your hand if you need to play guitar. "Challenge accepted", I thought. I hooked one of the metal bootlace hooks over a string and played a few phrases, then at the end of that night I told Bill we had to put the kibosh on that shtick. He laughed and never did it again.

There was a young guitarist hanging out at the club most nights, age 21 or so and still in music school, named Erkka Korhonen. We became good friends. He helped me find supplies in a foreign land where they speak one of the world's most difficult languages (actually most Finns speak five languages, including English, which made me feel pretty dumb), and I told him about the studio scene in Los Angeles. I didn't know it at the time, but we'd remain good friends and he'd go on to do big things.

After three weeks in Helsinki, I took the opportunity to extend the layover at Heathrow for a week of hanging out in England, which I had never seen. That month of living a European lifestyle, not driving anywhere and working out every day, made me the fittest I've ever been. For a few weeks upon my return, I could climb 5.12, my personal best. I bagged three of them. Then the effects of the American lifestyle kicked in, my body fat went back up above 15% and I was a 5.11 climber again.

And Dakota was unbooked, so I needed a gig. Having learned the cost and consequences of playing ugly music up in Alaska, it was with all the enthusiasm of a man forced to stick his tongue into a meat grinder that I answered an ad for a 70s cover band. It was literally the only lead on any gig I could find at the moment.

Lest you misunderstand things, there was of course a LOT of fantastic hit music in the 70s. It was truly an incredible decade. But when you see the words "70s cover band", you should know that that's code-speak for disco. That said, I was desperate. They actually required rehearsal (unpaid) to play that nauseating dreck, and to make things even worse, the rehearsals were an hour away. Though this was clearly unacceptable by any reasonable standards, my situation was not reasonable and I really needed the work. So I just sucked it up and conceded the tireless rationale: "Any port in a storm."

As I accelerated up the onramp to head west on the 210 to the first rehearsal, I felt a nasty pollution in my innards, and a deep sense of shame and foreboding in my soul. I turned on the radio just in time to catch the first Tympani hits of Copland's iconic masterpiece, Fanfare for the Common Man. A few seconds later, as the opening peals of the trumpets delivered their powerful, timeless spiritual exultation, the sun burst through the clouds right in front of me, with majestic multi-colored "What the fuck are you doing with your life?" rays and shafts of light piercing the world in a stunning display of beauty.

"Elevate yourself", I clearly heard the sky tell me. In tears—the good kind—I got off at the next exit, went home, unloaded and made the awkward phone call backing out of the gig.

When the bandleader answered, he heard something like "Hi it's Byron and I'm so sorry to do this to you because you seem like a really cool guy and I'm sure it's a great gig for the right cat but I just can't bring myself to do it because I just realized what an incredible honor it is to be alive on this Earth and to be a musician and I don't want to squander my time playing music I hate so thanks for hiring me but I'm sure it's best for both of us if I bow out now rather than later."

Then I listened to Copland for over an hour while contemplating what the hell to do next.

Chapter 23
Now What?

I remember seeing the pile of large concrete chunks rushing up at me and calmly thinking, "This could be fatal." It was July 28th, 1998, roughly 10:15 PM.

My dog Boone and I had just gotten back from a few days of climbing in Mammoth. I had been very slowly healing an injury in my right shoulder for two years, and though the injury was low-grade, it just wouldn't heal and I couldn't do pull-ups without setting it back, which is a problem if you're a climber. So I had forced myself to give it six solid months of rest. At the end of that time I had started working it gently, taking my time ramping things back up. Finally one day, I felt pretty good pulling down at the gym, and did three sets of pull-ups. It felt like I was good to go, so I called my climbing partner Howie, who by then had moved up to Mammoth Lakes. He said something along the lines of "Well, getcherass up here and let's climb some shit before you hurt something else!" I did some good climbing, flashing a pumpy, overhanging 5.11b on-sight, and Howie's comment from the belay was "He's baaack!" It was a great celebration for my soul, to finally be able to breathe fire again and really crank on some holds. Damn, it felt good.

Then Boone and I drove back to L.A. (never as pleasant a drive as when I'm going the other way), and when we got home at almost 10PM, Boone was antsy from the four-and-a-half hour drive. Ninety pounds of wonderful mutt, Boone was a bit on the high-strung side.

So I got out the mountain bike and off we went, down the suburban streets. Boone was trained to stay on the sidewalk adjacent to me as I rode in the street, but it took a lot of vocal commands. So after about fifteen minutes of that, I wanted to hop down from the right shoulder of a street to a dirt section of a county park parking lot, where I could give him a break and let him run around whichever way he wanted. The parking lot was about 8 feet lower than the shoulder, and the embankment between the two was in pitch darkness because of the shadow from a street light. But I knew the place well, we were all of five blocks from the house. What could go wrong? Pedaling fast in 5th gear, I was probably doing close to 20 mph when I chose a spot, thinking "This looks like a good place" and hopped diagonally down to my right into the darkness, and my third encounter with Kryptonite.

How else would it be: The spot I chose had the only boulder sticking out of the embankment within a hundred yards on either side of it. It deflected my front wheel with a loud "TANG!", sending it and the bike up over my left shoulder, upending me as well, as I described an arc through the air that would meet the ground at about 45 degrees. Keeping my hands on the bars, I thought maybe I could get the bike back under me, but physics was having none of it.

Then I had a last fleeting moment to notice the landing: A pile of about eight or ten jack-hammered sections of cement sidewalk that were roughly 2 feet by 2 feet by 6 inches, exactly where I was going to hit headfirst. The last image in my memory of that flight is of having both of my hands on the bars, up and behind me to my left, as a top corner of one of those blocks was coming directly at my right temple from a few inches away. "No shit, there I was, about to die..."

Then the impact. That corner drove into my temple, hard, while my head was forced toward my left shoulder to a degree that made noise, and my newly-healed right shoulder tried to set up house in my belly button as my body accordioned on impact. I suddenly knew what it felt like to be a bug on a windshield; my neighbor and friend, Cia, later called it my "splat maneuver". I wound up with my upper body chest-down on the concrete blocks, my right arm folded under me, my other arm and both legs waving helplessly in the air above and behind me, trying to get purchase—on what, air molecules?—I was in a lot of pain, having just injured several things, the bike was on top of me and a bit entwined with my limbs, and I was unable to get up. Lying there in the darkness, busted up with nobody around, out of sight of the road, what went through my head was "Help me! I've fallen and I can't get up!"

And I started laughing. Sometimes laughter is the only refuge, and the music industry is not the only thing that's tough on people who can't laugh at themselves. I have my Dad to thank for teaching me that. No matter what you do for your living, if you take yourself too seriously, you have my pity. That won't end well.

As I was lying in the dark, broken and laughing, Boone was barking "What the hell's the matter with you bipeds? Get the hell up!". Before I tried to move, I did a quick inventory of what felt like what: I could wiggle toes and fingers, I could breathe but it hurt (waitwait don't tell me, I know this one: broken ribs), my right shoulder hurt like hell and wasn't in the right place (probable fracture and/or dislocation, definite torn ligaments), my sternum didn't feel normal (broken clavicle?) my vision and the world was spinning violently and rampantly, at about 5 Gs. My head was trying to explode because my brain felt like it was bigger than the inside of my skull (legit concussion, shit!). Ideally I could call 911, something I had never in my life considered doing before, but like most people in 1998, I didn't have a cell phone yet. I hollered "HELP!!" a couple of times, but I knew that nobody was around or within earshot and besides, it hurt to do it. I took that familiar preparatory breath and rolled over my ribs (OW, GODDAMMIT), then cautiously got untangled with my good arm and tried to stand up. The world was pitching, yawing and rolling in an alarming way, I couldn't keep my eyes focused or even facing any specific direction, and there was a faint sound like ocean surf in my ears, but with a faster rhythm. I used the bike to steady myself, straightened the handlebars and tried to ride: I immediately started a crazy cycle of 180-degree zig-zags, nearly face-planting several times in just ten or twenty feet. GET OFF THIS THING NOW, a voice said.

Fortunately, my good friend Nate lived right across the street from the park. I staggered to his door, walking my bike with Boone following and watching me closely, and knocked on his door at 10:45. He watched me for about 45 minutes while we iced my temple, making sure the swelling was going down, not getting worse. The world gradually stabilized, and after 30 or so minutes I could follow his finger without jerky eye motions. When we both felt that nothing crazy would happen if I left, Boone and I walked home. In the clarity of hindsight, it's obvious that I should've let him call paramedics, as he offered to do.

Over the next five days a big lump developed on my shoulder and many things felt progressively worse, until I finally took Cia up on her offer to accompany me to the ER if things got bad.

If you're looking at being a musician, you should be prepared for the reality of sub-par health care, such as the county health system of Los Angeles circa 1990s. Things have improved greatly since the passage of the Affordable Care Act, but it's still worth considering that a life of scrabbling for your living in music probably means you won't have Gucci insurance and rock star doctors.

I've never been in a field hospital in a war zone, but I suspect it looks something like the LA County E.R. at Olive View did that day and night. Several gunshot victims were there, amid all kind and manner of sick and injured people. Docs and nurses scrambled everywhere with the harried expressions of the badly overwhelmed, and the triage nurse was necessarily more of a gate keeper. My own waiting time was six hours to get seen by a doc and get the X-Rays ordered, which was not nearly as bad as on some other occasions. During this wait, approaching midnight, we overheard the staff tell a guy who had a bullet in his calf, "Listen, you're stable, it's not life-threatening, we won't be able to get to you until 8 or 9 AM, so you might as well go home and get some rest. We'll hold your place in line." There was another guy who had had a heart attack and was brought in via ambulance, sitting outside on the curb smoking a cigarette. It was out of control.

And here was I—comparatively healthy-looking, able to walk, not visibly bleeding, not even in cardiac arrest--complaining about some kind of bicycle accident that hadn't even been bad enough for me to go to an ER at the time. When the X-rays came back, the doc met me in a hallway, held them up against the florescent light on the ceiling for a few seconds and said, "You've got a hematoma. You'll be fine. Go home." Hematoma is four-syllable medical jargon for a bruise.

It later surfaced from studies ordered by other doctors that I had compression fractures in four vertebra in my C-Spine, my right clavicle wasn't broken but had torn ligaments at each end, I had either severed or torn my right AC ligament (which connects your scapula to your clavicle, forming the top part of your shoulder joint), probably cracked several ribs and, of course, there was that concussion. The temple is involved with the imprinting of memory, and my memory hasn't functioned the same ever since that night. My suboccipitals—the group of muscles on the back of your head where your spine meets your skull—have been perpetually jacked since that impact, as has my atlas.

When I put the timeline together in retrospect, I realized there was about a half an hour that wasn't accounted for. It should have been about 10:15, maybe 10:20, when I knocked on Nate's door. Not 10:45. I asked a doc about it years later, and was told that when you get knocked out, the memory lapse could be from anywhere in your personal stream of consciousness, even before the accident, and it can obscure the moment of "coming to". So evidently I was laying there in the dark for a while, alone except for Boone.

About a week after the accident I went back to the scene in daylight to have a look at the mechanics of it all. It tickled my dark sense of humor to see how smooth that embankment was, everywhere but the spot I had chosen to hop down it. I looked at that boulder and that pile of cement blocks, and remembered cruising past all that nice smooth terrain then arriving at this fateful spot and thinking, "This looks like a good place", and I had to laugh at myself again. I clearly heard physics and spatial mechanics joining in and laughing with me: a familiar chorus. To this day, I'm as glad as I am mystified that my last thought in this universe wasn't "This could be fatal."

Mountain biking is actually pretty hairball, even for an adrenaline junky. This was brought home to me one fine day about six months after the accident, when I was finally ready to try climbing again. As I came walking up to my usual boulders at Stoney Point, I heard some buddies talking:

"I dunno bro, you think she likes me?"

"Bruh, she totally digs you. I saw her scoping you out."

I came around the bend and saw three regulars I knew—Dimitri, Angelo and I forget the third guy's name—they were three of the strongest climbers in SoCal. One was at the crux of Pink Floyd, a classic problem (route up a boulder) that required an iron cross of lateral opposing pressure between the left thumb on a wart and the right palm on a bulge, with "smedges" (more smears than edges) for the feet, 15 or 20 feet off deck in otherwise blank terrain, over a bad landing. He was talking with a guy who was pulling Crystal Ball Mantle's roof on Turlock boulder about 25 feet away, which involves somehow adhering to a blank face, and pressing up against a roof you're bunched up underneath with one hand, so as to increase traction with your crappy footholds, while blindly reaching over the roof for a wrist lock in a crack with the other hand, also 20 feet off deck. Falling off of Floyd at the crux would be a possible trip to the ER, possibly surgery. Falling while pulling that roof on Crystal Ball Mantle would be life-changing. Neither guy had a spotter or a pad.

They had done these things a million times, so really it was no biggie. I had done Pink Floyd once or twice, after many tries. It was a heady crux, and I didn't care to make too many attempts. I had attempted the roof of Crystal Ball Mantle a hundred times, but always backed off. I just couldn't unlock its mystery.

Upon noticing me, Angelo said "Yo! Haven't seen you in awhile! Where ya been?"

"Oh, I had a mountain biking accident. I've been out of commission for about six months."

All motion stopped and there was a moment of stunned silence as they stared at me wide-eyed, frozen in their positions.

Finally Angelo said, "Dude, you mountain bike?"

After another beat of silence, Dimitri said "Dude, you're crazy."

Chapter 24
Being Needed

Not long after that accident, I answered an ad for what was effectively a 5-piece Santana tribute band in search of a lead guitarist. They had some gigs coming up in the state prisons, which was something I had never done. I don't think any of us had. After we all passed some background checks and did a few rehearsals, we hit the road (these places aren't in the middle of town) and rolled up to the first one of two adjacent facilities in the middle of the desert outside of Blythe, a few hours east of LA.

Ironwood State Prison (ISP) and Chuckawalla Valley State Prison (CVSP) are both level 3 facilities. In California, there are four levels: 1 and 2 are both basically minimum security, 3 and 4 are both basically max security. Each facility had five yards: Alpha, Bravo, Charlie, Delta, and a minimum yard for inmates who were short on time and about to get out. We were booked to do one show in each yard, ten yards total, two per day, over five days.

When we arrived at Ironwood to do the first show, we were immediately in a different environment, with well-armed correctional officers (they frown on being called "guards") on battlements, roofs and in watch towers. After having the van pull through the first of two high-security gates, a small team searched the band's van thoroughly for bombs and drugs or other contraband, using mirrors, dogs and just looking each of us over. They stopped short of searching us. We were made to surrender all cameras and cell phones. That just got us inside the outer perimeter.

Next, we unloaded the van onto a trailer being towed by a golf cart. This got us through the next gate, which entailed an even more thorough emptying of our pockets into tubs, to store anything that could conceivably be dangerous. It wasn't until we rolled up to the first yard and started entering directly into it via the fourth gate that I began to realize what I had agreed to do.

"Wait a minute" I said, "I thought we'd be separated from the inmates, playing behind a wall, or plexiglass, or a fence, or something!"

"Nope," said our liaison, "you'll be playing right there on the yard."

"You mean we're going in there…"

"Yep."

"…with the inmates…"

"Yep."

"…with nothing between us and…"

"Come on, you've gotta get your gear inside."

"Ho-lee shee-it…"

At the time, I had crazy blonde rock star hair down to my belt. I had dressed for a show in summer heat, choosing a colorful muscle tank top. When I walked through the gate I was expecting to get the kind of reaction no guy would ever want, in an environment where no guy would ever want to get it.

What I got instead was nothing but kind-hearted, enthusiastic help: "Excuse me sir, can I get that for you? You know, my brother, he plays guitar. He has a Fender, a real one." Each one of us had several inmates offering to help with everything. It was unsettling at first, but after awhile we got used to it.

We set up on the yard with our backs to a building's cinderblock wall, facing across the yard sideways. All the yards I worked in the prison system were identical: Roughly 75 yards by 150 yards, with a semi-circle of multi-story cinderblock housing units around the perimeter, watched over by officers patrolling with guns from watch towers and rooftop walkways—who the inmates call "The Gummit"—and a large expanse of grass in the middle. Every yard was built for twelve hundred inmates but held at least twice that many.

Any prison comprises perhaps the most segregated population on earth, and the best indicator of how ugly and racist humanity can be. Before the show in each yard, the racial tension could be cut with a knife. I saw groups of guys roving around, defined completely and solely by race, each group keeping distance from the others as they walked: White, Black, Hispanic and what the system simply defines as "other", which is a catch-all that includes Native Americans and Asian Americans.

The remarkable thing about the music of Santana is the incredibly broad demographic it appeals to. Think about it: It's hard to name a group of people who don't like Santana, outside of maybe the most die-hard country or hip-hop fans.

When we were getting ready to play, a space of respectful distance formed between us and the inmates, which they maintained naturally. They were all standing together in one crowd now—I was hoping a brawl didn't break out—and we started playing. Before the end of the first song, an ancient shirtless geezer started dancing, a big toothless smile on his face, bringing laughter, cat-calls and hoots from the rest of the crowd. By the last few songs of that show, something incredible had happened right in front of my eyes: They were all dancing together. TOGETHER! Think of it!

It hit me pretty hard. For so many years, I had been so engaged with just finding gigs that paid my bills, that it never occurred to me that I could actually make a difference—that music can really have such a direct effect on people's lives.

While I was breaking down my rig after that first show, a female correctional officer made a point of coming up to me and saying, "I just want to thank you. It means so much to have you guys come in here and play like this. Y'know, we average about one shanking a week in this yard. After a nice show like this, we might go three or four months in peace."

That rocked me back on my heels even more. Music really does soothe the savage beast, and there are places in the world where it's badly needed to do just that.

With California's "Three Strikes" nonsense, someone who doesn't belong in that setting at all can actually get life. I was talking to a guy who wrote songs for and sang lead in the inmate band on one of those minimum yards. He said he had been originally busted for statutory—his girlfriend was 17 and he was 18, her dad hated him and turned him in. Strike one. Next, while on parole he got busted for not much over the "personal use" limit of weed, so the law prosecuted him as a dealer. Strike two. Having served his time for that and out on parole, he was riding down the street in a friend's car when they got pulled over and searched; one of his friends was carrying drugs, violating his parole. Poof, strike three. Twenty-five to life. The judge was powerless to rule otherwise.

Whether or not his story is true, the point is that it's even possible, which it is. Three strikes is an incredibly unjust law, championed by a California governor as a campaign stunt to get elected by the more reactionary element of his conservative base, and it has lasted for far too long.

When we completed the week of shows, I politely pulled the Artist Facilitator aside. She was a nice sculptor lady who oversaw the Arts in Corrections program at both facilities, and who had booked us and been our liaison throughout that week. I asked her if there was any way that I could be of further use in that environment. "I really like the feeling of doing some actual good in the world, not just keeping the roof over my head", I explained.

She immediately said, "Hell yes, we can use you! You can be what's called a Contract Artist for the state, and run the bands, teach music and stuff."

"Wow. That sounds great, but I should clarify that though I have a great musical education, I have no degree. Do you think that in the eyes of the state I have the necessary qualifications?"

"Are you kidding?" she scoffed. "Do you have a pulse?"

And so it came to be that I went legit. You'd be correct in thinking that a musician would require a lot of training before being allowed—paid, no less—to carry keys inside max security prisons, running the bands and teaching music, working alone in classrooms full of inmates without being accompanied by correctional officers. But there was in fact no special training that I ever got...they basically just gave me the keys and sent me inside. There were periodical weekend training things that all personnel attended about microbial safety, sexual harassment of co-workers and the like, but no useful law enforcement training for a musician.

The reason, as I discovered, was that I was naturally protected by an element with a far heavier hand than Gummit's could ever be: The inmates themselves. I was bringing something precious into their lives, and anyone who messed with me would probably get shanked within a week. Everyone intrinsically knew that.

Even so, I had to keep my head on a swivel and there were a lot of things that were at risk, including the AIC (Arts in Corrections) program under whose canopy I worked. Guitar strings were popular as tattoo needles, and would spread everything from AIDS to Hepatitis C to staph infections, all of which were prevalent in the population. So I had to police guitar strings in unlikely ways. If one drum stick got stolen and turned into a shank, that could close down the whole program. Inventory was carefully performed at the end of every class or band rehearsal, before I unlocked the door and led the inmates out of the classroom, back into the population. Again, the inmates' interests were aligned with mine and they did what they could to protect the program. But even so, AIC always operated under the sword of Damocles.

The reality for anyone working in that environment is that every inmate has a PHD in how to play you and the system. They've got nothing but time to think of ways, and you don't. Most of the correctional officers didn't like the existence of the AIC program. And I get it: It brought in a lot of variables. Their job is to maintain order in an environment where they're badly outnumbered at all times and, if they're working inside with the population as opposed to above in a tower, they're not carrying firearms.

But there was a powerful statistic that kept us up and running: Compared to the general population, inmates who were involved with AIC were 60% less likely to return to prison once released. To coin a phrase, that's not nothin'.

One of four facilities that I worked at was CRC (California Rehab Center), a level two out by Corona, just barely close enough to home for me to commute. I was there two days a week for a couple of years. This was very different from level three or four, because in level two, most inmates are getting out in a few years, as opposed to levels three and four being almost entirely populated by lifers. So the whole context was different. At CRC, I was helping guys find their way back to being the man they meant to be, so that they could return to their families and get their lives back on track. 80% were drug addiction cases, most sentences were two to five years. I had several really talented musicians and songwriters in CRC. In max security, I was basically there to give lifers an outlet so they didn't all kill each other.

Overall, there were a LOT of guys in the program who didn't belong inside (thanks, three strikes), including some very good men, which made me feel good about being there to help. With that said, though, make no mistake about it: There were a lot of guys who did indeed belong behind those bars, and who make me glad that the correctional system exists.

Early on, there was one inmate out by Blythe who was just a real pain to deal with. He had a prima donna attitude, needed everything to be about him all the time, and was disruptive to the teamwork atmosphere that I had to maintain in all the bands for obvious reasons. I finally brought it up to the Artist Facilitator, who did the paperwork to pull his file and see what made him tick. Maybe it would help us find a way to get him to be more of a team player. Thus did we discover, just once, what one of the inmates in our program had done in order to be there: He had stuck a gun in his girlfriend's mouth and pulled the trigger. We never pulled another file. From that moment on, I had to keep on working with that guy, having that knowledge in the back of my mind.

There's a level four up by Lancaster that I worked one day a week for awhile, where I realized how the passage of time is warped inside for lifers, and how insular things must be. An inmate off-handedly referred to the president, saying "Who's president now...it's Carter, right?" This was close to 2020. Carter hadn't been POTUS for over nineteen years.

One of the most powerful experiences I had while working as a contract artist was to have my recently-deceased Dad speak through me to an inmate, then through the inmate to a roomful of hotheads that was about to explode. What I had said to my class was "Opposition to your point of view is an opportunity to grow." This is the tenet by which my Dad lived his life, and which he instilled into my bones, though I never actually heard him say those exact words. My brother Gary said them at Dad's memorial, and I thought "Yep, that's Dad, through and through." It's one of the strongest pillars of my personal constitution, and obviously a valuable perspective for a prison population. So I had shared it to my class at CRC.

Later that week, that inmate—a great rock vocalist and fantastic lyricist in one of the bands—was in a group of about 200 men from diverse backgrounds who were in a class that put them in a room each week to work through their differences. Things got heated and it was all about to go south, when he jumped up and yelled "Don't you get it? Opposition to your point of view is an opportunity to grow!" He told me that there was a moment of shocked silence, then things collectively exhaled and mellowed right out.

Thus were Dad's insights proven to be so powerful, he could work magic on 200 men from beyond the grave. I had a lot of heady experiences like that, working inside. I'd drive home at night feeling something good in my soul that I haven't felt nearly as often since.

In 2002, the Contract Artist program was summarily axed by the stroke of a governor's pen. The "three strikes law", incredibly, still stands.

As you're crossing life's finish line—no matter what you do for a living—it won't be the brightest lights and tallest gigs that you look back on with the most fondness. It'll be the best things you did for the world around you. I consider the work I did as a Contract Artist to be some of the biggest points I've scored so far in the "plus" column of the universe's karmic ledger.

Chapter 25
You Are What You Negotiate

The soft tinkling of champagne glasses and chilled salad forks punctuated smooth ripples of poised conversation filling the ballroom. A quiet waterfall of affluent white chatter from 300 fundraiser guests blanketed the space: Real estate acquisitions, who's the best dog groomer, my kid just graduated Yale. In the background, a tuxedoed 17-piece big band softly played Bossa Novas.

Outside under the Arizona sunset, thousands of gallons of precious water sprayed into the air to keep a hundred acres of fairways and greens alive and lush, in a place whose climate should have barred any consideration of a golf course.

As the servers picked up the salad plates, the polished control of well-heeled musicians and sound crew kept the ten-thousand-watt PA to polite settings, ready to start cautiously letting things off leash once the meal was completed and it was time...but that would be awhile yet. As always with these affairs, the PA was big enough for an outdoor crowd of several thousand.

As investment brokerages were compared over brandy, and dentures furtively checked with tongues and compact mirrors, suddenly a noise erupted into the space loud enough to rupture eardrums:

[POP! CLICK] "HELLO?!? TESTING?? WYNN!! WYNN!!! I CAN HEAR MYSELF IN THE SPEAKERS, WYNN!! I CAN HEAR MYSELF IN THE MAINS!! WYNN!! WHAT SHOULD I DO?!?

The voice was that of a middle-aged female, yelling into a wireless mic from the back of the room, where she had been stationed to read the crowd and keep Wynn informed of its disposition. Wynn, the CEO and bossman of Wynn Pfeiffer Orchestras (not the real name), was at the moment playing piano and leading the band, smiling through teeth gritted so hard, I thought his jaw might explode. He was so determined to pretend he couldn't hear his wife, and that nothing was amiss, that I thought the whorls of his smile might freeze into his face permanently. While he hoped she would come to her senses, shut the hell up, switch off the mic, walk over to the sound man and take it up with him, she just kept hollering at the top of her lungs. Guests spilled Dom Perignon covering their ears and looking around for the offending party, as the sound man could be seen frantically scouring the board and wiring for the errant connection, in a presumably fruitless attempt to save his job. Wynn finally just hollered into his mic, "MARY, BE QUIET!!"

I had been working for Wynn Pfeiffer Orchestras for a few years at that point, doing the penguin gig thing for affluent white people all over SoCal and occasionally out of state, like this fundraiser gig in Arizona. It filled in the weekends and complimented my work as a Contract Artist, paying the rest of my expenses. Not needing the charts, I always had a climbing magazine open on my music stand. Those incredible pictures of climbers throwing everything they had at massive expanses of granite in places like Yosemite, Patagonia and Baffin Island gave me good juju and served to rebuke the psychology of the tux.

The Pfeiffer organization had a penchant for hiring great talent but treating them poorly. Their shows delivered good shock and awe for clients: They had great acrobats, professional tango, swing and hip hop dancers, and The Budweiser twins (remember them?) were hired as dancers on many gigs. The routine during a guitar solo was for the two of them to do sexy crawling poses, wrapping around the guitarist's legs and running their hands up and down his thighs while making sultry faces at the crowd. It took me totally by surprise on the first gig. "No shit, there I was..."

The musicians were fantastic of course, and since Wynn Pfeiffer charged a good deal more per musician than they paid the players, sometimes they managed to have more people on stage than could be considered musically respectable. Six lead singers was the usual, up to a dozen dancers was common on the larger shows...and I remember one show where there were two of every instrument in the rhythm section! Two guitarists, two drummers, two percussionists, two keyboardists, okay. Though it's reachy, none of that's unprecedented. But for the love of Saint Woofer, what do you do with two bass players? Regardless of how good they might be, that's a great way to make your bottom end sound like two elephants trying to squeeze through a door.

Wynn always had family wandering the room, reading the crowd and keeping him informed on the state of things. It should have been a slick system, and it was when it worked as planned: They'd report back on wireless mics routed only to his monitor, using a verbal color code to describe conditions. We'd be playing one style and hear something like "IT'S GREEN, WYNN, VERY GREEN!" and he'd abruptly start calling a different energy level of songs. He had a large A/B splitter switch attached to the piano in front of him that his mic cable went to, so he could opt to talk to the band through their monitors, or to the crowd through the mains. His wife's wireless mic was supposed to be in only his monitor, and though it almost always came through every monitor on stage, this was the first time I had heard it in the mains. Hell, it was so loud I could hear it bouncing off the back wall clearly, despite my being onstage playing in a 17-piece band.

Decorum and poise are expected on stage at all times among professionals working for casual contracting offices, but we're human, believe it or not. There are limits. Despite being a fairly disciplined lot, this was too much and we couldn't help ourselves. We were still playing our parts of course, but laughing like hell as we did.

Wynn was good with that A/B switch. I remember a few gigs where he was playing it like an instrument. Many of these stages are temporary plywood platforms sitting on top of a framework of metal scaffolding or two-by-fours, and when you get a 17-piece band up there then add 12 dancers jumping around in tempo, things can get a little trampoline-like and the whole band starts to go all San Andreas. Cymbal stands can topple over and gear can get damaged, as can players. Wynn, sitting at his big grand piano and taking a trampoline ride during the dance portion of the evening, had his hand on that A/B switch, repeatedly flicking it back and forth every two beats, at about 120 BPM (disco tempo): Smiling to the crowd, "Are we having fun yet?" then snarling at the dancers: "STOP JUMPING!!"...over and over, in rapid alternation: "Are we having fun yet? STOP JUMPING!! Are we having fun yet? STOP JUMPING!!" I couldn't help but think of the Mayor in Nightmare Before Christmas, who had that rotating head with the smiling face on one side and the monster face on the other. Like most musicians I know, it's moments like that that put a smile on my face.

* * *

New Year's eve is prime real estate on the calendar for any casual contractor and, in the right circles, if you're a musician willing to suit up in a tux and brave the drivers on the road and the puke on the floor during the drunkest melee of the year, you can make a premium. All the musicians in the talent stables of the

SoCal contracting offices had been comparing notes and theories about the rates that would be charged for us on New Year's Eve 1999, like so many sailors second-guessing admiralty. Some said triple, some said quadruple—I actually don't think they were thinking high enough. For that one night, every company, every wealthy household, every hotel, every civic organization, every casino, every nightclub, every restaurant and every dog's doghouse was throwing a "Y2K" bash to end all bashes—and the vast majority wanted live bands.

Casual contracting offices were on their back heels for want of enough qualified players. For once, musicians had some real negotiating power...if only as individuals. Wynn Pfeiffer had booked me in the band playing the huge high roller party in one of the biggest casinos in Vegas, in a two-stage, two-band lineup opposite a big pop star. I knew damned well they were charging thousands per player, but they initially didn't want to pay me more than 600. I dug in my heels. If I was going to take two or three days out of my life to travel to Vegas, play a gig and travel back during the chaos of Y2K, then dammit I was gonna be paid my fair share. Wynn blew his top on the phone—behavior for which he was notorious—but he reluctantly agreed to my price. We also both agreed that it would be my last gig with that office. I had had one foot out the door for awhile.

I brought my daughter and my girlfriend to the Y2K hang in Vegas—the gig itself was great and we three had a blast. I let a few days go by afterward while the contracting world recovered, then I made one phone call and was immediately working for another office, being paid more and treated with more respect.

The tip here, yet again, is this: You are what you negotiate.

* * *

Playing for that new office, I found myself among a new and even better cadre of players. It wasn't long before I met Angela Carole Brown, one of the most incredible vocalists I'll ever work with. ACB, as she's known in local musical circles, is a Soul / R&B and Jazz singer where she really lives, but she was classically trained on piano and sings just about any style--including opera--and is known for wearing some other hats which cumulatively make her completely unique.

We hit it off immediately. Having been formally trained and being a singer, she's literate and can discuss musical things more like musicians do. So talking to her is not like talking to most singers. In fact, nothing about her is like most singers. She's a prize-winning published author, accomplished in sculpture, doll-making, painting and alcohol inks, and brings a level of enthusiasm to experiencing existence that makes me envious. And her voice is amazing: Full, gutsy, rich and projecting, capable of all the drama and nuance that any arranger / producer could ever want.

And she was involved with some really interesting projects. During a break on a tux gig over a well known staple known to musicians as "bandwiches"—bologna on white with kraft cheese, mayo and a limp piece of lettuce, whose presence in the workplace is testament to a client's having spared no expense—she told me about a progressive fusion orchestra she sang for called Elvis Schoenberg's Orchestre Surreal.

"If you think 'Stravinski meets Zappa at Hendrix', with some narration in the vein of Rod Serling and Hunter Thompson, along with a little sado-masochistic rap in German, you're on the right track."

It might strike you as odd that to my sensibilities, her description of this band made it sound like it not only made sense, but was inevitable: Sravinsky, Zappa, Hendrix, Serling and Thompson are all very audacious minds. Bringing their influences together on one project sounded like something naturally bound to occur, and here I had found out that somebody was doing it. During my lifetime, no less.

"I have GOT to see this!" I said. "When are you playing?"

And so it came to be that I went and saw the coolest, hippest, most inventive, hilarious and musically dumbfounding show I ever had. I drove away from it having met most of the players—all very respected musicians among the LA musical community—and thinking to myself, "Man, how cool would it be to actually play with that band? Maybe someday."

When I described the show to James Hurley on the phone afterwards, his immediate response was "Ah! So it's music for jaded musicians."

* * *

For the first couple of years in the new century Koz and I were busy on and off, scoring things at the Centrum Building. That, along with the tux gigs on the weekends, helped alleviate the financial stress when the Contract Artist work went away.

In late '02 I got a call from Chris Hardin, one of the most wonderfully competent arranger / MDs I've ever worked for. He's an alum of my alma mater Grove, and wanted me to be in the band he'd be directing for a massive event called "Synagogue 2000" in October of '02, playing to a packed Universal Amphitheater—people from something like 42 different synagogues would be there. We'd be backing up a long list of pop stars, mostly Israeli, playing 36 songs that none of us had ever heard.

It remains the most perfect book of charts I've ever played, for reasons a bit technical to set down here and which aren't the point of this story. But kudos to Chris for having arranged a book of 36 flawless charts—no mean feat, that—and it's a good thing he did too, because we only had one rehearsal and, after one more brief opportunity to brush up a couple of things at sound check, we'd be performing it to over six thousand people.

As you might imagine, a gathering of that many synagogues in one place, a little over a year after 9/11, required a lot of security. Pulling my pickup into the back of the venue to unload was almost exactly like getting through the two outer gates at the max security prisons I had worked. I was expecting something like that, and pleased to see that they had their act together.

The actual load in, on the other hand, was interesting: I was prohibited from carrying any of my own gear from the truck to the stage, by some overtly zealous members of IATSE (International Alliance of Theatrical Stage Employees), who were very defensive of their jobs. Pronounced like the game "Yahtzee", IATSE is the union that represents almost everyone in Stage, TV and Film production who isn't a writer, director or some kind of talent. It's a massive union, and fairly powerful. Many of its members are highly qualified professionals, such as the wizards in charge of special effects, rigging and stunts, whereas some others are more suited for grunt work. These guys at the amphitheater were the latter type—they looked more like comfortably dressed mafia muscle than anything else. I was concerned they'd accidentally break my gear, so I kept a close eye. After some back and forth, they reluctantly agreed to "let me" set up my rig, since none of them had a background that remotely qualified them to do it.

Unions are a great thing. Not to belabor the obvious, but as a lobbying group unions have been the keystone force without which we Americans wouldn't have many of the things we take for granted: weekends, overtime pay, worker safety laws and OSHA, child labor laws, maternity leave, health insurance, retirement packages, and on and on. Basically, many of the prerequisites of the American dream—such as remains of it—are thanks to the efforts of labor unions, regardless of however many Americans have been led to believe otherwise. This is why large corporations and ultra wealthy power brokers are constantly trying to cut them off at the knees, and doing bad things to those who are trying to form new unions. This isn't a digression, I'm just setting the context for some things you should know about the Musician's Union.

The AFM—American Federation of Musicians—is a mixed bag. I've belonged several times over the years, and might rejoin this year (2024), since the union hall is just a few minutes away and offers great deals on nice rehearsal space. But I wouldn't be joining with any notion of being represented in the way you'd expect in other unions (or towns), and here's why:

Local 47, the Hollywood local that serves LA County and most of SoCal, exists primarily to represent orchestral players who do a lot of film work. And in fairness that's a lot of people and they definitely need representation, because of the clout of the film industry.

But for the rest of the musical workforce in SoCal— also a large number of musicians—making their living through "gig work", wearing tuxes, playing nightclubs, teaching or doing recording sessions, the majority of which are non-union—there's no meaningful representation. If you're a union member and a nightclub owner or producer stiffs you, Local 47 won't go lean on him for you unless it's a union gig. And union gigs are actually pretty rare outside of civic orchestras, film shoots or film score recording dates. If an indie artist or the mother of the bride hires you for services consisting of A, B and C, then gets the notion that that includes X, Y and Z for the same pay, again: Local 47 won't help. They'll have some good attorneys to recommend no doubt, but you'll be on your own.

This is sadly apt, though, since musicians are nothing if not un-unified, creating a spineless lobby when it comes to negotiations. Local 47 has made many attempts at being the champion for us all, lobbying to congress and negotiating with the big studios during strikes, in hopes of securing the necessary adaptations and concessions when a new medium threatens to starve our families. Alas, every single time the AFM has joined SAG (Screen Actor's Guild) and The Writer's Guild in going on strike when a new technological threat reared its head, SAG and The Writer's Guild both got far better deals than us. There have been many such battles: The Digital revolution, Cable TV royalties, VHS rental royalties, streaming royalties, and now A.I. is coming for us. SAG and the Writers' Guild have both negotiated better deals with the big studios than AFM every time.

It's not that AFM doesn't care—they just need more clout. So it doesn't help that the AFM's membership isn't higher. The snowball has rolled down the sad side of that hill over my entire career so far, in a sort of logistical feedback loop: Musicians are intrinsically un-unified, so membership is low, creating a weak union, so bargaining power suffers, lessening incentive to join, creating low membership...'round and 'round it goes.

I've been trying to get musicians to stick up for their worth for decades, whether individually or collectively. We're in a race to the bottom—too many of us are willing to underbid our musical brethren and sistren. Some of us, unbelievably, are even willing to render services for free. If the trend continues to gradually worsen, as it has for decades, music will cease paying anything at all. It can go away entirely as a subject in school and as a career, if we don't unify and dig in our heels.

Musical gig workers in SoCal and many other places need a union of their own, and it's been tried several times, but never caught on. We should be more like the Teamsters: The drivers working for local 399 fare much better than us. In negotiation, we're more like that cow in the brilliant book by Douglas Adams, "Restaurant at the End of the Universe", when she walks politely up to the diner's table and recommends her different parts.

All in all, it's worth joining the union. It doesn't cost much, you do get some concrete, immediate benefits, and the networking is undeniably valuable.

* * *

That show at Universal Amphitheater went off without a hitch, to a past-capacity crowd. The arrangements and charts being perfect, every song sounded like a hit single. And the band was incredible; I was truly honored to be a part of such a collection of talent, playing such an event. Yet another lineup of cats that could happen—you guessed it—only in L.A.

Chapter 26
The Reality About the Dream

The ugly truth about scoring for TV is that you often have no time to actually score. Better production leadership understands the value of a great score, and allows the budget and time for it to happen. Michael Giacchino—an incredibly fine composer and the next John Williams, I expect—first got on my radar via his work on a TV series called "Lost". I knew I was listening to a major new talent, and told my wife as much. "You mark that name, he's gonna win a Best Original Score Oscar someday, before he's done."

Before he's done, hell. It was the next thing he did. "Lost" ran until 2010, the same year Michael Giacchino won the Oscar for "Up".

But regardless of how incredibly brilliant the composer, if he hadn't been given the time and budget to work with, "Lost" might as well have had a Chimpanzee doing the score. And that's our problem: In many cases, with many companies, there's a blatant disregard for the time it actually takes to write, arrange, record and mix a tailored score that actually enhances storyline. Many shows with one-hour episodes literally have a 48 to 72-hour turnaround, and some companies even have a policy of continual music.

To put that into perspective, consider that outside of film and TV, people commonly spend months or more writing and producing an album of a dozen tunes, or over a year writing one symphony. Imagine being expected by some bloviated studio suit to pull 42 minutes of composed, arranged, recorded and mixed music out of your ear in 48 or 72 hours. Sometimes you only get one day.

That's enough time to jot down the start and end time of your cues with the director, sketch the ideas involved and get a good start on the writing, but nowhere near enough time to get the writing actually done, to say nothing of pre-production, soundscaping, scoring, arranging, recording and mixing. This is why TV scoring against tight deadlines gives composers heart attacks at young ages. It literally kills good people.

It's also why you hear things that can't actually be called "scores" at all...it's more common than not these days for a show to actually have zero writing: there's a total absence of any coherent musical thought whatsoever. It sounds like some midiot (a guy with a midi lab) just turned on the drum machine, hit "record" and left the room with his cat sleeping on the synth keyboard, holding down some kind of wooshy-sounding noise. I can see you nodding your head as you read this; you know that of which I speak. It's not the composer's fault. He might or might not be good, but it doesn't matter because he had zero time to do it any other way. And as a viewer, it's hard to endure such a horrible soundtrack, but it's no surprise. Studio suits are as ignorant of music as the rest of society.

In case you're wondering how we got here from the iconic, fantastic TV scores of the 50s, 60s, 70s and 80s, it bears mention that this all ties into the itinerant defunding of arts in the American educational system. Over the course of my lifetime, musical training in the public schools has gone from every student learning the major scale and doing sing-alongs starting in the first few years of grade school—along with semi-realistic funding for band programs—to nobody getting any musical training at all, unless they're in band class—if their school even has a band program—and even then, only if they can get in. Many times, they have to provide their own instruments because the school can't afford to.

Likewise, music programs are always the bottom-rung priority for funding, the first thing to be cut, perpetually dangling over the abyss and holding on by their fingernails, held together and above the waves by bake sales and other last-ditch efforts to keep the entire program from falling into oblivion. They are championed, categorically, by the most selfless, saintly, driven public servants in all of education: Your school band directors. Meanwhile, athletics departments are eating steak and lobster.

* * *

In '01 and '02, I was scoring a lot for film and TV, mostly TV, mostly with Koz. This is the type of work I had always wanted to break into, the hallowed ground. But as I hurried through the process—always hurrying—I became more and more aware that it wasn't creatively gratifying: it was more a fight to survive the race against deadlines than anything else.

I scored several hundreds of minutes of footage in those two years, and out of all that work, only one cue of around two minutes comes to mind as being something I actually liked, and that's due to my having forced myself to spend the time on it.

It was in that Discovery Channel TV series of ten one-hour (42 minute) episodes, hosted by a South African wildlife biologist named Jules Sylvester. If you think along the lines of Jeff Corwin or Crocodile Hunter, you're on the right track. In the segment, Jules is sitting next to a massive African vulture, talking about the species and feeding it strips of meat at intervals as he speaks.

It's a huge, comically weird looking bird, and it's striking pretty violently at the meat as Jules holds out the pieces. So I made a moody, sardonic and darkly comedic thing, with a spooky sound playing an actual melody, and I punctuated the bird's strikes with giant stings featuring pizzicato strings, snare flams, cymbal chokes and some other things ("Pizzicato" is when the string players pluck with their fingers instead of bowing). The cue works really well, has a nice build to it, and I tied it all up with a pretty little bow knot at the end just as he finishes speaking. Everything dodges the dialogue nicely. I spent about an hour taking it from nothing to finished mix, which is hauling ass by normal standards of course, but still far too slow for the conveyor belt we were feeding.

As always seems to be the case nowadays, the post-production audio engineer was evidently deaf. And astonishingly, he was incapable of lining up a cue's starting frame number with that of the video's—a very simple task that any seven-year-old could easily perform. Then the whole score got mixed into the show at such a low level it might as well not exist.

* * *

My daughter, visiting me from out of state for a few weeks of her summer vacation between 9th and 10th grade, noticed that I really didn't seem to be enjoying the scoring process much. I had been going at it even harder than usual, trying to get ahead before she arrived so that I could take her up to Mammoth and Yosemite for a few days. As it was, she had to watch me pound noises into the world for a couple of days before we could leave. She was super cool about it, because she's amazing that way. Koz had to absorb some of my workload as well, and he was very cool about it too...I was ghosting, after all.

Then as now, my time with my daughter was a precious thing because we had a lot of lost time to make up for. We tossed Boone and some camping gear in my Toyota pickup and lit out up 395 to the Eastern Sierras.

A few nights later, we were sitting on the tailgate in a turnout off of 120 overlooking Tioga Lake at 9,700 feet in the High Sierras. It was the last few minutes of dusk, and the alpenglow was silently fading on Mount Dana. Yosemite's high country never disappoints—the air was so crystaline and pure in our lungs, we could smell a pinecone drop a mile away, and the stars were already putting on a show. The biosphere was gently exhaling into its nightly repose, traffic had died for the day and it was completely quiet. There was a lull in the conversation as we both just sat there and drank it all in.

After a minute or two she said, "Dad?"

"Yes, m'love?"

"You know how you're always asking me to come move in with you?"

I was instantly two hundred percent alert. I had been careful not to make her feel pressured, but had made it clear that I would love nothing more than if she lived with me.

"Yeesss...?"

"Okay, here it is." She took a breath, readying herself for her next sentence...I could tell that she knew she was about to take an important step in her life.

"If you're living in Mammoth Lakes by the beginning of my Junior year, I'll come live with you."

I didn't even have to think about it. "Done deal, m'love!!" And that's how I lined up the best seven years of my life. And kudos to my daughter...she knew damned well I was dying to move to the Eastern Sierras. I had told her about a twelve-week period during the preceding year, when I had headed up to the Eastern Sierras eleven different times. My patience with living in L.A. was clearly wearing thin.

And so it came to be that I planned to be a single dad in a resort town more expensive than Beverly Hills. The only thing that remained was to figure out how the hell I was going to manage that.

Chapter 27
Anchors Aweigh

Looking for work is always a crap-shoot, usually a tricky one. The basic premise is that if you're enough of a badass and you've been keeping your face in the right people's minds by doing the right gigs, showing up at the right hangs and throwing down at the right jam nights, your phone will be ringing. But if you fall off the radar, getting back on it will take some effort. For the last couple of years I had been concealing myself inside tiny studios working on Film and TV scores, then wearing a tux and playing private shindigs on the weekends. Not really the right presence around town to put me in people's minds for larger gigs.

The perfect thing for me at that time would have been some big tour or other, ending just in time to make the move to Mammoth happen with my daughter, my pockets happily bulging with cash and plunder. I made a few calls to my more connected friends, very tactfully letting my availability be known. Regardless of how tactful and professional you come across, this practice is called "groveling" in the ruthless comedy of musical vernacular, so I only called close friends. I knew it was a long shot and sure enough, I had no luck there. So I hit up the listings at MCS.

There are times when you know right off the bat that things are thin for everybody. Sometimes MCS will have lots of viable gigs, other times there's nothing better than out-of-town two-nighters with cover bands, or the ever-present listings from lost pilgrims expecting players to throw in with them as they endlessly tilt at windmills: "Hollywood-based original melodic rock band with lockout rehearsal space seeks guitarist, must be dedicated and committed, no posers, pro gear only. Must contribute $40 a month toward rehearsal space. Owning a P.A. and knowing a good bass player, drummer and keyboardist is a plus. Will be booked soon".

De-coded, that reads "Singer / songwriter wishes he had a band to rehearse with in his apartment endlessly, while chasing an errant dream based on a bloviated sense of talent and fictional understanding of the record industry. There will be no bookings. Ever."

That "pro gear" language is always good for a chuckle. I'm currently endorsed by PRS Guitars and Amps, DR Strings, Danelectro Guitars and Pedals, Egnater Amps, Kopo Guitars and Levy's Leathers Gig Bags...and as Jesse is my witness, I have no idea what the phrase "Pro Gear" even means. I don't know anyone who does.

There was one listing that caught my eye, for a cruise ship gig. The timing of it was right: 16 weeks, ending just before I was to go collect my daughter and move to Mammoth with her. So I called the number and lined up the audition. After meeting with Dave Romeo, the bandleader and also an excellent drummer, I was hired on the spot.

Thus began my odyssey through a corporate vetting and testing process that was more involved than anything I went through when hired by Universal, or even when California Department of Corrections hired me to carry keys around max security prisons: There was a physical exam that included a cardiac stress test on an exer-cycle, an EKG, a hearing test, blood work, psyche evaluations disguised as "questionnaires", geared to determine if I was mindlessly obedient enough for the absurdities and cheerleading of working for a large corporation (I gave the answers I knew would placate them), legal background checks, and my standing with the DMV was even looked into, though one might wonder why.

The one thing I was never asked by the cruise line, and which I doubt they ever researched, was whether I was any good as a musician.

Many players in LA's upper echelons have done time on a ship. I wouldn't call it a rite of passage, but if you can hang with it, it'll be established that you have the discipline and professionalism to tolerate high levels of bullshit—a valuable attribute on many other gigs—while smiling and performing as reliably as the ice cream machine. And it lasts awhile. Working for casual contractors, a lot of the clients are corporate. But you drive home after the gig. This was to be 16 solid weeks of crawling around inside the very bowels of a corporate environment.

The cruise industry is of course massive. The largest players are multi-billion dollar companies owned in the States, whose ships are operated by Norwegians, registered in the Bahamas and operate in international waters much of the time. These companies retain the best fire-breathing corporate attorneys known to humankind, and are almost completely indemnified from accountability to worker's right's norms as we know them here in the states. In terms of how they treat their employees, they make the big studios look like mom and pop hardware stores. If you work for such a thing, you're effectively a conscript in every way except for a couple of legal technicalities, which for all practical purposes disappear when the bow line is cast off. When you board, they literally lock your passport in a safe and force you to use your ship's ID tag when you go ashore in foreign ports. Too many would jump ship otherwise.

In case you've never been on a cruise ship, here's a brief rundown of how massive these things actually are: The ship I was on weighs 69,130 tons, is 867 feet long and has a beam (width) of 117 feet, known familiarly as "panamax", or the widest thing that can fit through the Panama Canal. It's eleven decks tall, an average cruise will have 2,000 passengers and 735 crew, give or take. That's not even the largest class of cruise vessel. These things are giant floating hotels. Even in rough weather, you get almost no sensation of being on a ship at sea.

Our contract had us sailing out of Galveston, doing three long cruises around the Caribbean, then crossing the pond and doing nine laps, one week each, around the Mediterranean.

Our last time through the Panama Canal, we added an overnight stay in Panama City to try to fix an engine problem that had us limping along on one propellor. Ever the good-timing opportunists, my band mates and I asked around the port to find out where the good live music was. We wound up having a great time jamming with a local band in a packed nightclub and getting treated like visiting royalty.

The starboard engine needed a new circuit board that nobody could lay hands on, but they did get it semi-useable. So off we limped on one-and-a-half props, one engine running and one walking, leaving an asymmetrical foam trail behind. We tagged Nassau for one last afternoon, and crossed the pond in that state. Barcelona was our new home base, where we restocked and picked up new passengers each week—and where we rendezvoused with a new circuit board.

Not long after I got on board, I got a clear indication of the brutal nature of the industry, when I fell into a conversation with a ship cleaner polishing the brass railing in one of the passenger stairwells. These are the people you see cleaning windows, vacuuming and polishing the brass all over the ship. Like all ship cleaners, she was hired from one of the most impoverished third world countries, worked twelve-hour shifts, seven days a week, for $135 USD per week in 2003 money, and her contract had a minimum of 6 months. If she got sick she could get fired and let off in the next port with no airfare home, if an officer took the notion. That last thing was actually true for us all, and there's a ridiculous list of rules that nobody is equal to obeying. She also said that she was glad to have the work, because it was better than anything available to her at home. Of course, the corporation knew that and took advantage with all due ferocity, in accordance with the level of humanitarianism taught in business schools everywhere.

That's what you have to admire: These cruise ship companies know exactly how little they can get away with paying everyone—from every class of society in every country, for every different job—and how much abuse they can get away with as far as job duties and work environment is concerned. There are occasional class-action things shaking things up, but not enough. The industry's work force badly needs a Cesar Chavez. One can always hope.

The pay scale of personnel is arrived at according to supply and demand of course, so it's not as crazy as it sounds if you look at it from the de-humanizing math of an accountant's ledger, or the boardroom in corporate America's penthouse. At the time, we had doctors from broken eastern bloc countries clawing their way to a better life by working contracts on that ship as waiters and maids.

And here was I, speaking only one language (despite the Emmanuel tour, my Spanish still sucks), amidst a crew of 60 nationalities, only 6% of whom were American, and pretty much all of whom were overqualified multi-lingual world travelers whose station on board had them calling me sir, and waiting on me. I worked four or five hours a day, playing music. I never got used to the dichotomy, but I was in good company, and lots of it. Everyone in the crew was smart, hard-working, disciplined and, for the most part, the musicians were of high caliber. The ship had 13 musical acts on board, each performing in its own niche. We were the 4-piece Top 40 variety band.

* * *

There was a jazz trio of Romanians whose venue was a 6-deck deep atrium in the middle of the ship called The Centrum. And they played their asses off: pearls of beautiful organic expression reverberated off the hotel-chic plastic, fake ferns, glass, chrome, brass and semi-lucid passengers each day, starting at around sunset. I sat in with them only once and wish it had been more often, because the keyboard player and the drummer were seriously great cats. Unfortunately for me they shipped out halfway through our contract, but before they did, I wound up at a table with them and a couple of guys from the ship's orchestra one night in the crew bar. Altogether, we were three Romanians, two Poles and a Yank. And they told me their tale.

These guys were around my age, so they had been musicians under Russian rule. I asked them if it was really true that until the wall came down, none of them were allowed to practice or perform anything but state music. I had heard things to that effect over the years, but could never really get my head around the reality. Hearing them tell me about it was a different thing. Try to imagine running a risk of political imprisonment if you play anything but whatever music the government says is okay. The national anthem is fine and dandy, but if they overhear you playing Beatles or Bach or Ellington, you're going to a gulag. No wonder those guys played like the wind, and with such feeling—and drank like they were still chasing liberation. I have deep respect for them, for having won their way onboard that tub, and for the incredible noiseletting that came from their souls. I feel broadened as a human for having met them.

* * *

The band I was in had a solid bass player and singer, Paul Foti, who could sing the country stuff on country night and the 50s stuff on 50s night, so that I didn't have to. I owe the man my life.

The biggest saving grace was Dave Romeo's excellence on the drums and, being a fellow fusion hound, his willingness to join me in firebreathing and noiseletting on a regular basis, to keep the carbon from building up in the cylinders. The drummer is the engine under the hood and the most important element of any musical act that has drums. I could never have survived that gig if he hadn't been a great player.

Otherwise it was a very loungy gig, and would have had a high potential to drive me off my hinges or over the railing. The keyboardist—also named Dave—held down a very serious role, in that he was the cruise director's boyfriend and kept us from having to tear down, move, set up and soundcheck in a new place every day—a nightmare scenario that could otherwise have happened. All three guys were good hangs and easy to get along with.

After a while, the band started getting that level of comfort with the gig that feels a lot like cobwebs. I felt the louginess starting to degrade my chops, so I broke out Frau Metronome one afternoon in a low-traffic crew stairwell behind the stage. I felt my chops rebound, like a predator awakening and stretching its claws.

Fired up and enthused by my newly rediscovered glory, I was able to bring some passion to the gig that night. It was 50s night, and I really didn't want to play it "stock". I strode into the lounge carrying the hope of offering something useful, something real, something I actually desired to deliver, and which had been lacking in recent weeks.

This was like building up a big head of steam and momentum on a bike, then pedaling straight into a tar pit: my enthusiasm was no match for the louginess of the gig. My passion lasted about 15 minutes, then the plowshare had its inevitable effect. Hee-haw.

But soon after that, after another good bludgeoning from the Frau, I again carried my desire with me into the lounge on 50s night. This time I had more resolve, and the gig went better as a result. Passion won and I kept up the momentum, cruising over the top of the tar. Instead of my being dragged down, elements around me were elevated. I visited the same old worn out trade routes and discovered new lines. The band was getting inspired too, like rings from a pebble thrown into a pond.

The lesson here is this: When the music is crap, don't castrate yourself by trying to suck badly enough to sound the part. Bring that shit up to your level and set it on fire. With enough irreverence, you can transmogrify just about anything into a meal worthy of a salivating, fanged beast. Two months on that gig is what it took for me to realize that I just wasn't irreverent enough.

There are plenty of musical situations where music needs to be played in its stock form, and plenty of musicians doing that. Dog knows I've paid my dues kowtowing to the expected part. But for a live band to be exciting, it needs to show some game, and not be a faceless human juke box. If it's a high-profile, rehearsed show touring large venues, then okay. You need to play your role and part and trust to the lighting, pyro and sound to provide the shock and awe. But in lots of situations, such as nightclubs, it's different. How far things can be taken, and how often, is a matter of factors ranging from the state of the crowd to the club owner to your whimsy. I've gotten really good at reading the "what can I get away with" meter--another benefit of being an arranger--and I find that it often makes for a much better performance if I'm strutting around the china shop like a bull.

Us humans are imbued with a sense of existential duty to ascend to the highest possible pinnacle, be it within the bounds of reason or not. It's our genetic job to clamber our cosmically irrelevant way to the top of the crap heap, proclaiming ourselves underneath the night sky. This applies to musical endeavor too, if you don't want to perish from the mix.

If you have to play something that makes you feel like you're licking a toilet bowl, just elevate the music. Make it something you can stomach by trans-substantiating it into its sweet sister or evil twin. I've always done this when I thought the room and band were hip enough.

And in that cruise ship lounge, I discovered that people either didn't notice that their music had mutated into something burlier and grown fur, or they did, and they were "in on it" with me. Invariably, the minions in charge of killing the vibe—managers, directors and such—didn't even notice that Peggy Sue had become 5/8 fusion ska with blistering 16th-triplet pyro-technic guitar. I set my nozzle on spray, professionalism be damned.

When you lose the mousiness and play like a lion, you have more to offer a situation, if you can do it musically and without getting fired. And of course it helps when the drummer is a great player and easy to get going. David and I took those lilting little 50's tunes and injected steroids, turning emaciated limp noodles into muscly things benching 300 pounds and breathing fire. "Dream" by the Everly Brothers with double kick drum that could cure constipation at a hundred yards, and a guitar depicting anti-aircraft artillery. "All Shook Up" with a rhythm bed like Toto's "Rosanna", but more muscular, like it was being played at The Spud, with thunderous drum fills and rock fusion guitar histrionics with full afterburners blazing.

Paul, bless the man, did a great job of tolerating this hooliganry while crooning and holding on to the bass line for dear life. I actually started looking forward to 50's nights, if only for the perverse pleasure of taking those despicable lilt-fests and turning them into Frankenstein's Monster. Whether out of spite or to facilitate my survival, it became the new law.

***

Ship life was very different from my schedule at home. There was no daily talking with family and friends, just a weekly e-blast and check in via email. No networking, no multiple musical projects, no casting about for work, no racing deadlines, no cooking, no driving, no doing dishes or housework...I had many hours of free time every day. Also, there was no hitting the trails, or crags, or mountain bike with Boone, who I missed greatly. I knew he was in great hands with my two housemates back on the horse ranch we all shared in Sylmar, so I wasn't worried. But I missed him.

Besides lighting the afterburners and cruising the tar, there were three other things that kept me from going stir-crazy:

The first was scotch, which was affordable and in copious supply in all directions, at all times. My drinking increased markedly over the course of that contract. For passengers and crew alike, cruise ship culture is basically a life support mechanism for drinking and eating.

The second was fine cuban cigars, which I took to quietly enjoying under the stars on top deck along with my scotch after the gig. I found a great tabac on La Rambla in Barcelona who carried my favorite Cubans: Cohiba Corona Especiales. Those were great at massaging my forehead and saying reassuring things after a tough night placating the clueless abstract of corporate directives.

The third was writing. It was during those sixteen weeks that I discovered my love of creative composition, not via sculpting sound against a framework of time, but with words. I found that I love the process.

And for good reason: with music, there's a lot to it. In its full-blown form, the workflow is this: First, you create your basic theme. This is one or two, maybe three very simple, very basic motifs (also called "germs", "riffs" or "hooks", in modern vernacular). It's counterintuitive, but the larger the body of work you want to create from these fledgling motifs, the smaller and more brick-shaped they have to be, so that they can be adapted into more variations.

Next you develop those motifs into phrases and sections, then you develop that into your sketch, and your roadmap through the piece's sections. Then you take all that and score an arrangement, which is the most important part of the whole shebang if you're thinking about it clearly enough. You might spend 30 to 80 hours just on arranging one song—some arrangers will take months on one piece.

The next thing in most production workflows is called pre-production and soundscaping, where you get all the virtual (synthetic) noises to exist that won't be played by actual instruments, plus whatever virtual noises are needed as guide tracks, to give players an idea of what you're after with the real tracks, which they'll be providing. Depending on genre there may be none of that or nothing but that, and typically it's a mixture. Then, after your arrangement is done and all your virtual stuff is on board, you go into the tracking phase and get all the "non-virtual" stuff in the can (recorded). Then you do the inevitable editing—which should bring the thing to life, but if you're not careful, will file off too many warts and suck the life right out.

Then finally, you go into the mixing phase. Mixing is a promise to no man, to paraphrase one Bard, and to paraphrase another, "mixes are never finished, only abandoned." Once it's mixed, it's still not done: It needs to be mastered for consumer use.

Every producer's career is littered with fiascos of heartbreak, and sagas of homeric length, springing from each and every one of those steps. In the writing phase, some people struggle on a note-by-note basis, agonizing over every fraction of every beat that you'll hear. Mixing a song might take three weeks, it might take a year, it might take 3 hours. Unless you've done a lot of bringing music into this world, you really can't have any idea how involved and time consuming it can actually be.

Now, compare all of that to the logistic of composing with words: You write the word, and that's the final product. Boom. Notwithstanding edits and rewrites, you're done. My having typed that particular "you're done" just now is likely to be the last time I'll deal with that. It kind of blows my mind.

The first manifestation of my new creative tumor was a compost heap of rants about the absurdities of life on board, and several parodies of it. All but inevitably a play started to emerge, based on the characters around me, and there was the weekly e-blast to friends and family. Collectively, I called it "Knucklehead's Log". Knucklehead was born in my bunk on a wheezy 14-year old laptop borrowed from a housemate back home. The thing was so old it had a wind-up crank sticking out of the side, next to the manual choke for starting it on cold mornings. But as long as I babied it, it did the job.

* * *

Our gig was so undemanding of our time that even though I went ashore almost daily to see the sights of whatever port we were in, I still had hours to kill. So Frau Metronome came out on a regular basis, and not only did I practice, I crawled around inside the whole chop-building process and did a ship-bound forensic analysis of how it all actually works, this thing I had been doing with my entire life.

What surprised me is how my chops are tied to my passion. When my chops are up, my mind, body and soul are all breathing fire. I shake the ground when I walk. I have more passion not just for music but for life, and more desire to do something with it, in the same way that having a really nice bike or a new pair of skis makes you want to hop on and go for a ride.

But do I get my chops up because of re-ignited passion, or vice-versa? Chops aren't passion, those are two very different things. Passion can't be practiced, or improved through use. It's either in you that day or it ain't. So are chops maybe talent? Closer, but no. If only I could count the players I've worked with who had chops up the yin-yang, but no talent. Talent is something else, and like passion it can't be taught, sort of like a bright sunny smile on a little kid.

I define "talent" as the ability to pull fresh ideas out of your skull. Call it imagination, or originality, or inspiration. Talent and passion are close relatives. But hooking all that up via physical discipline and know-how is where chops come in, and where the rubber meets the road.

That means that chops are neither talent nor passion, but the mechanism that removes the barriers between talent and passion on one hand, and the expression of what they have to say on the other. To me, what's being communicated is the talent. How well it's being communicated—how well it strikes the heart—that's the passion. Chops are just the prerequisite skill set enabling that communication to take place.

So if that's all that chops are, why do I get so impassioned and fired up when mine are a notch or two above the norm? My passion should come from something beyond my grasp, not time spent sparring with The Frau in the woodshed. It should come from my emotional state, or my circumstances, or from the universe itself...a Passion-Distributor Fairy.

I can just see her: A chubby little old lady, grotesquely spackled with Tammy Bakker make-up, wearing a cheesy yellow princess outfit and a glittery plastic halo wobbling around on a wire frame. She dangles from some cables, descends on me in my sleep and beans me with a wand. The following day I wake up with an extra bit of passion and write or play something good.

Maybe passion comes from anomalies in the gravitational field, or bio-rhythms, or divine intervention, or wind direction. Maybe it's the right diet, tea leaves, astrology, tarot cards, or just dumb luck. Whatever it is, I shouldn't have any influence over my own passion and inspiration just by shedding. That puts the ball entirely too much in my court.

But like it or not, that's what I arrived at in my dissection of the woodshedding process: I reclaim some physical chops and gain a stronger drive to resume work on the records I was making before life interrupted—a renewed desire to ascend the stair, mount the dais and assume my rightful place on the throne of The Almighty and Omnipotent Guitarist / Composer, majestically reigning over the smoldering ruins of the digital apocalypse, radiating brilliance to the numbed indifference of the general public for several feet in every direction. Look upon me and tremble.

* * *

If you've ever been to or on the ocean and looked at the state of anything metal that lives in that environment, you've seen the moisture and salt plastering everything with a hoary coating that might resemble anything from spray adhesive to frost to barnacles. I won't bore you with how hard it is to play guitar with that gluey salt-munge all over the neck, the fretboard and your fingers—but just try to imagine what that does when it encrusts the circuits of musical gear that lives on a ship or at a coastal venue. Unless you've done time trying to use that gear, you can't appreciate the tragic comedy of how truly bad it is. Cue primal screams and horror music here.

There were half a dozen guitar amps on board, two or three of which worked when I arrived, but by halfway through the contract every amp on board had stoically croaked its goodbye as its innards were devoured by air-crustaceans and other sea creatures. One day I had had enough and got permission—more like I laid down the law, if I'm being honest—to get every amp on board in one place at one time, along with one or two of the other guitarists and a sound tech. We scavenged tubes, fuses and other parts from several amps in hopes of bringing just one of them to life. The mission was successful. By any normal standards that one working amp belonged in the ER, but it got passed around as needed for the next few days. The next Barcelona, we repeated the scavenger hunt in every likely shop in the city. I put a lot of miles on my dogs that day, and brought my plunder of tubes back to the ship in a plain brown bag. We got some amps working, sort of.

Roughly halfway through our contract, the ship got a new sound engineer named Corey. Corey was a young American sound tech, pretty fresh out of school, and hell-bent on doing good. Nice kid. Real bright-eyed and bushy-tailed type, and Dog help the poor lad, he cared.

The gear that lived outside on top deck had long since had half its innards consumed by the salty demons of the sea. Connections were made by the oxide monsters that created circuits no drawing board had ever seen, whereas connections that belonged had gone the way of a fish carcass. Amps didn't even power up half the time, and there was live music up there pretty much daily. We played up there once or twice a week, and always wondered what unknowable the non-gear was going to contribute that day. The PA's mixing board, bless its little digital heart, was an aging Yamaha 01V. If you think of a wheezy mid-1990s computer with audio connections, sliders and an LCD screen, you're on the right track. The thing would have been challenged in the best of environments, and here it was in atmosphere so salty and humid it might as well have lived underwater. Strangely enough it usually powered up, but beyond that, using it was like climbing into the half-buried, rusted bones of a wrecked airplane and expecting it to start up and fly.

The day after Corey tried to run sound on top deck for the first time, it was on. He spent an entire day dismantling and cleaning every connection in the mixer and every amp, then reassembled them. He re-soldered half the cable ends. He re-patched the entire PA, setting it up in a different, better position. He optimized wire management, checked every speaker and cleaned the tartar off of every connector with emery cloth. Had I known he was doing all that, I might have saved him some trouble, but the exuberance and hope of youth probably required him to find out for himself.

We had the honor of being the first band using the gear up there after all his heroic efforts. We were amazed at the difference and quality—hell, the existence—of sound, along with the vocal monitors having something that sounded like our vocals coming out of them. The keyboard amp even powered up. So went the sound check. Downbeat arrived and we counted off the first tune, wondering how long it would be before something blew up and bummed the vibe. Somewhere around the end of the introduction of the first tune, the bass amp got possessed by the farting ghost of Jabba the Hutt, and by the first chorus our vocals sounded like a cell phone signal breaking up. System after system reverted back to normal dysfunction, until halfway through the first set, the mains and guitar amp inevitably died entirely, and we were forced into our familiar default "gear-free" mode: "DRUM SOLO!!"

I expected Corey to pull out his hair or toss himself over the rail, but to his credit he just laughed. The kid was gonna be alright.

Sometimes that gear worked alright up there, though. It was luck of the draw. One of the coolest gigs I've ever played was on top deck of that damned ship, believe it or not. I had set up for sound check with all the enthusiasm of a lamb being led to play on a stage with no functioning gear. We had left Naples that afternoon and passed close to Capri at sunset. We started playing around 9PM. It was some kind of ship's gala, and because of all the brass and management in attendance, we actually had to play things straight. I was wallowing in the tar pit, and in self-pity. Poor me. Then somebody said "Is that a volcano?" I looked off to starboard and saw a glorious, bright orange-red river of lava flowing unbroken down the flanks of Stromboli into the sea, a few miles away. "WAY COOL!!" I thought to myself. Then about two minutes later, someone said "Hey, is that a lunar eclipse?"

And just like that: "No shit there I was, playing a raging, howling guitar solo to a thousand people under a total lunar eclipse, while sailing past an erupting volcano." My imagined hardships were vaporized by Ma Nature's very real majesty—not the first or last time She's pulled my head out of my ass. And I clearly felt my Dad's presence: He who made sure that I inherited his love for the night sky and all natural wonders.

* * *

The ship had some seriously great guitar talent on board. Most of us felt like racehorses pulling apple carts on our respective gigs, so one day in Malta we made something really cool happen: We got permission to grab a soundman, use the stage and PA on top deck, and have a sprayathon with electrified classical guitars. It was an official show in every way except for existence on paper.

Luis was a great flamenco guitarist who played a weekly show in the theater with his act "Ole Ole". Nazzereno was an incredibly good classical / flamenco / jazz cat, employed by Manuel as the ringer to fill out their duo, "Azatlan". Brian was the fretmonster in the ship's orchestra, whose strong suit was fusion and who had recently bought a really fine classical axe in I-forget-what port. Manuel played rhythm, but usually sat out so I could borrow his axe.

In searing 100-degree heat and 97% humidity, surrounded on all sides by the yellow stone cliffs and the yellow stone buildings rising up from the yellow stone beaches in the yellow stone port city of Valletta, we used our favorite Latin Jazz tunes as race tracks for solo trade-offs and headcutting sessions. We hit "play" on a mini-disc player providing percussion tracks through the PA, and away we went, nozzles on "spray".

To say it sounded busy is an understatement, and in that blistering heat and wilting humidity, the guitars and players suffered and sounded accordingly. But the people loved it. Malta was the second-to-last day in the weekly cruise, so by that point everyone had seen Luis, Nazz, Brian and me highlighted on our respective gigs, and they knew this was something special. Many would run and get their camcorders (this was '03, before cell phones were also video cameras, calendars, navigators, mail carriers, auto mechanics and dishwashers).

We were sometimes joined by Dave, one of the best bass players I've ever known, who was on that ship playing in the orchestra. Dave was Brian's roommate, and the three of us had many impromptu fusion jams in the cramped confines of their cabin. Dave was mentored by Jaco Pastorius—in fact they had been good brothers. He said he was Jaco's son's godfather. And MAN, that guy could play.

It became a weekly thing and one of the most popular shows on the ship, according to the "passenger entertainment poll". Despite being so infested with 32nd-note flurries, it always drew a crowd of hundreds—no mean feat on top deck, in heat like that. One week, it polled as the most popular show. And there's a good lesson there:

Don't underestimate your listeners. Sure, the record industry may have agendized the oversimplification of music so badly that even now, with the recording industry's classic business model all but gone, that old "dummy-it-down" pathos still persists. But that doesn't mean that lay-listeners can't appreciate sophisticated music. And people of all walks will always get excited by irresponsible displays of virtuosity.

Musically, that was the highlight of the cruise gig for me. I've chewed a lot of mud since then, but I still miss spraying with those guys.

* * *

The ship's orchestra was made up of nine harried and sleep-deprived staff musicians whose coal mine was the main showroom, either in the pit or on the stage. The term "orchestra" might be an aggrandizement for a 4-man rhythm section, 3 brass and 2 winds, but they were good. It was their thankless lot in life to back up the "headliners", and to perpetually be in rehearsal to accommodate the steady stream of new shows rotating through. I always invited Brian and Dave along when I was headed off to a port to see some sights. It usually went something like "Heyman, wanna go kick around Rome for a few hours?"

"Don't I wish. We gotta rehearse."

It sort of kills the main upside to a ship gig of you can't go see the places you're visiting.

A headliner is a luminary—or someone who can be passed off as one—booked onto the cruise to bolster sales. They're short term, usually just there for one cruise. Some are faded-glory stars, some are would-be and wannabe celebs who are great at leveraging their promotional savvy into touring the cruise ships as a "somebody", and some actually graduated themselves up through the ranks of ship life because they're just that talented and driven. No mean feat, that.

According to my buds in the orchestra, some of the headliners failed to achieve the humility you'd expect their stature to inspire. Add to that the horrible charts they usually had, and it made for a badly under-paid, over-rehearsed band. At the helm of all this was an individual stuck between the interests of the headliner, his players and the cruise line, namely the ship's musical director. The MD was also in charge of all musical acts, including the band I was in. Not surprisingly, he was by far the most harried and miserable.

So if you must get a gig on a cruise ship, either be a headliner or in a contracted band, or in a band just doing a couple of shows on a themed music festival cruise of some kind. Avoid the orchestra. It pays too little and works you too much.

* * *

One night in the crew bar, way down in the belly of the beast, on bottom deck far below the waterline, something happened that blew my mind. It bothered me then, and it bothers me now. About a half a dozen of the ship's musicians—some guys from the orchestra and from the Romanian Trio—came up to me when I walked in, and said, "Byron, we have something to tell you."

"Oh?"

"Yes. You will like this. We held a poll of most of the musicians on the ship, to decide who most of us think is the best musician on board."

"Really? I never heard about it..."

"We decided it's you."

I just stared at their faces for a second, waiting for the punchline. None came. From their expressions, they weren't messing with me.

"Waitaminnit, what? Are you serious?"

"Yes, no lie. We are here to honor you and buy you a drink. You won the poll!"

"Guys, no. I strongly disagree...this is a huge honor, and I clearly don't deserve it. C'mon, the talent on this ship is way better than me..."

They insisted it was true. This wasn't anything organized or official, and I have no idea who was actually asked. But even if it was only those guys there in the bar hoisting drinks with me...well, shit. Considering the company I was in, it was the finest and most undeserved compliment I've ever received. And the wrongness of it really grated on me then, as now.

For most serious musicians, there's a toxic psychology to compliments. For one thing, we're wired to never be happy with our craft. Even after our best showing, we drive home imagining having done things better, and wishing we had. We all, every one of us, long to play that perfect note someday that beckons from just beyond the horizon, on the golden sands of a promised land we must never, never actually reach. The day one of us thinks we're there, game's over. It's exactly that striving—the swimming upstream—that makes us good.

For another thing, imposter syndrome is very real. I've talked to some of the best musicians on earth here in LA about it, and we all get it to some degree. And it's not like any one of us can accurately assess how we stack up. In the brilliant words of the great philosopher Alan Watts, "it's like trying to bite your own teeth."

So any time I get a compliment, of any kind, from any quarter, something inside me recoils and I'm instantly struggling not to be awkward as I'm pursued around my attic by a horde of barking monkeys. The more legit the source of the compliment—like those badass cats in that crew bar—the more it irks me. And it still bugs me: Why the hell did they do that? Why me? Nazz was way better than me. The keyboardist in the Romanian band was better than me, and he was sitting right there. Dave Wilkinson, bass player with the orchestra, was better than me...hell, at least half the musicians on board were better than me.

If you have a musician in your life who you're finding it hard to relate to, all I can say is that you have to accept our quirks, and you have my every sympathy. If you can't allow us our differences, then good luck with that. We're just not wired like other humans. Idunno why we aren't, but we aren't. And if you're a musician who has discovered these difficulties with accepting compliments, you're not making it up. You're in good company.

* * *

From aboard that ship, it seemed impossible to me that I'd ever be able to balance a musical career with the role of fatherhood, which I'd be assuming as soon as the contract was over. It was a mindfuck. I discovered something, though: Because I had been so close to my dad while he was alive, I always knew what he would say about any situation I was in, and his advice was always golden. So although he had left this earth a couple of years prior, I could still talk to him sometimes while lying in my bunk, to pick his brain. I wrote about one such conversation in Knucklehead's Log:

I had a talk with Dad last night. He appeared in my mind's eye as the all-powerful superman he always was to me—still is—we were in the High Sierra, his favorite stomping grounds. It was a calm, temperate summer night on the banks of Snow Creek in the Yosemite back country, not far from Mt. Watkins, and right across Teneya Canyon from Cloud's Rest. Sitting around the fire after the first day's hike in, we were relaxing like always, talking of great things big and small; he was savoring his pipe. His pipe always tasted better to him when lit by a burning stick from the fire...all the more in the High Sierra. For this purpose, he used to engage us all in a search for just the right stick to be ordained as The Lighter, and it would function as such all night, and proudly so. On a good night, when conversation kept us up, there might be a Second Lighter. On a 'two-lighter night', even as a kid I knew things in this life couldn't get much better.

Of all the conversations I can remember having in my life, the best, the most powerful, the truest and the most influential to my character were with Dad. Of the conversations I had with Dad, those that took place around a campfire were by far the most memorable, and it's those that I miss the most. I'm sure he was no more profound, insightful, funny or draped in greatness in that setting than any other. I was probably just more open. And it makes me wonder what I might have learned, had I been that open all the time.

We're looking up at the stars through the breaks in the trees, smelling the pine needles on the floor cooling down after a hot summer day, and smelling the remaining snow-pack, not far away. Good smells—the absolute best. In all my travels, I've come across none better. The soft, timeless rushing of Snow Creek is nearby, providing aural wallpaper to our exchange.

I kick things off: "Dad, I've decided I want to live here, in these mountains. Britt loves it here more than anything else, and I just spent 23 years in LA. I feel like I've earned it, and I really need to get grounded again." These words float off into space under the stars that were there when I was 6, the first time we were here. The stars look on in sparkling indifference.

Dad's whole comportment changes instantaneously, from one of vacationing and reveling in the wilderness, to Father / sounding board. His eyes show more brightly, more intensely, as he filters this information through that incredible machinery in his head. My words, their portent and the firelight reflect off the bark of the pines nearby: "I know I need to be settling into a job that's solid enough to set Britt up—and I want that, I really do. It's just that I have to have this. THIS." Waving my arms around me, as if he doesn't know what I mean.

And the man who instilled such a love of nature in me leans back a little, working that mind, figuring a way to make it all work and to set me up to win. "Hmm" is all he says...it sounds more like 'hmmph'. His consternation is plainly visible in the knitted brow, the busy way he works the pipe. "Well...I don't suppose you've made this decision lightly....that Cal State thing, you know..."

He was talking about an offer I had gotten to be faculty at Cal State Monterey Bay. I had been agonizing over the decision between that and another offer in Reno at UNR, as opposed to living in Mammoth and just winging it.

"That Cal State thing can't start before a little over a year from now at the earliest."

He nods acknowledgement of the new info: "mmHmm..." Two puffs on the pipe go rebounding through air molecules, carrying the soulful aroma of Old Hickory tobacco through time.

"Well, buddy boy, I hate to see you struggle, you know. You seem to have had so much of that...you'll need for that to be over, for Britt's sake. Any idea how this is all going to work? Where is it you want to be, precisely?"

"Mammoth."

"Mammoth. I see."

"Yeah, Mammoth...." I say the word with some reverence.

"I've got friends there, and I..." I take a second to collect my thoughts about this. There's a lot to it, and I don't want him to be disappointed. The bark of the pines glow patiently in the firelight along with Dad's eyes, along with the stars, along with the brilliant liquid crystal water of Snow Creek. They've all been patiently timeless as I've squandered my stupid existence on city life. My tide is finally turning: "Dad, I've looked at housing in both places, Monterey and Mammoth. It's doable. Mammoth High is a great school, and there's work there. The ceiling's lower, sure...but how many times in my life am I gonna learn that lesson about doing what I love being the most lucrative thing? And Mammoth is going through a major growth spurt, right now. There's gotta be a good, stable job in all that, somewhere. Maybe something with retirement and all that..."

The pines, the creek and the stars graciously tolerate my discussing such things in this setting, this context. I plow on: "My friends there are keeping an eye out for ways to open doors for me in advance, in the job market and looking for a place, both. If I don't do it now, I probably never will..."

I stop, realizing I'm prattling, tumbling one half-formed thought after another like some panhandler in front of a 7-11. I don't need to justify this move, this change of direction, I realize. I just need to explain it, to make it make sense. The thought of trying to 'sell' Dad is absurd.

"Well, hot shot" He says, "okay, let's look at this: First, you say you've got these friends there, and they're trying to get you situated...?"

He's cautious about accepting this. Some of the friends I had during my upbringing gave him arrhythmia.

"That's right, and they're great people. You'd like them a lot."

He puffs twice as the pines weigh the truth in that remark. It holds. No better jury in all creation.

"All right, and you say the school there is good...what about work, buddy? What are your ideas there?"

And so we arrive at the crux, the hardest question to answer in all of this. He is the very picture of Dad: left hand grasping the pipe, glasses firmly regarding me, infinite love radiating from within, the way a diesel puts out horsepower. His barrel chest humbly shrugs off his accomplishments, his power, the same way his old canvas backpack shrugs off the notion of modernization. It's the basic things in life that matter most: what about work, indeed. I'm pinned.

"Idunno.." is the most articulate thing I can manage at first. "I won't know until I go there. I've talked to everyone there, Dad, even the guy that founded the town. They all say the same thing: ya gotta go there first...but ya know what? I believe, Dad. I believe there's a good life for me there, and for Britt, too. I just gotta go, and see."

This seems to make an impact. As shaky as it is, it's a powerful statement, and it's not until it's out of my mouth that I realize why: Belief, real belief, the kind that lives in the heart, is a powerful thing. Belief, in self and in possibilities, is how a man becomes who he needs to be.

"Well," he says. He leans back a little, beholding this power of belief, and how it looks on his youngest. He looks proud, accepting, even pleased: "At the risk of sounding like I ever had any choice in the matter, this sounds good. You know, there's worse places one could want to be...I wonder if you might not 'go the distance' in Mammoth. How big of a town is it?"

He's warming up to the notion, despite himself. I find words more easily now: "At present the year-round population is around five thousand, I think. It's a resort town, though, so it dies in the fall."

"MMmm, I see." Two puffs..."Yes, I remember being there with Randy. Not far from here, as a matter of fact. Beautiful place, buddy. HAH!...So the trick will be finding permanent, year-round work."

A short but endless, breathless silence, during which the cosmos rotate on their axis imperceptibly, the fire burns towards its death, the old pines age while the saplings grow. Snow Creek moves a pebble in its bed, the baby currents from which will be amplified with time, and change the boulders at the bottom of waterfalls downstream in years to come. I wonder how much less or more this whole "time" thing affects him, in whatever form manifests his energy now.

"Think you can?" He asks.

"Huh?"

"Find year-round work in Mammoth, you twerp."

"Oh. Well, I'm sure as hell gonna give it my best. We'll see…there's only one way to find out." My words and intent, my love, go floating out over the flowing waters of Snow Creek…that water, where Dad watched me swim in nature's own clothes as a 6-year-old and as a 9-year-old, marveling that I could stand the temperature. That wide blanket of liquid crystal, flowing over its smooth, glowing slabs of golden granite, so cold that we used it to stanch the flow of blood from a hatchet wound on the back of my left hand when I was a kid—it took all of 15 seconds.

I realize that this setting, Snow Creek, the place of my first-ever backpacking trip, has been the witness, the means, the end and the progenitor of several defining moments in my life. This moment is just one more. And it occurs to me that Carlos Casteneda might have had something after all, when he said we all have a place of power in this universe, each individual. Mine is in the High Sierra, and I happen to have been shown this, and felt this, at a very early age.

As I sit with Dad, I see and feel our words and intent become our history and our future, floating out over the golden water, mingling with the currents that flow downstream to whatever end awaits them, us, me. Whatever end I earn. I look to Dad for some profound realism about all this and he says, "MMmm. Could you do me the greatest favor, buddy boy, and hand me the lighter? You're closer…"

As I reach to hand it over the fire to him, his MIND is working, that MIND, figuring out how to find me the right job in Mammoth. And it occurs to me that not many knuckleheads in this life could hope to have such a powerful one in their corner.

I'll forever live in a world where Dad and I spent the best moments here…a world where he forever smokes his pipe by the fire at our spot on the banks of

Snow Creek, nonchalantly tossing out wisdom to any who'll have it. My brothers and I returned there the year before this conversation, and Dad's presence was as tangible as the ground I sat on, the stars, the pines, the golden granite creek bed, the golden water and the High Sierra air. He will always BE.

I leave him there, sitting at the fire, the very image of power, his pipe coming into better form with each puff, the pines, the creek, the golden rocks, the cosmos themselves a part of him and of his mind. I don't leave, but simply go off far enough to pee...in the Mediterranean. And when I return, to reside in Mammoth, his presence will be around me all the more. And then we shall see.

* * *

By the time the contract ended, I had gained over twenty pounds and was drinking about twice my normal amount. I returned to LA and had a wonderful, frenzied reunion with Boone that kept erupting for hours. He kept a very close eye on me for several weeks.

Having been unable to keep my butt planted on the ship while in so many fascinating ports around the Carib and the Med, I failed miserably to save up the funds I needed to move my daughter and myself to Mammoth in good form. My good brother Eric Potruch—a brilliant vocalist and songwriting partner of mine, turned banker—loaned me the funds I needed to pull it off. I feel deep gratitude to him to this day.

There have been so many times I would've gone belly up if not for good friends. If not for a solid, trusted climbing partner who held my life in his or her hands as a belayer, or rides to the hospital, or timely advice that headed me in a different direction at a pivotal moment, or taking great care of my beloved pet while I was on tour, or a place to crash in tough times, or a loan at a crucial juncture like moving my daughter into my life, my story would be very different. And most likely a brief one.

Whether you're in music or not, life is all about having your friends' backs, so that they'll have yours. I really can't overstate it: You won't get far in music, or any other area of endeavor, without having earned the trust of those around you. To reiterate what Dick Grove said: Money doesn't make the world go 'round. Relationships do.

Chapter 28
Seven Years in Paradise

It might surprise you that some of the most noteworthy musical things I've done, measured by both a professional and a creative yardstick, happened in the breathtaking middle-o'-nowhere majesty of the Eastern Sierras. But living there is very different from visiting, and some things took some getting used to. One such thing is how laid back everything is compared to LA.

Local musicians refer to blue jeans and T shirts as a "Mammoth Tux". A 9:00 PM downbeat means any time between 9:30 and 10:00, whereas being just a few minutes late in Los Angeles will quickly get you fired, blacklisted, tried, convicted and keel-hauled—assuming you survive the pelting with rocks while your wrists and neck are locked in the pillory.

Having played in so many countries and cultures, I can tell you unequivocally that Los Angelenos comprise the most calloused and jaded audiences you'll find anywhere. It's a thing: Whenever a performer or band gives a stunningly great delivery of something and gets little or no applause, players on stage look at each other knowingly and say "LA audience." Angelenos seem to regard music as a commodity, more like toilet paper than art. And this in the city with the finest musical talent pool on Earth.

The good news is that if you drive away from LA for a couple of hours in any direction, audiences are far more appreciative. There's just something in the water or the air in Los Angeles that makes LA crowds the most culturally desensitized and difficult to impress.

Living in Mammoth was an eye-opener on many levels. Playing around in my ad-hoc fusion / variety bands of the best local talent, it was almost jarring to me to garner the genuine appreciation and attention of listening, grooving crowds. I wanted to say "Why are you all bobbing your heads, staring at us and smiling?" It reminded me of that joke about the paranoid comedian, who said "Why're you all laughing at me?". It took some effort for me to pry my mind open to all that appreciation after all those years in LA—a town that seems to regard music as toilet paper.

The musicians in Mammoth get it, too. LA crowds are not an unfamiliar thing up there. On the big weekends when the town fills up with Angelenos, the difference in the audiences is jarring.

* * *

Being a single Dad in an expensive mountain resort town—where I had no job lined up upon our arrival—turned out to be more of a joy than a panicked rush. In a continuation of the freakish good luck I've had over the course of my lifetime, things did indeed work out, as I believed they would. Credit for that also goes to my daughter's character and personality. Every neighborhood has a problem child, and my daughter was (and is) the diametric opposite of that person. She was 16 going on 40, and very much a team player. That's something you can't say about very many teenagers. When I look up at the night sky and thank the cosmos for the good things in my life, she's always at the top of my list.

Don't laugh, but the first job I immediately scored was a phone sales gig, selling listings on a website for vacation rentals. It was actually a decent job, and nothing dishonorable. That got us established. I actually had a second floor office, with a glorious view of the Sherwins, Laurel Mountain and Bloody Mountain, all of which ignited with alpenglow every late afternoon. If I had to have an office job, I really couldn't ask for a better environment or view. My daughter got hired there as well. It was her idea to get a job, not mine.

I gigged on the weekends and was already known among local musicians before I arrived, so I fairly quickly became the big fish in a small pond, pretty much the go-to guy for musical services for Bishop, Mammoth and June Lake.

There was a guy teaching guitar in town who had a great approach to the private instruction business, and around 35 students most of the time. Since it was such a small pond, I called him to discuss the separation of labor upon my arrival, so we didn't step on each others' toes: he was the go-to guy for lessons, I was the go-to guy for musical services. He appreciated that and we were both happy.

Six months or so later, I lucked out yet again when he moved to the UK and sold me his business and student body for about the amount that it brought in per week. I quit the sales job and pivoted into teaching free-lance full time, creating symbiotic relationships with some local business owner friends for teaching spaces in Mammoth and Bishop.

Thus began my physical downturn: It turns out that it's very hard on your body to sit on your ass 5 days a week for hours on end, teaching little Jimmy where the D string is. Every day, I felt like I had gotten in my car and driven for eight solid hours. This could not end well.

Being a musician in a small town is a really interesting nut to crack. It surprised me to find that it's very doable, and not just because of remote work over the 'net, which I did a lot of. The coolest thing to me was being a part of a community. I had never felt that. I'm a part of the musical community here in LA, but that's different. I'm talking about an entire community—from outdoor sports enthusiasts with disposable jobs, to blue collar workers, to the professional crowd: restauranteurs, doctors, lawyers and judges, reporters, every walk of commerce—everybody knew everybody. And like many locals, I did a lot of business on trade, for professional services from chiropractic adjustments to advertising—things I probably couldn't have afforded otherwise.

Living in a place as heartbreakingly gorgeous as Mammoth, it's almost impossible to stay indoors if you don't have to, so the average Mammoth resident is very fit. This is a huge contrast to LA, where only five or ten percent of the general public are in that level of health. There are a lot of professional athletes living in Mammoth and, as a town, it has the highest per-capita number of Olympians in the country. It's at roughly 8,000 feet, so running teams and swimming teams go there for high-altitude training. That way, when they compete in lower elevations they slay the competition.

It was almost surreal to me to live where I could just bop up to TJ Lake and be at the bottom of Crystal Crag, any time I had an hour or two to spare. I could hit Tamarack or Mammoth Creek on a lunch break. In the winter time, I could hike around east of 395 by Hot Creek, and have that incredible view of Mount Morrison, or go snowshoeing pretty much anywhere, just to burn a few minutes. These things were all around me there at all times, right where I lived. I couldn't even walk out my front door without getting smacked in the face by incredible beauty.

Chapter 29
John

John Bachar lived in Mammoth, and became a good friend of mine. You might not know the name, but if you're a climber that name is royalty, and inspires awe and maybe a little fear: He's the father and inventor of free-solo climbing. Long before I ever met him he was a big hero of mine, as he was to most climbers. He was featured in TV shows and in Life magazine when I was in my teens and early twenties, with heart-arresting images of him dangling his life out over the void. I remember thinking, "Man, I wish I had the balls to live such a life!" In retrospect, I'm glad that I didn't chase that particular demon. John was the most calculating individual I will probably ever meet, while I inhabit the opposite end of that spectrum. I've free-soloed a few times, but only when the vibe was right, the rock was solid and I knew I had things well in hand. And I wouldn't have lasted long if I'd made a habit of it.

In the 70s, before most of the climbing community had a very good understanding of exercise physiology at all, John noticed that the Russian gymnastic team was routinely kicking our butts in the Olympics, and figured it must be for a reason. He read up on their approach, and what he discovered was specificity training, among a lot else. This led to his development of very specific strategies that transformed the entire sport of climbing to a pretty massive degree—not the least of which was the "Bachar Ladder", a training concept employing wooden holds bolted onto the underside of staircases, which eventually blew up to become what we now know as the climbing gym industry.

The son of a UCLA math professor and a great mathematician himself, he also developed a way of calculating how much you can expect out of your guns (pulling muscles), and for how long, under how much of a load. This is of course great information for any free soloist who doesn't want to die. He had a much deeper running inventory of numbers in his head while climbing than anyone else before him, and I'm sure that all who have followed, up to and including Alex Honnold, will tell you that without John Bachar, free soloing would still be decades behind where it is. Those who are still alive, that is.

John also played tenor sax, and though he wasn't to music what he was to climbing, I enjoyed many great jam hangs in his garage with our local player buds. The irony wasn't lost on me that I met him when my body was starting to fall apart from all the sitting and teaching, and it didn't help that I was still drinking as much scotch as I had on board the cruise ship. While onboard, my level of fitness and sobriety fitted right in with everyone around me. In Mammoth, not so much. I was surrounded by people who looked and felt the way I had before I ever met kryptonite.

John liked his alcohol, too—though he could turn it on and off at will, depending on what climbing endeavors he might be training for at the moment—and we became great drinking buddies. Many was the night we sat out under the magnificence of the night sky, discussing everything from climbing to music, mathematics, politics, business and women, over scotch and cigars. And stories. He had been at the spearhead of some truly visionary first ascents, which are well documented. To have him tell me those stories in person was a high honor. If you're interested, you could do worse than to get a book by another climbing legend, John Long, called "Rock Jocks, Wall Rats and Hang Dogs: Climbing on the Edge of Reality". It's a great collection of climbing stories, mostly by John Long, and all of which are very well written. It's a really fun book. You'll understand why John Bachar's name inspires such respect and awe among climbers.

Chapter 30
Noiseletting at Altitude

Not long after I moved to town, I got a call from a retired gent who wanted me to arrange and produce an album of outdoor-sports-themed songs. I did. The budget was fairly tight, so I handled everything "in-house", i.e. all tracks by me, no hired guns. Being an indie project and lacking promo machinery of any kind, it went nowhere. But it enabled me to make some important upgrades to my studio gear.

I usually had an enjoyable weekender gig, on which I surrounded myself with the cream of local talent. There were some surprisingly good players for me to abuse, and abuse them I did. Marty Burgenbauch was a fine drummer, and the father of three incredibly smart and musically gifted mutants. He was always my first call, as was Brian Ogawa on bass, the best cat in the eastern sierras. We did a lot of funked-up Jazz standards, some old Motown, some classic rock and the inevitable blues tune or two. With the Jazz standards, then as now, I tended to change the time signatures and grooves into something hipper and more suited to more modern, younger crowds. "Rhythm and Blues and Funky Grooves" was the catch phrase on the promo blurbs for one of the bands.

The local club owners all knew me and would call me with the occasional last-minute "Help, the band I booked broke down on 395 and I need a band in an hour!" Some of the rooms had great sound, and for a minute there was a Jazz club in town—an Irish pub actually, but one night a week it was a Jazz listening room, so I'd add my own pieces to the song list.

I had a house gig, one night a week for two years, as half of a duo with Eddy Evans. Eddy is one of only a few de-facto professional musicians in the Eastern Sierras who gigs locally. He's a sax player—a Bari player where he really lives, which is kind of rare—who spent most of his career in the pit orchestras of Reno. Ours was a very low-key restaurant gig, and great for maintaining my comping (accompanist) chops. I also had Eddy on pretty much every other gig I did, whatever its nature.

Eddy was one of four great woodwind talents that just happened to live in the area. The other three were from the classical camp: Kim M. played English Horn, John Weihausen is a world-class oboist, and his wife Carolyn Tiernan is a world-class clarinetist. John and Carolyn are both top-shelf in their respective professional fields, too: John is a wildlife biologist and the world's leading authority on the Sierra Bighorn Sheep, and Carolyn is an E.R. doc of incredible diagnostic skill. Carolyn had recently branched out into Sax and jazz when I moved up there, and she was on most of my gigs with Eddy. She got better and better over what I call my seven-year sabbatical in the Eastern Sierras.

Howie Stern, my climbing partner until I became too modified to climb, is also a wonderful guitarist. We originally met in LA while bouldering at Stoney Point, a sandstone crag in Chatsworth where many legends have cut their teeth. We hit it off as climbing partners, since we had two different styles, and different strengths and weaknesses. It wasn't until our third or fourth outing, driving up Angeles Crest Highway to another climbing area, that the conversation turned to other interests. Before long, we arrived at "Waitaminnit, you're a guitarist? I'm a guitarist!"

Howie had studied with Paul Gilbert and had some of those insane 8-finger tapping tricks. He wound up studying from me for a few years, and I delivered harmonic understanding to him a la Grove. He took to it like a fish to water. Once I moved to Mammoth—a couple of years after he had—we got a reputation for turning gigs into sprayathon sessions. If you can imagine two shredders trading off on Strats, trying to out-spray each other while the dance floor clears, you'll understand why it wasn't the most popular thing in some situations. With the right crowd, though, it went over great. We learned to pick and choose carefully.

My daughter got the lead in the high school musical, and the pit orchestra needed a guitarist, so I got to back her up. Having so little time with her before she'd be grown and gone, my agenda was to be with her as much as I could, without cramping her style or her teenaged exploration of life. Backing her up in the pit band for that musical was pure gold to me.

I still got calls to come down to LA for gigs and sessions. In '05, Koz called me for a film score that he had started, but whose deadline he was going to blow because he had too many other irons in the fire. So I headed down to the Centrum building in Universal City and quickly made some great dough, the operative term being "quickly": In a sleepless blitz, we created a finished and mixed score in three and a half days. I won't say it was a masterpiece, but we did it and the director was happy. Mercifully, "Frostbite" (ironically shot in Mammoth Lakes) went straight to DVD. I took the money and bought a used Subaru Outback before the next winter, and never had to put on tire chains again.

Chapter 31
Inclement Elements

It would be wrong to write about living in Mammoth without mentioning the reality of the winters there. Mammoth is a meteorological oddity. The town's founder, an Olympic gold medalist skier named Dave McCoy (an absolutely wonderful guy, a fierce proponent of arts and education and beloved by all) had been a hydrologist for the DWP, paid to wander around the high places measuring snowpack. He had noticed something anomalous about Mammoth Mountain, in that its placement relative to prevailing weather patterns consistently gave it more precipitation than the surrounding range. He obtained the lease, founded the ski area, opened it in 1953 and the rest is history.

Living there is just different than other snowy places. You're usually not shoveling just a foot or two, and occasionally there are insane storms that dump three to five feet per day, for up to five days. After heavier winters, the ski area is open as late as the Fourth of July. The house whose bottom floor I rented for my daughter and myself was just a few hundred yards from the bottom of chair 15, so we were right up there in it.

I got a New Years gig in SoCal at the end of '05, budgeted in a compelling enough way that made it make more sense to do it than not, so I did it. I knew that the band would be slammin'. I had good reason to trust in my daughter's being safe until my return—now 17, she was probably more level-headed than myself, and we had a strong infrastructure of friends whom we both trusted impeccably if anything crazy happened, like the mountain erupting or a cometary impact. Short of something like that, my daughter was solid. Fate timed my departure perfectly for me to be in the very last group of a dozen or so vehicles escorted south on 395 by the CHP in near-whiteout conditions, before they closed the highway for one of those insane dumps. It was the snowiest drive I've ever done on 395, which is saying something. I was still seeing patches of snow on the ground under the sage bushes in the desert over 200 miles south, just outside of Mojave. This obviously wasn't a normal storm.

The gig was with one hell of a band of LA dignitaries and was led by Ralph Dudley, a friend of mine with pipes so good he can sound like Luther Vandross when he wants. He's a great frontman too, and we took no prisoners. Fate timed my return so perfectly that when I drove up to the closed gate at the bottom of the grade in Bishop, I got there at the same time as the CalTrans crew who opened it and was the first car through. Bishop is in the rain shadow of the Sierras and might get six inches of snow in a heavy storm, if any. A foot is a lot for Bishop. This storm had buried the town under four feet. I could only imagine what Mammoth must look like.

The short answer was that it looked like nothing. When I drove into town, it was an abstraction. This was my third winter living there, but I hadn't encountered anything like this before. The roads were deep corridors in the snow with walls fifteen feet high, and very little else seemed to exist. Single lanes of pavement had been exposed by the efforts of the town's snow removal crews and machinery (they're truly incredible), and I could only see buildings whose driveways had been cleared in such a way that they opened a brief line of sight through slits in the wall.

When I turned onto my street, all of the houses were gone. There almost weren't even any visible trees—just a very deep, narrow and blindingly white corridor with so little contrast, there was only the strip of blue sky above and a narrow strip of pavement below. Everything else was white on white; topography was for all practical purposes imperceivable. I had to follow the ribbon of pavement under the ribbon of sky, and count what I thought might be driveways. I noticed a dent in the height of the wall about where I thought our driveway was. There was a cul-de-sac across the street that I parked in, and from that vantage I had my bearings.

    Looking at it from the end of the cul-de-sac, about 35 yards away, I could make out the roofline of the house under the snow. In knew the apex of our roof was about thirty five feet off the ground, but the snow just kind of gently sloped up to it and back down. The dent in the top of the wall in front of our driveway still left over twelve feet of wall. I started swimming from the neighbor's driveway. It took me some time to get to the front porch and dig out the front door with my hands—it had a big eve, thankfully—and get inside. The driveway was too full of buried, invisible cars for the snowblower to be used and besides, that blower's cage was all of two feet high. What the hell was anybody gonna do with that? So it was all manual shoveling—my daughter, our two housemates and myself. It took many hours a day for several days to get a handle on things.

    And the snow just kept coming, all the way through March and April. Mammoth Mountain eventually recorded over 56 feet of precipitation that winter. For everyone in town, shoveling became not a matter of having a clear driveway, but of survival. Most of us shoveled for several hours every day...getting behind wasn't an option. The hospital gave free clinics for elbow tendonitis. A lot of long-time Mammoth locals finally moved before the following winter: enough was enough. Incredibly, there have been even heavier winters in Mammoth since '05 - '06.

Humanity seems to be incapable of understanding the difficulties that outdoor gigs can present to musicians and gear, and all musicians have horror stories about playing outside in inclement weather. Mammoth's weather is a big factor for booking gigs, and any musician does his or her gigging thereabouts at the mercy of Ma Nature.

One January in the late nineties, booked into Mammoth from LA, I took a spill that lasted thirty seconds if it lasted one, in front of an applauding audience. No, I wasn't on stage. It happened while carrying two leather guitar gig bags, one in each hand, as I walked very gingerly across the greased ice of the Whiskey Creek parking lot on my way inside to play. I was about 35 feet from the dining room, illuminated by the light coming through a long row of picture windows where the choicest booths were. I could see that as always, the whole dining room was packed. Then my foot slipped. I quickly saved it with the other foot, in sort of a Russian Cossack dance move. Then that foot immediately slipped, and I did the same maneuver in mirror image. This started a Cossack dance that went on for a truly proud duration—HOY! The ice was so absolutely frictionless, it was a scientific oddity. Nothing I did would stabilize any part of me, not even for a millisecond. I might as well have been trying to get purchase while floating in an interstellar void.

Gravity was gradually winning and I kept getting lower and lower—just like the actual dance—then one foot went a little too far and I went down on one knee and was dancing on one foot and one knee. Then both knees, still dancing, HOY! I would have gladly conceded defeat and stood motionless on my knees if physics could have allowed, but that frictionless medium wouldn't have it and the dance continued, HOY! Just by chance I happened to glance in the direction of the dining room at about this point, and saw some diners standing up and crowding along the windows while some others pointed at me. This was lasting way too long. I had started laughing almost immediately, and that wasn't helping my coordination.

Next, my guitars started becoming outriggers, not because I wanted them to, but because I couldn't hold them high enough. They were trying to get purchase on the same frictionless ice, and had no stabilizing effect of any kind. Gravity continued its steady victory march, and then I was dancing on one knee and the other butt cheek, then I found myself dancing alternately on the outsides of my thighs, squirming around on the ice in some sort of writhing snake dance (vaguely erotic and decidedly non-Russian). Next my lower body was prone on the ice, and even just trying to use my elbows to keep my chest and head up became another dance. It went on. And on. I couldn't get motion to cease.

Gravity and zero friction weren't done with me until I was literally lying chin down and spread-eagled, head towards the dining room with my arms fully extended to each side, each guitar's gig bag also lying face down in its flattest possible orientation, as far from me as possible. Even then, motion seemed like it ceased begrudgingly. I had become something resembling a puddle, or Wile E. Coyote after he gets run over by a steamroller. Then I heard the applause. Very carefully, I raised my eyes and saw a crowd of diners crowding along the windows and clapping, laughing and giving me the thumbs up.

The coldest gig I ever played was on the back deck of Main Lodge at Mammoth in the middle of winter. It was tied to a sweet gig that night for an awards banquet inside the main hall that paid well, but to get that booking, the mountain's booking manager—Jim V— made us play outside in a blizzard that afternoon. Ambient temperature was ten to fifteen degrees fahrenheit, but the wind was howling, and the chill factor made it minus five or lower. The band was Howie, the wonderful local bass player Brian Ogawa, a visiting LA drummer with wonderful pocket named Chuck Sparks, and me. Howie, Brian and I were all keeping our hands in the pockets of our parkas and jumping up and down to get the strings ringing, then letting our rigs feed back in "E". Chuck had to have his hands exposed to hold sticks and play, and was yelling rhythmically with the beat, "You guys SUCK! You guys SUCK! You guys SUCK! You guys SUCK!"

We were doing our best to laugh about things, but it was the kind of cold that cracks guitar bodies and does real damage. We should've just said no. I don't know what Jim V. was thinking, but like every local, I have found myself perpetually wondering that about most of the mountain's management ever since Dave McCoy retired and it all went to corporate.

We took a break and crowded around under a propane patio heater's aluminum dome, but it was no match for conditions. We were standing about ten feet away from the drum set when we heard someone slam the snare drum really hard. We turned and saw nobody near the drums; the top head had spontaneously exploded. We tore down and bailed.

Not all outdoor gigs on the mountain were like that, though. I generally didn't like booking out of doors in Mammoth at all, because I've personally seen it snow above 8,000 feet every month of the year in the Sierras. The axiom around Mammoth is "Don't like the weather? Wait five minutes."

One Memorial Day when I lived in Mammoth, a friend's band was booked to play the patio at McCoy Station—that's "mid chalet", halfway up the Mountain—and he invited me to do the gig at the last minute. It was a gorgeous day, so I took a breath, crossed my fingers and said yes. The snowpack was still in great supply, like it was February, but there was no wind and the sun was blazing, as it only can above ten thousand feet. People were skiing in tee shirts and shorts. The patio was on the side of the lodge that faced up the mountain, and I remember looking up at the gorgeous view as I played the Star Spangled Banner a la Hendrix at Woodstock. The sound went up and spread out over the blinding white expanses, bringing cheers from skiers and snowboarders within earshot in all directions. So under the right conditions, playing outside can be fine, it's just that Mother Nature is nothing if not unpredictable in Mammoth.

Chapter 32
Empty Nest in Paradise

My daughter headed off to college, but I stayed in Mammoth rather than to return to LA. The next winter was almost as heavy, and after I had another adventure swimming through a white void to uncover what I hoped was the right house—this time from over a block away, as my street hadn't been cleared yet—my roommate and I were both feeling like we had had enough of shoveling. We knew we made a good team as roomies, so in the Spring of '07 we scored a really nice house in Bishop, about four thousand feet lower. It was the nicest place I've ever lived.

My part of the house in Bishop had exposed rafters breaking up the ceiling, rough barn wood paneling and deep carpet: It might not have been designed as a recording studio, but you'd be hard pressed to design a better sounding space for one. I put it to good use and it served me well. The house was in a neighborhood called Rocking K, a magical little enclave of a couple of dozen houses a few miles north of town and well over a mile off of 395. It was dark enough at night for serious stargazing right there in the driveway, and it was the quietest, most peaceful place I've ever lived. Surrounded on all sides by miles of open sage near the Tungsten Hills and not far from the base of Mt Tom, which towers almost ten thousand feet above the valley floor, Boone and I enjoyed several walks every day in a setting that I still miss every second that I'm not there.

It was in that setting, walking Boone out through the sage, that I met my wife. It would be a couple of years before we'd become romantically available and interested in each other, but she lived right next door, so we ran into each other walking our dogs almost every day. She was intelligent, low key, attractive, definitely not high-strung or an "LA woman" of any kind, an easy conversationalist, and her company always felt very comfortable.

Being as quiet as it was, that enclave of houses outside of Bishop was the most conducive environment to writing music I've ever inhabited. I thought back to the moment in my twenties, driving back to LA in my '68 Mustang after my first gig in Mammoth, heading down "the grade", southbound on 395 just above Bishop, looking out at that heart-breakingly gorgeous view of Round Valley, Mt Tom and the Sabrina skyline and thinking to myself "Maybe someday". Well, now that was exactly where I was living.

The only hardship related to dealing with snow in Bishop was the pangs of empathy I felt for my friends who still lived in Mammoth and were shoveling for their lives, as I strolled up and down the driveway pushing a snow shovel in front of me with one hand, once or twice a year.

Not long after moving into the Bishop house, I got a call from Michael Hamdorf, a prospective client who had heard my name around Mammoth as the "go-to" for musical services, and wanted me to meet with him and his wife Violetta Martin at Roberto's, a popular Mammoth eatery with fantastic tacos. Upon sitting down at their table, the first thing Michael did was to look furtively around the room to see if the coast was clear, then pull out a fat manilla envelope—the size they use for stacks of money—and slid it across the table to me, like some kind of drug deal. It was almost an inch thick. I was thinking "what the hell's this guy all about?"

"Go ahead," he said, "look inside."

I did, making a conscious point of not looking furtive. It was stuffed with bills. I looked closer, and they were mostly ones and fives! They both busted up.

Mike said, "I've always wanted to do that, just give someone a big envelope stuffed with cash like some big drug deal. Thanks for playing along!"

Thus went my introduction to Mike and Violetta, two fun-loving people who had already checked me out thoroughly and decided they wanted me to produce her album, and who were indeed giving me a production deposit. They brought some fun into the game. Violetta had recently discovered a love of singing, and though she was a tad inexperienced at the time, she had naturally great pipes. I told them I could definitely work with that. It also turned out that she could write great melodies, and I could easily fill in the chords by playing a couple of likely choices and having her choose. I'm fairly accustomed to working that way, so we had a pretty good writing flow.

Mike ran a thriving local water damage repair business, and business was good. Mammoth has a lot of "second homeowners", which is real estate code-speak for rich people who live in LA, own another house in Mammoth and are seldom there. In the more neglected "second homes", the winter cold freezes and bursts the pipes, flooding the houses. Mike was no dope.

The budget for Violetta's album was good enough for me to hire my upper-echelon buddies in LA for remotely-recorded tracks. Accordingly, the project turned out great. It had elements of Salsa, lots of Latin Pop in the same genre as Emmanuel, a little Brazilian Jazz influence, and the tiniest pinch of Norteno. Mike's antics kept things fun throughout the process. After the album was done, we traveled south to do a live showcase at a big Latin music convention in downtown LA. I had John Pena on bass, Otmaro Ruiz on keys, Richie Garcia on percussion, Walter Rodriquez on drums, Bill Churchville on trumpet, Terry Landry on sax and Eric Jorgenson on trombone: Basically my "A" team throughout the entire band. The kind of band you can put together—you guessed it—only in LA.

A couple of days before the show, we were sound-checking for rehearsal in one of the big rooms at Third Encore (one of LA's premier rehearsal facilities) when Terry Wood walked in, stopped dead in her tracks and exclaimed, "My God! LOOK at the talent in this room!!" Considering who was saying that, it made me feel pretty good. Terry had been hired at John's and my suggestion to coach Violetta in the art of live presentation. Like everyone involved, she did a great job, as did Violetta. The show went great.

Alas, Boone left this earth one August afternoon while we were tracking Violetta's vocals in Bishop. I knew he was suffering from kidney failure and that his days were numbered, so I was trying to spend as much time with him as possible. But I failed to be there with him as he crossed the finish line, and he died alone in his doghouse. It haunts me to this day that I wasn't there for him.

He now resides among friends in the most beautifully situated pet cemetery I've ever seen, commanding a view of the East Side's wide-open majesty, just about a mile from the old house, out on the sage where we used to hike every day.

* * *

The finest school that ever had me as a teacher is a beautiful dichotomy perched on an unlikelihood. To appreciate the reality of what this school is, first think of everything that's wrong with the typical American college, whose application and admission process is so overweighted with bureaucratic red tape that it requires a college education just to navigate it; whose teachers are overburdened and unavailable because of overwhelming student-to-teacher ratios; whose cost puts higher education categorically beyond the reach of a tragically high number of us; and—worst of all—whose curricula is for the most part content to be recited for tests, job interviews and professional life.

With few exceptions, these schools don't place emphasis on the teaching of critical thought, or service to the community here on Earth.

Now, imagine all the finest ethos and philosophies of higher education all being applied in a utopian environment, where people learn how to think—how to research facts, how to scrutinize and reason independently, how to achieve rational opinion, how to devise and implement plans according to needs presented by circumstances and by the world, how to get traction for their ideas through hard work, and how to become leaders.

Everything about Deep Springs College is different. It's an academically elite two-year boarding school with a student body of less than thirty, whose labor keeps it going. Founded in 1917 by L.L. Nunn—who put the hydroelectric dam at the bottom of Niagara Falls—it's a Truman Scholarship school with some very dignified alumni.

And these kids are smart...I can't put too fine a point on that. When I was teaching there, they were studying quantum physics, philosophy and hydrodynamics right out of high school.

You'd be forgiven for thinking this place is somewhere in Massachusetts or Connecticut, maybe Northern California, built with stately stone and covered with ivy. But to get to Deep Springs College, you take 395 along the Eastern Sierras into Big Pine, hang an east on highway 168 and drive out a narrow, isolated road that winds up into completely desolate emptiness for 26 miles. The road itself is an indicator of the remoteness of the place. Sixteen miles of the drive is non-stop S-curves, and it squeezes down to one lane through "the narrows". When you find yourself on a long straightaway crossing the wide-open solitude of a beautiful desert valley, you're getting close to the only human presence within many miles in any direction: The oasis on the right in the distance is the school.

Students there operate a successful functioning cattle ranch and dairy, growing their own alfalfa. And with the minimum possible oversight from faculty, the students also run the school, from daily minutiae to decisions that guide its direction. It's a full scholarship for every student, and they earn their way through with their labor and stewardship of the land and the legacy, while handling what is always a heavy and heady curriculum. App Comm (applications committee) is just one of many student committees. Its members have to take hundreds of applications and decide which dozen or so applicants will be given the honor and the weight of studying and living there the next year. It's a big process, and one they take very seriously.

Graduates tend to go on to finish their undergrad degrees at a variety of prestigious schools, and they all leave with a strong desire to help the world around them. It is truly an incredible school, and one whose ethos, academic and business models I'd like to see catch on in our society at a grander scale.

As to how a knucklehead like me wound up teaching music there, I'd like to say that I'm just that smart. But the humbling truth is that the school's offering me a post was more likely due to a lack of alternatives than to choice. I perpetually felt intellectually outclassed by everyone I met, with the exception of one or two cows. Full-time faculty lived on campus, but I commuted 168 each day that I taught, making me "outside faculty"—with a really fun commute. I taught there until one year, the next new batch of students lacked enough interest in music to justify my post.

Deep Springs and her students remain an unchanging, timeless element in a rapidly changing world. The way things are done thereabouts are largely unchanged from a hundred years ago. Looking at pictures of students doing this job or that, you have no idea what decade or century the photograph is from, without looking at the date. It soothes me to read the quarterly newsletter. It's a refreshing voice of reason in a world going mad.

* * *

If you're eyeballing a career teaching music in academia, good on you--planet Earth needs good music profs. But she needs them not to perpetuate lies, so please be careful where you study and what you believe. As you've read and hopefully learned in this book, there is a lot of curricula being being passed off as true in the bloviated firmament of higher learning's power structure that doesn't stand up to even rudimentary inspection in the light of day. Also—not for nothing—you need to be wary of putting all your eggs in one basket, because music departments tend to get funding suddenly yanked out from under them, leaving faculty abruptly unemployed and insolvent.

And if teaching music is your main objective, you'll want a college degree. Teaching is one of the only sensible reasons to get such a thing, degrees being largely irrelevant in the working corridors of the industry. My being non-pedigreed has made being on faculty at many schools a non-starter, but it's had zero effect on my professional career. I have high equivalency, which gets recognized at many schools, but most have a hard policy of hiring only holders of advanced degrees. And in many cases, the degree doesn't even have to be in music. If you're hired with high musical equivalency, you'll earn less than you would at the same post with a sheepskin in mechanical engineering. Such are the things that make me say "BAH!" Regardless, whether or not teaching is your main focus, teach at least a little. It's badly needed higher-calling work.

* * *

When you own a home studio it's impossible not to record an album, if only for the simple reason that you can. Likewise, when you own a home studio and guitars and amps, it's impossible not to record an album of excessive wheedly-wheedlies, in a genre called "shred". Much of shred is a delivery mechanism for brainless noodling in E minor—the like of which assails you from all sides when you walk into any Guitar Center—but there are several exceptions. One is "Truth in Shredding", an iconic album of trade-offs between Allan Holdsworth and Frank Gambale, and another is "Centrifugal Funk", which features Frank Gambale, Shawn Lane and Brett Garsed. Both albums were produced by Mark Varney, whose name will accordingly be esteemed by the guitar collective in the vaulted firmament on high for all time.

I had a delicious and unlikely accident on my calendar while living in Bishop: Pockets of spare time. It wasn't long before I found myself recording an album of stuff so self-absorbed and heedless of listeners' druthers that it struck me as flippant, rude and just wrong. It felt almost sarcastic. But I had the time, and the studio—and guitars and amps—so why the hell not? I had spent almost my entire career in the service of music whose purpose was to sell some specific thing or other, so why not do something aimless, whose point is specifically to please no one but myself? I had earned that, dammit, and besides: who the hell would ever hear the thing?

It came together in the spare moments over a two-year period, amidst other projects and dealings. Writing is something I do every day just to maintain sanity, so material wasn't a problem. Thus was "Combustible" born, a surprisingly well-received album that has gotten close to three million organic plays on one internet streaming service—almost enough to buy a good hamburger—and whose follow-up album "Explosive" landed both albums on Steve Vai's now-defunct "Digital Nations" label (both albums are currently available via Apple Music, Amazon and CDBaby).

Having set about to please no one other than myself, I had inadvertently produced my most genuine and honest work to date. Maybe I shouldn't underestimate the patience and understanding of listeners. It got flattering reviews, due in one case to a recommendation from a powerful luminary in that genre who I happened to have met about that time, namely Mark Varney himself.

It turned out that he lived just a few miles away from me in shit-you-not Bishop—a small desert town of less than 4,000 people, four hours' drive from the nearest city—you can't make this stuff up. He and I became good friends and remain so. Besides his successes producing guitarists, Mark was a school psychologist and counselor whose focus was helping at-risk children with learning disorders and aberrant behavior—the parallels between that and dealing with guitarists presumably not requiring comment. A saintly glutton for punishment is our Mr. Varney.

In all seriousness, I should clarify that Allan, Frank and Brett don't fit those parallels. I have good personal familiarity with all three guys, each of whom is kind, intelligent, articulate, hard-working and disciplined, as you'd expect the finest players to be. Otherwise, how would they have gotten that freakishly good? But there's a well-earned stereotype that paints guitarists in general as childish, illiterate and undisciplined prima donna gunslingers—and outside of professional circles, it's not like the shoe doesn't fit often enough. You know who you are.

Mark suggested one day that we do a video of one of Combustible's songs. My imposter syndrome started raging, I thought of who this man is, and the massive commitment of time he was probably letting himself in for, and I found it hard to say yes. But at the end of the day, it was harder for me to say no, so we did it. And it was serious fun for both of us.

We shot me finger-syncing things in likely and unlikely locations around Bishop, such as atop a 70-foot boulder by Bishop Creek, whose footing at the top was so sketchy I almost fell off. And it didn't help that I had broken the hell out of the fourth toe on my right foot slipping in the shower that morning. It made a lively "SNAP", and colors of all hues were climbing up the foot within minutes. I knew from past experience that broken toes are no big thing, so I "buddy" taped it to the toe next door and was more or less good to go.

Mark wanted to learn how to do animation, and our video was the guinea pig. He spent a lot of hours on a beginning and ending sequence, and we called the whole thing "The Fairy God Shredder". It features a song called "Monster Jam".

* * *

Anyone who tells you that rock and roll has died hasn't been paying attention to Scandinavia. Hard rock and heavy metal is pretty much the mainstream pop over there.

One day around the time Combustible was coming into being, I was driving up the grade on 395—yet again, the stunning view of Round Valley, Mt. Tom and the Sabrina Skyline next to my shoulder—when the phone rang. It was my old friend from Helsinki, Erkka Korhonen. We had stayed in touch, and since his school days about a decade before when we met on my gig in Helsinki, he had gone on to become a multi-platinum producer and noteworthy guitarist in that part of the world. He worked for a major Scandinavian label called IVK.

After catching up on family news and the like he said, "I'm actually calling because I have a project that I'm hoping you will want to be a part of."

"Oh? Do tell!"

"IVK just signed Michael Bates, the winner of 'Australia's Got Talent'. He sings his ass off, and they've assigned me to produce his debut album. It's going to be pop/rock."

"Very cool, congrats my man!"

"And here's the thing: We need songs, so I was hoping you'd want to contribute some material."

He continued to read me in on the thing: The artist was in Australia, the label and production facility was in Finland, I'd be contributing via making demos in my home studio in Bishop. Almost everything would be handled over the 'net. About this time, I remember looking over my shoulder at that view, then looking at the phone in my hand connected to the other side of the world, and allowing myself a rare moment of gratitude for the miraculous technology making all this possible.

"I'd be honored of course, if you're cool with my bringing in one or two lyricists. Lyrics are a weakness of mine."

"Sure, who do you have in mind?"

"Well, Barry Coffing is obvious, if we can get him. And my old writing partner Eric Potruch writes incredible lyrics as well."

"Go ahead and ask them and let me know. I'm sure the label would be cool with that. They'd be crazy not to be."

We hung up and I called Barry as I reached the top of the grade.

"BeeCee!!"

"Yo Byron, what's up?"

"I've got a thing to run by you, in hopes you'll want to contribute some lyric writing."

"Oh? Do tell!"

I ran it all down to him. The thing you have to understand about Barry is that he has the most incisive mind for the business of music out of everyone I've ever known. Any time he's going to weigh in on something, you're well advised to pay very close attention. So when he paused like he was thinking, I said "What's up?"

"Oh, I'm just thinkin'...this artist is coming from Karaoke, and this is his first album, he's got no track record. Plus, this needs to be a good launch for his career, so we need something that'll give him legitimacy in the eyes of the critics. I'm thinkin' maybe a Rock Opera."

"Oh hell, YES" I immediately replied, "That's some good thinkin', compadre. Lemme float this to Erkka and get back to you."

Before I reached Mammoth I had told Erkka what Barry had said and why, Erkka called the president of IVK and called me back in less than 45 minutes with the label's decision: Hey presto, it was a Rock Opera.

So, we had a multi-national, multi-continental, multi-hemispheric team: Erkka and two or three writers in Scandinavia, a couple of very good lyricists and me as composer / arranger in America, and a very talented vocalist in Australia. We all wrote a storyline collaboratively in an email ring, then set about to assign what songs were needed for this and that in the plot. We needed 17 songs total including the overture, which I would do. Then we rolled up our sleeves and got to work.

We all agreed to just Lennon / McCartney the whole thing. That's code-speak for an equal writer's royalty split of every song, between all parties involved, regardless of who did or didn't do what. I highly recommend it for any collaborative situation, if only to avoid all the confusion of trying to do it any other way known to man, not to mention any head-butting. Either returns will be small and dollar amounts won't matter, or it will be good and there will be plenty for everyone. The only thing you really can't afford to do in this industry is to fuck up your relationships, so really: Just Lennon / McCartney your projects.

We split the writing load evenly between Team Scandinavia and Team America, at eight songs each. Michael Bates couldn't be talked into contributing as a writer, but being the artist he got a cut anyway of course, as should be the case.

The working logistic that emerged was that I'd get a lyric from Barry or Eric, write the melody and chords, then sketch an arrangement and produce a pretty full-fledged "guide production" and chart, which Team Scandinavia would follow very closely in production, notwithstanding where Erkka would make occasional enhancements to arrangements, to serve needs he knew more about at his end than I did at mine. He's a good arranger too, so things were turning out really well. And the production quality was over the top: They were locked out at what Erkka described as the premier recording facility in all of Scandinavia—a three-story megaplex with a swimming pool in the basement—using the best studio cats in that part of the world. Some of these songs wound up having 72 tracks...just of backup vocals. So it was also becoming a big noise.

It was a really enjoyable process, mostly because of where I lived: Between hikes up in the mountains or out on the sage with Boone, I'd sketch, arrange and produce ditties in my home studio in the middle of that incredible paradise, then send them off and they'd get replicated by a crack team of yo-cats in Scandinavia's premier production facility. I had to admit, it was a nice way to work.

Once we got all the songs done, I arranged the overture, borrowing thematic excerpts from each song. It took almost a week of focused effort to get that exemplar production to completion, then I sent that mix and charts over to Erkka, and I was pretty much done. Some of those songs were massive freaking hits, there was no doubt about it. I felt good about the project as a whole--what Eric and Barry had contributed, what I had brought to the table and what the entire team had accomplished overall. We had a multi-number-one-hit writer involved (Barry), a multi-platinum producer with a proven track record, and a major label in Scandinavia with the resources to make something meaningful happen with it all. I actually dared to entertain notions of checks in the mailbox.

Not long after that, once all the vocals had been tracked and the whole thing was heading into the mixing phase, I got another call from Erkka. He sounded pretty down.

"Hey brother, I'm afraid I have some bad news."

"Oh? Do tell."

"IVK is also a big producer of karaoke tracks, and the president's wife is in charge of that wing of the label. She talked the president into making IVK an all-karaoke label, because they've been selling more karaoke tracks than their actual music. They're dumping all their artists, just like that. The rock opera is scrubbed."

"Waitaminnit, what?"

And so it came to be that we had a paperweight worth many hundreds of thousands of dollars, representing thousands of man-hours of work, and with the potential to make some very real money were it to ever launch in the right manner. As of this writing, it remains a powerful rocket without a launch pad.

The label gave us the project and all rights, out of consideration for Erkka's history with them, which was really cool. It has yet to be mixed, though Erkka has taken some stabs at mixing it in his spare moments here and there over the intervening years. It's a massive undertaking to mix the thing at a level that will do it justice, so I have no idea if it ever will see the light of day. Barry, Eric and I all hope it will, as does everyone who contributed musically to its creation. That's one hell of a fine album just sitting there in the digital birth canal, waiting for a good delivery team.

If there's a moral to that story, it is yet again, to encourage recording artists of every stripe to be indie. Handing your reins to something as sketchy and unpredictable as most record labels is to jump off a cliff and hope there just happens to be water at the bottom.

Chapter 33
Fry's First Symphony

Musical excellence can rear its lovely head in unexpected places. For one week of the year, some of the finest classical talent in the Pacific timezone gathers in Mammoth Lakes to present the town with a windfall of great performances. For the players, it's basically a working vacation. For that one week, Mammoth sprouts a symphony orchestra rivaling anything on the west coast.

The Eastern Sierra Symphony Orchestra (ESSO) is an 80-or-so-piece collection of dignitaries from the LA studios, some principles from civic outfits such as San Fransisco and LA Philharmonics, and a handful of players representing the cream of local talent. A number of performances are booked, from smaller clinics to a chamber music program on Friday night, then on Saturday the big 80-piece plays in the only space large enough for such a thing, which is main lodge.

When I lived in the area, it was directed by Bogidar Avrimov, a very tall, skinny, brilliant and sweet Bulgarian octogenarian who also directed the Beverly Hills Pops and the Monterey Symphony Orchestra. It was musically my favorite week of the year on the Eastside. Financially, ESSO was always hanging by a thread and was even pronounced dead on a few occasions. Somehow though, it always rose from the ashes. I don't know ESSO's current medical prognosis, but hopefully it lives and this August will see incredibly fine music visited upon Mammoth.

Among the local talent featured every year are my friends Carolyn Tiernan (clarinet) and her husband John Weihausen (oboe). In '08, the idea was floated and green-lit for ESSO to feature "local composers" in the chamber music program. At the time, Carolyn had been studying from me for a few years, and "local composers" consisted of two people—Eddy Evans and myself—making this a suspiciously flattering move. I asked Carolyn if she had anything to do with it. She just grinned and said "I can neither confirm nor deny."

Any composer will tell you that the writing isn't the hard part. Sure, all that arranging, orchestrating, scoring and copying of the individual parts is sometimes challenging and always time-consuming, but none of that stuff is the real difficulty in bringing music into the world; what's hard is getting things played. For every piece that gets performed by a good orchestra, there are thousands of new pieces that aren't getting played. It's so difficult for a modern composer to get anything performed that even Frank Zappa wound up having to cross the pond to get his orchestral works played in Europe, because he couldn't find an American orchestra willing to entertain the notion. So this was a golden opportunity for me, and one that would probably never have happened living in SoCal. And like many of the best things in my life, it just landed in my lap.

I had only six weeks to write a new three-movement symphony for a 30-piece chamber orchestra, which sounds like a tight timeline on the face of it, and for a lot of composers it guess it is. But here's the thing: A symphony is broken up into movements for a reason. Sitting down to write 20 or more solid minutes of new music is impossible to get your head around, unless you break it into smaller chunks which can be organized by their nature. If you do that, things drop into manageable proportions and it all starts to look doable. Writing a book looks like a monumental a task if you look at the whole thing, but a chapter is no problem. It's like that.

I aimed at three movements of six to eight minutes each, which is basically double the length of your average arrangement of a song. Suddenly the timeline made perfect sense for my normal rhythm: One movement every two weeks, or one song's worth of writing, arranging and orchestrating per week.

I put off using notation software for well over a decade after the technology emerged, because of how natural (and portable) it is to use a good pencil, stave paper and a drawing board. This symphony was just before I begrudgingly admitted that I had to make the change or get left in the dust by my competition.

At the time, I was living in that incredibly quiet neighborhood outside of Bishop, and we had a covered patio out back with a table where I sat and wrote at night by porch light and headlamp, using my favorite 21-stave score paper from Valle Music, my trusty Pentel Twist-Erase 0.9 mechanical pencil with HB lead, scotch and cigars. The only accompaniment was the tree frogs and bull frogs in our ponds. It was a thoroughly enjoyable zen. For daytime writing, I also had several favorite rocks and perches where I liked to sit and write, up in the high places by waterfalls or creeks. The sound of rushing water does a great job of masking noise pollution, while not being tonal or rhythmic. I could hear my thoughts much more clearly up there than I can down here in SoCal, surrounded by all the noisy failed experiments of civilization. I decided to hire out the drudgery of copying, not only to humor my preferences, but because there wasn't enough time to do otherwise.

Suffice to say that there will never be an action / adventure film about composing and arranging. Inside the composer's head it might be any sort of environment—the chaos and explosive violence of a battlefield, the exultant bedlam of a political liberation, some frolicking animals, a chase scene, the spooky intrigue of someone sneaking around a corner, or a breathless moment of whispering and mystical beauty. But on the outside we just appear slightly unhinged, like we're silently having an argument with ourselves.

The only time I've ever seen this depicted accurately in film is in "Amadeus", when you see the actor portraying Mozart sitting at the table alone in the middle of the night, and you hear what he's hearing: an orchestra and choir absolutely exploding with one of his iconic pieces, so loud it almost blows your speakers. He's quietly going "tum-tum, ta-dum.." as he feverishly, fervently and madly writes, sweat dripping down his brow punctuating the incredible music that's erupting into being as he drives his pen relentlessly across the staves. Then suddenly there's a horrendously loud "click" as a doorknob softly turns, the music meets sudden oblivion and there's a stunningly abrupt, deafening silence as his wife pokes her head in the door and says, "Voofy?". When I saw that scene in the theater, I was barely able to stop myself from jumping to my feet and hollering "YES!!! YES!!! IT'S LIKE THAT GODDAMMIT, IT'S EXACTLY LIKE THAT!!" Kudos to whoever put that scene together. I wouldn't have though it possible to get it across.

As a composer, the biggest enemy to my creative process is noise pollution. Regardless of how massive and grand things may sound in my head as I write, all it takes to derail my thoughts is the soft buzz from a light fixture or a mosquito, because the softest noise that actually exists is louder than the loudest dream. A single engine Cessna innocently passing overhead will derail me until it's passed out of range of all hearing. I usually wear earplugs while writing.

I must be a very strange thing to live with. My wife has my deepest sympathy...not being musical, she'll never understand. I'd like to say that I've arrived at a place where I don't require that of people, but let's just call that a work in progress. And I thank my lucky stars that my wife is of the accepting sort.

The next hurdle of premiering new music is rehearsal time: You won't get much. Having that many qualified professionals in one room is of course expensive, so it's one thing for an orchestra to dust off and perform music the players are familiar with, but putting 20 or more minutes of new music on the stands that no one has ever seen is a different thing entirely. This tends to kill new orchestral music, along with your competition being the greatest composers of all time--no pressure there at all. There's a reason the world likes the music of The Masters, and why it's survived in our repertoire for centuries: It's very, very well penned.

What I was trained to do at Grove, and what I've spent most of my career writing and arranging, is music that can be performed fairly easily (the fiendish talents who have played in my progressive fusion projects might disagree, but that's a different animal). Music doesn't have to sound easy, or be predictable or pedantic, in order to actually be easy to read, learn and perform. There's definitely an art to that. Every film score you've ever heard was written in a way that didn't require much rehearsal, and just think of how involved some of that music sounds.

The secret is this: You use the characteristic strengths of your specific instruments and instrument families, you avoid their weaknesses, you keep your winds and brass breathing, you don't go into extremities of range, you orient your rhythms around a clave (a repeating rhythmic sequence), and write by piecing together rhythmic and melodic phrases--comparable to words in English, say--that aren't unlikely and are simple to play. Then of course you hire the very best cats you can. If you do all that and have a great copyist (so that it isn't nonsense that you're putting on the stands), you'd be surprised how quickly you can bring forth music that sounds a lot more difficult than it actually is.

If you write stuff that's actually difficult--like piecing together letters rather than words--it had better be a commission for a very specific purpose and player or ensemble, and you had better know their actual abilities. Otherwise, you'll deserve to have it sound as bad as it does when it gets recorded or performed in public with insufficient rehearsal.

Your reputation is at stake with every note you write, so really: don't be that writer. But even if you're tasked with writing a show-off test piece for virtuoso so-and-so, if you learn how to write things a certain way, you'll find that you can always get your idea across, in the way you actually mean creatively, without making the band sound like they're falling down a flight of stairs.

All of that said, my first symphony—three movements in 3/4 time, called "Three of a Kind"—could have used more rehearsal. I only had a little over an hour with the whole band, much of which was spent chasing down typos in the first movement. For the second and third movements I had switched to a retired union copyist from LA who lived in Bishop, played flute in the orchestra, and whose work copying the charts on the last two movements was impeccable.

Overall it went down fine, despite insufficient time in rehearsal to address typos. And as any creative will tell you: If I had it to do all over again, I'd change everything.

Igor Stravinsky once said "Music, in its purest form, is the interplay of musical elements, not subservient to images on a screen, or to a lyric, or to choreography." I couldn't agree more. After my decades in SoCal making music that was subservient to one, two or sometimes all three of those things, this was different: I was writing music just for music's sake. It felt like pure liberation.

Chapter 34
Chickens Come Home to Roost

On the 5th of July 2009, John Bachar fell to his death while free-soloing at the Dyke Wall, an outcropping of gorgeous white granite above Lake George in Mammoth. I was rocked, as was the entire international climbing community, the town of Mammoth Lakes and many of the East Side's inhabitants. We don't know how it happened, he wasn't in view of any other climbers at the moment. But I've been up where he was, and it's much easier terrain than other things he could easily cruise on that wall. So maybe he was using it as a downclimb and hit some flaky grains under foot, or a hold broke off, or maybe some rockfall got the better of him. We'll never know. Two climbers around the corner of the cliff band just heard him say "Oh SHIT", then they heard him hit.

His service was on a beautiful day at Lake Mary, on the deck of Lake Mary resort. The crowd overflowed into the parking lot. "He died", said his long-time buddy and fellow climbing god Ron Kauk, "living the dream."

The same afternoon that John left us, while at home alone in Bishop, I experienced my first ophthalmological migraine. My vision, which has always been excellent, was replaced by an opaque letter "C"-shape of little whirling, prismatic fan blades, as if somebody took several dozen 6-inch fans made from rainbow tape, all blowing in the wind on a sunny day, arranged them into a 6-foot letter C, then plastered that inside my skull so that it was mostly all I could see out of either eye, whether that eye was open or closed. It scared the hell out of me—I had no idea what was happening. There was no pain, no dizziness, no hypersensitivity to noise. It lasted about 20 minutes, during which I called my good friend Carolyn (Dr. Tiernan, who ran the local E.R.), who put me in touch with an on-call neurologist, who breezily said on the phone "Ah, you had an optal migraine, eh?" He said not to worry about it, they often present for the first time after 35 or 40 years of age. I confirmed all that with subsequent visits to two other neuros, just for due diligence. I've had only one or two other optal migraines since, not nearly as bad.

But this was combined with some other things that had been piling up. While quadruple-tracking an electric sitar figure of rapid-fire, aggressive "hammer-and-chisel" 16th notes at 165 BPM that appeared in several places in one of Combustible's tunes, I had given myself a bad case of De Quervain's syndrome in the right hand. I had no idea what it was at the time, I only knew that it was so bad that I had to stop playing, until whatever it was had cleared up. So work on the album, and everything else, was at a standstill. I also had growing neuropathies down both arms, more my right than my left, that were getting so bad it was becoming hard to even ride my bike. And when I looked up and extended my arms upward, as when changing a lightbulb, I felt like I was going to black out every time. There were pains in my right elbow when I played guitar that weren't my usual climber's tendonitis, and my entire C-spine had felt permanently jacked up ever since that mountain bike accident in '98.

All of these conditions seemed to be getting worse. I had half-joked for years that this lifestyle of sitting on my ass and teaching was a slow suicide, and the drinking hadn't abated since the cruise ship gig, six years prior. It was becoming obvious that the path I was on had to change, and I took the events of July 5th as a courtesy warning from the universe—maybe the only one I'd get. I chose not to ignore it.

***

What followed was a series of events that would have never happened without some great friends. First off, I quit drinking. I didn't know if I would go into DTs or not, so I made Carolyn aware of what I was doing so that it was on her radar. Then I called my good buddy Robin T. in Mammoth, who was a 12-stepper, and asked him if he'd sponsor me in the event that I needed it. He said yes.

This was prior to the ACA being passed, and medical insurance wouldn't cover pre-existing conditions unless it was corporate-style coverage, through an employer. So even if I could have afforded the $1600 or so per month, most of my problems still wouldn't be covered. Fortunately, there was a way forward that got me into some great corporate insurance, thanks to a working arrangement with a friend who had a company and traded me for lessons for him and his son. Just like that, hey presto: I had gold-plated Gucci health coverage.

As it turned out I didn't descend into shakes, DTs or other symptoms of withdrawal from alcohol. And I didn't need to go to meetings, though I gladly would have if it was needed. As of this writing I'll be 15 years sober in a few days. My friends in sobriety circles—of whom I have many—tell me I'm what they call a "normy". But I still take it as seriously as anyone else whose life depends on sobriety, and I mark the anniversary each year, along with the poignance of losing my good brother John.

As for getting the body fixed, that was a more involved journey, which I call my 100,000-mile overhaul. I had spent my entire adult life without health coverage while hosting a strong addiction to adrenaline outdoor sports, whose livelier moments are sharply punctuated in my memory because I lacked the athletic chops to honor the checks that my spirit tended to write. I had gone to county E.R.s only when I might die if I didn't, so I had a long laundry list of things that needed qualified scrutiny and probable treatment. At the moment, the most urgent ones were between the base of my skull and the tips of my fingers on both arms, so I started with those.

A gifted spine surgeon and one of the state's best certified hand and elbow specialists had a practice together in the same office, four hours' drive south in Westlake Village. I did several days of fastidious research, and from every point of the compass, every qualified source I spoke to pointed to them.

When I walked in with my laundry list, conveying the inventory was a funny exercise. I'd tell them about a problem, they'd think that that was all, and start to synopsize.

"Okay, so..."

"Wait, there's more..."

This process repeated for awhile, their eyebrows raising higher each time I added something. Eventually I had conveyed the whole picture, and a flurry of activity ensued as things got underway. There were some funny conversations after the first round of MR images came back.

Dr. R., the spine guy: "Did you know you have several broken vertebrae?"

"Nooo, but I can't say I'm surprised."

"And I can see where your vertebral arteries are a bit impinged by some stenosis."

"Mmm. Probably explains why the world starts to go away when I try to change a lightbulb."

Dr. C., the hand guy: "Good gawd Byron, your right elbow alone is conclusively positive for six different things! You've got De Quervain's where your right thumb meets your wrist, an inoperable torn brachial radialis, tendonitis of the biceps tendon, lateral epicondylitis, some beginnings of arthritis in the elbow and wrist, and the nerve conductivity test comes back as a conclusive positive for radial tunnel syndrome—

which is bad news—as well as conclusive positive for carpal tunnel." He took a deep breath and puffed his cheeks out as he exhaled, then looked more directly at me..."so I'm gonna begin by just throwing a grenade on the field to see what it kills. By that I mean we're just gonna put your right arm in a cast for a few weeks."

And so began the overhaul. The De Quervain's responded nicely to cortisone, as Doc C. said it would. That was by far the easiest thing. Putting me back together after all my shenanigans, it turns out, took another seven surgeries—eight if I count a spinal epidural. My radial nerve (the wiring harness that goes from your neck around your shoulder and down your arm, then splits out to your fingertips) had impingements in the C-spine, the right shoulder, the right elbow and the right forearm. "Other than that," Doc C. joked, "the nerve path is fairly clear."

The first C-spine fusion was anterior, followed a few months later by a successful right shoulder repair. A year later, a second C-spine fusion was done posterior, because one of the levels hadn't fused.

Doc C. got me back to playing guitar in pretty quick order, but that radial tunnel syndrome was stubborn as hell. After two years of trying lots of highly-qualified physical therapy and some cortisone shots, we were up against it. Doc C. said "Y'know Byron, for every 1,000 cases of carpal tunnel I do, I see one case of radial tunnel. And I was at an annual luncheon recently of the five best hand guys in California...we polled each other about what our least favorite surgery is. Four of us said radial tunnel repair."

"Holy crap. Why's that?"

"It only gets about a 40% success rate."

"Ah. So, lemme ask you this: If we do this surgery, other than a 60% chance of not improving, what do I need to be afraid of? Side effects or other risks, I mean?"

"Nothing, other than the usual risks associated with any surgery. It's just that it may not work."

"Sounds like a no-brainer, then. We won't know if we don't try, and I'm a very long way from not needing to play guitar as best as I can. Let's do it."

So we did it, and he also repaired the right elbow's lateral epicondylitis at the same time. After the post-op PT, the radial tunnel pain was reduced by about 70%, so it went in the win column.

There was more to the overhaul--a half-successful knee repair and a third C-Spine surgery to remove the posterior hardware because a screw was where it didn't belong and threatening a nerve--and if I'm being honest, some things on the list never really got addressed. But in big-picture terms, I got my career back and returned to life, and to doing great gigs.

Without my having been a part of the Eastern Sierras community, without great friends, talented docs, a host of incredible PTs and of course nurses—and without my wife, who was there through thick and thin helping me through every step of the process—I don't know where I'd be right now. But I doubt it would be pretty.

* * *

I was able to start playing again within a few months of starting the overhaul, and after a few weeks of gingerly dusting off my chops, work on "Combustible" resumed. I finished the thing and released it on several online sales and streaming platforms via CDBaby, plus a few that I loaded it into myself, certain that all of this was so much tilting at windmills. But what the hell, it didn't cost much money or take much time to just put it out there.

Before too long, something very strange was happening: it was getting a high number of organic (un-promoted) plays online, and receiving flattering reviews. At first I thought I was being pranked, then I was gobsmacked. The positive response to "Combustible"—an entire album of me trying not to please anyone—was hard to process, but the facts were undeniable, as facts tend to be.

My surprise was matched only by the encouragement I felt to do a follow-up album of similar folly, so I started tilting at "Explosive". Bolstered by this encouragement—always a dangerous thing in my history—I set about to make Explosive less of a lark than Combustible, more of an actual effort.

Before Explosive was completed, though, its inception and realization would be interrupted by a move.

Chapter 35
Southbound Again, Again

If there is one central theme to my life and to this book that overshadows all others, it is the immutable power that music has over the musician. I can think of no clearer illustration of this than a decision I made with Roni in 2010.

Living in the Eastern Sierras and being perpetually awed by nature's majesty every time you step outside or turn around has a value that's impossible to quantify. Living hand-to-mouth in such a breathtaking place is a good deal better than owning a McMansion anywhere in Los Angeles as far as I'm concerned, and every single day I felt intense gratitude for my quality of life, and having realized my dream of "maybe someday" living there. And being made to feel like a valued part of the community by those who lived there was an honor I've experienced nowhere else. I had, then as now, great friends there and a deep love of everything about the East Side.

But living hand-to-mouth is a young person's game. Having recently turned fifty, I had more of my life behind me than was in front, and despite my itinerantly behaving like I'm immortal, I had to begrudgingly admit that time would eventually win. At some point I'd be unable to maintain the scrabbling, burrowing and hustling existence of a musician, and on that day I'd need to have squirreled away enough to retire, whatever that word even means. Accomplishing that would require greener pastures for my last couple of decades of professional viability—someplace where the professional ceiling was higher than six inches off the floor.

I ran this by Roni and discovered that for her own reasons, she also felt hamstrung by the limitations of the tiny local business pond. After mulling it over for a bit—that's code-speak for several weeks of agonizing over a short list of possible locations—we opted for a move back to LA, where "the only limits to which you can rise are those of your own wits", as Ben Franklin said of the United States. It didn't guarantee that I'd succeed in amassing a retirement, but staying in the Eastern Sierras pretty much guaranteed that I wouldn't. And in LA, I'd have connections and be back among the finest musical talent on earth.

The sky to the south was that old familiar piss-yellow and there was that old familiar gnawing in my gut as we drove south on 395 with everything we owned. Moving back to LA was returning to the devil I knew—another recurring theme of my life—but I couldn't deny that in front of us lay limitless possibility, while behind us was a place that would keep us working until the day we die.

* * *

Once we were moved into our new 'hood—a quasi-rural enclave tucked up against some hills by Burbank—it wasn't long before I was back in the class-five rapids, playing with some top-shelf musicians and getting involved with some very cool projects. The cooler the noiseletting I took part in, the less I felt the gnawing in my gut.

My business plan this time did not include playing nightclubs around SoCal as a means of making money, because most gigs were over an hour away from Burbank and still paid the same as 20 years earlier. Hourly net pay, driving time accounted for, was maybe 10% of what any good professional was now worth.

Playing listening rooms around LA for music's sake, on the other hand, was something I prioritized. If you don't get your mug out there playing cool stuff with good cats, you won't get called for the important gigs that are worth doing, like tours and recording sessions. Such is the imperative of networking with your instrument. Good listening rooms like Vibrato, Alva's, Spaghettini's, Catalina, Vitello's and Typhoon were among the prime places for noiseletting with great cats. I happily made a point of treading their stages.

When you go "off the res" and come back like I did, you've got to win your way back into things. I was gratified to find some new doors opening and old doors re-opening when I called, and some of the noises I was a part of were truly proud on the coolness meter.

One of the first such projects was Dogg Mansion, which was the fault and brainchild of a trumpeter / composer buddy of mine named Larry Williams. His music was unhinged enough to be both challenging and really fun, and his lineup of players was as proud as the legacy of the space where we rehearsed: a venerated and much-storied place known to insiders as Magruder's.

Inside those walls, many of the more noteworthy players in the LA studio scene regularly got together to hang out and play challenging charts to keep their chops honed, in continuation of a tradition: Many had actually cut their teeth there. Magruder's was hallowed ground, where the default level of talent and difficulty of charts made for legitimately tall grass, and if you were going there you brought your A-game. Many times I found myself surrounded by some of the world's best, playing their asses off on some really oddball charts, having a great time and availing themselves of Joy Magruder's wonderful plates of cookies, strawberries and the like. "Magruder's" was the living room in her house.

Joy was like a den mother to incredible musical talent, maintaining the tradition built by her late husband John, who had been the band director of a local high school. A disproportionately high number of his students graduated from his class and went on to become well-known and respected musicians, doing noteworthy gigs. John and Joy had hosted band play-downs every week for decades, and though John was gone by the time I came along, the power of his legacy wasn't lost on me, nor the love that Joy perpetually poured into us and into that scene, to keep it alive and thriving. I'd be thrashing, sweating and cussing my way through impossible charts—usually Larry's—surrounded by players known for their work on things like the Tonight Show Band or some seriously major tours, and all the while Joy would sit in her chair listening and smiling as she unofficially presided over it all. We all felt a tangible imperative to play well enough to please her. When she finally sold the house and moved, it was lamented by many as the end of an era.

I made several important acquaintances there, not the least of whom was a drummer named Jay Setar, one of LA's beastly mutants, who would become a good brother of mine and pretty much my go-to guy for drums on many, many productions. The son of LA sax legend John Setar, Jay was raised on substantive music from the get-go, and is more comfortable with strange, technical terrain and changing meters than perhaps any drummer I've ever known. And that's saying something. I asked him once why he's so weirdly comfortable with weird rhythms. He said "I grew up listening to weird Hungarian music around the house." Go figure.

* * *

Progress on "Explosive" resumed as soon as I had the studio set up in the new house, and of course it was the first thing I set up. My usual rhythm is to write, arrange, track and mix one song, then rinse and repeat.

You might think it odd that I always write things for a project if it needs music, rather than dip into the massive pile of orphaned music I've already written. And it's true that the pile is legitimately proud, filling several totes gathering dust in the garage, getting so heavy that it's threatening the structural integrity of the house's foundation--and this place is built on a thick concrete slab--but I'm a writer. As any composer will say, writing is what I do. It would actually take me more time to sift through all those orphans for something that might be appropriate than to just pen something new and custom-tailored for present needs. So the pile grows, and stuff almost never gets used. Every composer worth his or her salt has a large pile. If we meet with mad success, then after we die things from The Pile might get pitched to big names, or auctioned off at fundraisers as framed works of art. If we're nobody, it either gets donated to a school somewhere or tossed out with the egg shells and coffee grounds. I'd have it no other way.

Fiscal success will never be a good yardstick for measuring the quality of a musician's work, but if a song sees the light of day—gets recorded, say, or performed someplace that matters—that's indicative of good work. And I'm not superstitious, but I've had a lot of experiences that made me feel like a puppet dangling from the universe's strings as mysterious forces chuckled overhead, so for reasons that cannot be explained, I just sort of trust those forces to make things happen for music that deserves it. Call that strange if you like.

Once Explosive was done, the fiasco that hobbled it was that I signed with a brand new indie label who gave me a friendly contract. I was the second artist they signed. Being so new, they spun donuts of indecision about how to operate. For awhile they changed the plan almost daily, then just sort of evaporated.

They let me out of the contract, but the damage was done: when I resumed shopping Explosive around, it was beyond consideration as a matter of most labels' policies, because it was no longer a "new release", despite not having really been released.

Well and good, I hadn't really expected the thing to see much daylight. The digital wing of Steve Vai's label, Digital Nations, was willing to add it to their catalogue along with Combustible, and was a fitting home for both albums. When Digital nations went away, I put Explosive out on some of the other outlets that Combustible was on, which brings us to yet another thing to watch out for when dealing with labels:

Nothing is more impermanent than an online music outlet. To give you an idea of how bad it is, I'll have to re-check all my online label info as the very last thing I do before handing this book over to the publisher, because some things change perpetually. It's a good idea for those who sell things online to check the vendors and their links once in awhile.

While doing a periodic check of my sales links to make sure all was up and running, I searched "Byron Fry Combustible" and the same for Explosive. Lo and behold, I was on more than a half dozen labels I had neither heard of nor talked to, let alone signed with. "Good golly" I said, or something to that effect. It turned out that the fine print in the agreement with one of the online outlets I had signed with allowed them to make secondary deals. Thus I'm featured on several labels—some as a part of a collection— whose deals I had nothing to do with, whose terms I still have no knowledge of, with unknown individuals who are of unknown honorability, and the funds from whose sales will almost assuredly never reach my hands, because: Money does not intrinsically want to flow to the artist.

With each pair of hands your money passes through, the odds of your actually receiving it grow longer. About the time this was happening (but before I discovered it), I had a sandwich and a cuppa with a great entertainment attorney buddy of mine from the Jackson camp, to talk about this and a few other things.

He assured me that the problem of artists not getting the money they're owed is far, far worse than I could ever imagine and, as cynical as I am, I'm not nearly cynical enough.

Granted, these two albums are guitar-driven world / jazz / rock fusion, so who cares. Not exactly Billboard Top40 material, no big loss. But if I had spent a lot of money and time trying to make some kind of pop project that people might actually buy, this would be a problem. So I say, yet again: Count your silverware when dealing with anyone—ANYONE—who wants to sell your music for you. Even if they're innocently doing business correctly as it's intended to be done, you're almost definitely still getting screwed.

* * *

While I was efforting all of this with Explosive, I had to maintain a good stream of paying work. While preparing to move back to LA, I had gotten an inquiry from someone who had seen my profile on social media and was interested in having me produce some stuff for her. Christina Lynn Martin was an indie from Oregon, happened to be driving down to LA soon, and could take 395 so we could meet up and discuss things. So we met in a parking lot and she sang right then and there. She had great pipes. She would be the first paying client in my new digs in SoCal.

Producing indies is sort of a specialty of mine. I like the simplicity. There's a direct connection between arranger / producer and artist, and of course I like the lack of labels and their bosses being involved. I can make any deal I want, and be creative about it---typically half up front, half on delivery, but it can work lots of ways as long as everyone's happy. And the bid is mine to screw up.

Given the nature of the industry, faulty business models such as "spec" deals have long since fallen by the wayside for me, simply due to the nuts and bolts of fiscal attrition. That's code-speak for hard-won lessons. "Spec"—short for speculative—means you don't get paid for your work unless the project generates the funds from which you'd theoretically be paid. It's never been a good idea, hence my refusal to work for "spec" dating back to about 1992. But with things the way they are now, I've become such a cash-on-the-barrelhead thinker that I shy away from anything containing language that's even remotely speculative. If you want to hire a plumber, you pay him. If you want to hire me, you pay me. It's that simple. And my work smells much better than a plumber's, or so we can hope.

Since moving back to LA I've arranged and produced about eighty songs so far, all for indie clients of various types, stripes and budgetary robustness. My point is that you don't have to be working for a big name in order to be making some great music and paying your bills. With the miniscule nature of royalties in the post-digital apocalypse, the stature of someone's public persona is not as relevant a metric as it used to be. But that doesn't mean working with big names doesn't have its perks.

* * *

Ronnie Ciago is one of the greatest drummers around, and has been a good brother of mine since John Pena introduced us in the nineties. We've chewed mud on a lot of different gigs, from things with John and Dave Garfield, to Dogg Mansion at Magruder's, to a couple of my own fusion projects playing the Spud. Ronnie's gig history is truly proud. He's worked with the iconic fusion band Brand X, toured with The Meters and toured one-on-one with Patrick Moraz...if you know these names, you're probably a musician and your eyebrows just went up. If you don't, well, just take my word for it: Ronnie's a world-class badass.

When Ronnie showed up to play some of Larry's insane charts at Magruder's, it was a great reunion for us. In getting caught up, he told me he'd been playing in Frank Stallone's band. "What's that like?" I asked, in the usual manner of players wanting to know how their friends are being treated.

"Great," he said, "Frank's a solid cat and a great guy to work for. It's a fun gig."

A couple of years later, Ronnie called me to tell me that Frank was looking for a guitarist, and asked me if I wanted him to toss my name in the hat.

"Heck yeah," I said, "I'd be honored! Thanksman!" The audition was arranged, I got the gig and we started rehearsals in the West Side at Frank's pad, surrounded by walls adorned with gold records and boxing memorabilia. Frank and I hit it off on several levels, not the least of which is guitar. Besides having legitimate talent and great pipes, Frank is a great host, makes a mean espresso, always asks if you need anything, treats his players with dignity and respect at all times, and hands you the check before downbeat without fail. Many is the time I've wished that more of the people I've worked for were more like that. He's an honorable guy who, like many of my best friends, occupies the opposite end of the political spectrum from me, but we never butted heads about it. At the end of the day, I think we both intrinsically get that as Americans we have far more in common than not, despite the wedges our news media might try to drive between us.

Frank's a natural teller of stories, and like all great entertainers he's got a lot of funny ones. As Ronnie had said, he's a great guy to work for. With all the storytelling—which the crowds always love—I was getting entertained on stage almost as much as I was taking part in the entertaining. We played only the best listening rooms in SoCal, his audiences itinerantly consisting of pretty Hollywood women, sprinkled throughout with his big-hit-producer and songwriter pals. Frank always knew how many records were sold by each of his buddies, and would bring it to the crowd's attention as he pointed them out—Frank is no dope. We were treated far better than if we were some scruffy fusion band and Frank wasn't involved.

He's a strong songwriter, singer, player and performer—as evidenced by all the hits and awards—but perhaps more than anything, Frank's just one of the guys. Like many stars in this industry, he and Sly came from nothing. It's a proud story.

Jonathan Butler was and is keyboards / MD, bass was and is either Baba Elefante or Larry Antonino, so it's one hell of a band. We only played two road gigs when I was in the lineup—one was at the other end of the country in Florida, the other was at the other end of the world.

If you've ever flown from LAX to China and you think like I do, you might've started to wonder, as you passed over Hawaii or thereabouts, "Where the hell is all this fuel coming from?" Suspending that much tonnage in space with hundreds of passengers and their luggage for fourteen solid hours while propelling it forward at over 500 miles an hour is a technological marvel to me. I tried to make the math work a bunch of different ways, but failed. Evidently, aerospace engineers have better math skills than me.

Upon landing in Macau we were treated like heads of state: A heavily-armed escort met the plane and hustled us through customs to the curb, where we were loaded into a large black Caddy SUV, then rushed to the casino in a full-on motorcade with lights and sirens: "No shit, there I was, riding in a motorcade with my bros like we were friggin' heads of state." Thus did I get to check "motorcade" off the list for the first time. As we climbed out of the Caddy at the hotel, we were hurried into a somewhat glitzy meet-and-greet with the hotelier, with cameras and press. Fourteen hours on a plane isn't the best prep for a photoshoot, but we made it work. I thought that I pulled off the "haggard-looking guy in raggedy sweats surrounded by Armani" look very convincingly.

The thing that struck me about Macau is that visually I was in Vegas, plain and simple. There was almost no sense of being in a foreign country. And you may think that Vegas is a boom town, but it's got nothing on Macau. The growth is out of control, literally—it's a runaway train. So many buildings are going up, there's nothing to fill them with. Property developers don't achieve any balance with need. I don't understand the economics of it, but it's not sustainable.

Another thing that any westerner will notice while visiting China is the size and nature of the population. Individuality isn't so much the thing in that culture, at least not in the way westerners think about it: power is derived from the capacity to think and act as a collective. And China is nothing if not quite a large collective.

This was brought home to me as we were setting up for soundcheck in the casino's showroom, and I had a tightly-packed scrum of seven young hotel sound techs standing in front of me, every one of whom was desperate to help. Some manager had told them "Go help the guitarist", I guess. I turned on my amp, got no sound, looked down and realized I hadn't plugged a cable all the way into one of my pedals, and bent down to plug the thing in. On that cue, all seven of those guys lunged in the direction of that cable end, literally elbowing each other out of the way in the effort to be the one to plug it in for me. It was an awkward moment: There was a hidden desperation in the air that had allowed itself be seen for just one second, and whose genesis I couldn't fathom. Maybe I'm just a westerner who can't understand eastern thinking, or maybe all seven guys were trying out for one job. Maybe both, I'll never know. But I want to understand it.

After a couple of years I had to reluctantly part ways with Frank's band. For him, playing live wasn't the main thing and the booking calendar was too slim to justify a commitment that kept me from being able to commit to other things, so I needed to free myself up and pursue a busier booking schedule. I introduced him to my good brother and a great guitarist, Rick Vitallo. Thus was Frank covered in very good form.

* * *

Also in the twenty-teens, I was part of a delightful unlikelihood: A large ensemble of amazing talent that included a grammy-winning pop icon, multiple grammy-nominee hit songwriters and the odd rock icon or two, on a brief grass roots tour of the Pacific Northwest. It remains one of the funnest tours I've ever done.

Chapter 36
Caravan of Gypsies

For several wonderful weeks in 2013 I wandered the Pac Northwest as a member of a beautiful family of fellow howlers-at-the-moon, comprising the maiden incarnation of a show called "Romancing the West".

It was one of the most eclectic things I've ever been involved with, and that's saying something. The show tried to be so many different things—succeeded in being so many different things—that it was very difficult to market in that first year, not being established among talent buyers.

The nature of the show was totally unique: A narrated history of the western United States, in a format no one had ever heard of, called a "documentary concert". The storyline started just before the arrival of the first Europeans and ended in present-day, and was illustrated by video and live performance of the music from each era. From the 1950s on, we had people on stage who had been responsible for some of the hits being played.

The show was written and directed by Christina Lynn Martin, she whose songs I had produced around 2010-2011. It was a truly great show, featuring 18 fantastic musicians and myself, representing a wide variety of backgrounds and cultures.

Whether you're hawking downloads, or trying to place your songs on film and TV, or selling tickets on a tour, you have to be able to pigeon-hole what it is you're selling. Humans are nothing if not very easily confused, and that goes double when you're talking about music. When asked to buy a ticket, even those who actually do understand music will respond better to a recognized category than something that looks like this:

"Waitaminnit, run it by me again...what kind of tickets are you selling? Is it a Rock concert..."

"Yes..."

"or Folk..."

"Um, yeah, and..."

"or Jesus Music..."

"well, yeah..."

"or Jazz..."

"yeah, but here's..."

"or 50s Surf-Rock..."

"y'se, here's the..."

"or Cowboy Poetry..."

"yeah, but here's the thing..."

"or Gothic Rock on a pipe organ rising up out of the stage..."

"whatcha need to underst..."

"or blistering Shred Guitar trade-offs..."

"yes, but understand th..."

"or a narrated Historical Documentary? Which is it?"

"Okay, yes. Just...yes. It's all of those."

It was confusing to people. It was hard enough to get across what it was in person, let alone with ads or foot-tall lettering on a theater marquis. But once inside, people always loved the show and its message of cultural respect.

Treading the stage together was the following talented gaggle of diversity:

- Melanie Safka, she of the 60's Woodstock-inspired hit "Lay Down / Candles in the Rain", and Billboard's #1 Top Female Vocalist in '72,

- Chuck Girard, founding father of the "Jesus Music" genre,

- Pam Mark Hall, grammy-nominated hit folk songwriter and artist,

- Bryan Duncan, vocalist extraordinaire and multi-#1-hit artist in the "Jesus Music" genre,

- Martin Gerschwitz, an incredibly talented keyboardist who played and sang with Iron Butterfly, Meatloaf, Lita Ford and Walter Trout, and with whom I had chewed mud on a hundred stages starting with our time together in one of the wilder cover bands in the 80s & 90s—in fact he was the occupant of the lower bunk the morning I woke up with those crushed ribs,

- Cilette Swan and Roman Morykit, two of the most magnificently talented and wonderful humans I'll ever know, whose unique indie duo "Gypsy Soul" will bring a smile to places you don't even know exist inside you,

Nick Garret-Powell, a horrifyingly, terrifyingly good guitarist and vocalist, and who would be a megastar if this world made any sense at all,

John Elliott, an extraordinarily good songwriter and performer of Americana / Folk,

Jacque Nunez, a wonderful Native American educator and singer,

- Beau Safka, Melanie's son and a savant multi-instrumentalist,

- Monte Byrd on Sax, a great player whose perpetual smile and spreading of love always kept the vibe right,

- Paul MacIntyre, a seriously burning fiddler,

- Patty Moran McCoy, a jazz pianist of such great ability that she played with Duke Ellington back when women weren't allowed in the "boys club",

- Southern Oregon's great Jim Sitter on drums, and me—hired ringers rounding out the rhythm section.

Most of these talented parties could hold an audience in awe single-handed, so to have them all on stage in one tour was an incredible accomplishment. The whole shebang was emceed by Christina (vocals and narration) and a cowboy music duo of Butch Martin (vocals and fantastic cowboy poetry) and Skip Bissonette (vocals and folk guitar).

Believe it or not, we actually did manage to have a natural flow through all of those genres and presentations because they represented, in music, that timeline of settlement of the western US—delivered by some of the actual artists, to boot.

Despite the difficulty of getting the idea across in a two-second world, the theaters where we spent a normal amount on marketing actually did well, but we only had about half the funding needed to market the whole tour. Consequently, having amassed all that star-power and talent, and having made such a splendid show to utilize it in such a cool and unique way, that first tour wasn't as lucrative as it could have been. "Seizing defeat from the jaws of victory", as the saying goes.

We were accompanied by the seats of our pants and an ad-hoc collection of our own vehicles, rented vans and one seriously cool vintage 1950s-era greyhound bus, resto-modded into one of the most vibey tour rigs I've seen. We stayed at colorful, historic hotels and B&Bs, we mixed and matched rides and we had each others' backs. We experienced things in a more personal way than we would have if we had been insulated by the mechanical logistics of a well-run major tour. This felt much more human, more organic. We performed for each other, and loved doing it. It made us into more of a family, and burned a lasting fondness of the tour into our collective memories.

Butch dipped into his savings and kept the paychecks coming, even after it became obvious how much it would cost. The tour was short enough and his sense of honor and duty strong enough that he just took the hit for us all. It remains one of the most selfless acts I've witnessed, bless the man. Christina made him a full partner, and they tell me that they've long since recouped their money, they've learned how to capture the essence of the show in marketing, and it's been touring around successfully now for over a decade.

* * *

There's a good lesson here for you if you want to build your presence among the touring acts of this continent: If you're going to tour your own act, don't be your own entrepreneur, putting your own money on the line for the venue, the publicity and promo, and relying on ticket sales in order to not lose your butt. There are talent buyers and promoters who do that for a living, they're much better at it than you or me, and they've got established pipelines, systems and machinery already in place with which they routinely succeed.

You'll always be relying on ticket sales, but the numbers involved will be far better if you let the people who are good at that stuff do their thing, enabling you to focus on doing yours, which is making your show great. There's a fairly direct way to meet and make your act known to these buyers and promoters, and I'll lay it out for you later in these pages.

Chapter 37
Be Careful What You Wish For

As I struggled with the unlikelihoods in some of the hardest charts I'll probably ever play, I found myself looking to my left, a few feet away: "No shit, there I was, playing in a rhythm section right next to Keith Emerson." It was just one of many such thoughts generated by the oddities happening all around me, thanks to the musical audacity and eccentricities of a man named Ross Wright.

I thought back to the night in the early aughts when I first witnessed a performance by Elvis Schoenberg's Orchestre Surreal, and how I had wondered what it might be like to maybe, someday, actually play in that band. Now that day had arrived. In the intervening years, it had grown to 30 pieces and sprouted a male tenor opera and rock singer, to join The Fabulous Miss Thing in fronting the spectacle.

For her part, The Fabulous Miss Thing requires some explaining insofar as it's feasible. She is the persona donned by Angela Carole Brown when she fronts the orchestra. You may remember Angela from a conversation I had with her over bandwiches in a green room at a tux gig, when she first told me about this band.

Miss Thing is a steampunked-out and monocled, platinum wig and thigh-high leather boot-wearing Afro-American / German Dominatrix. She uses Angela's blinding talent to whisper, sing and belt Rock, Soul, R&B, and Operatic melodies over complicated chords, rhythms and arrangements, interspersed with sado-masochistic rap in English and German. And as musically challenging and unlikely as that sounds, it's the visual spectacle and theatrical command of Miss Thing that ices the cake. Elton and Gaga have nothing on Thing.

Elvis Shoenberg is Ross Wright's stage persona, who delivers hilarious narrations in the style of Rod Serling when he's not conducting. Ross is a brilliant and very bold composer / arranger, and ESOS is entirely his fault. I was trained at Grove to paint within the lines, to avoid challenging an orchestra too much or writing stuff that requires too much rehearsal time. Ross has become a good brother of mine and is my polar opposite as a composer, which is why I love the man's writing. He's quite insane, itinerantly writing stuff I would never ask nor expect an orchestra (or guitarist) to play. But the band is comprised of some of L.A.'s finest studio cats who feel, as do I, that being a part of such unlikelihood is an honor. So we basically make it work.

Dangerous Dan is the bare-torsoed, bombastic viking persona assumed by Dan O'Callaghan, a fantastic tenor of legitimately respectable range, projection and versatility. He turns from Operatic high C to belting Rock to Rap on a dime, often within the same phrase or the same note. Besides vocal gymnastics, he brings great antics and theater to the front line. Between Dan, Thing and Elvis, the audience is usually too distracted to notice the lineup of world-class gentry occupying the stage behind them, some of whom are respected recording and touring artists, many of whom have been featured in musical periodicals and every one of whom is duly respected among the LA musical community's "constantly working" cadre.

Performances are typically two or three times a year, usually in theaters or listening rooms around SoCal. I've played eight or ten shows with that band now, one of only a few guitarists to be tapped by Ross. The nature of the music played by ESOS defies explanation by words—or logic—and might just be the coolest noise I've ever been a part of. Like Angela had said in that green room: "If you think 'Stravinsky meets Zappa at Hendrix on the set of The Twilight Zone', you're on the right track."

I couldn't fully appreciate the actual depths of Ross's musical depravity until he called me to play in the band. I arranged to pick up the guitar book from him five full days before the first rehearsal, just to hedge my bets a little. I had never done that for any gig, but I knew this book would be a handful. I figured five days was plenty of time to shed. Having picked up the book, during the drive home I thought "Hell, if anything I'm probably playing it a bit too safe." A mile later I thought, "I shouldn't have gone to all that trouble, driving to all the way over to Ross's to get the book. It's not like me to need to do that." And so my drive went, building my confidence mile-by-mile like an ornately embroidered quilt of complacency, until it was so big I could wrap it twice around my shoulders. By the time I turned up my street, I was riding on a gold-filigreed throne of musical ability mounted on a royal litter borne by Scandinavian blondes, and I was laying plans for what to do with all the spare time I'd have before rehearsals. Then I got home, opened the book, and all the air was sucked out of the room.

As I leafed through it, my mouth gaped farther and farther open. The problem wasn't the physical difficulty of the lines—which are indeed difficult—or the rhythms, which are indeed really odd. The problem was, and is, just how utterly weird some of Ross's ideas are. He writes stuff that is so unlikely that even years later, there are parts I never have gotten my head or hands around. I cut my teeth on progressive stuff, remember. I like it weird and challenging. But this was a whole new level.

What followed was several days of solitary confinement in my home studio while my wife Roni tiptoed about the house, repeatedly startled by sudden blasts of expletives through the door as I repeatedly failed to play some phrase or other. The poor woman dared open that door only twice a day, to gingerly push in a dish of raw meat with a stick. When it was bed time, she had to get the drop on me with a tranquilizer gun then winch my limp form into the bedroom, while I incoherently mumbled something about musical propriety. Now we know: every time I tell Ross I'll play a date, we're losing a week out of our lives.

I eventually got to where I could play about 95% of the parts, and that's as good as it's ever going to get. There are lines in that show that are so nutty, I've literally spent hours at a time trying to get my mind and fingers around just a couple of phrases, and I've still never been able to play them. Don't tell Ross.

I've compared notes with a few other guitarists who have had that chair, and we all agree: In all of our careers, it's the single most intimidating book any of us has ever played. To give you an idea, Ross sometimes calls a Zappa chart, and it's one of the easiest charts in the book. We sometimes do Elfman material from Nightmare Before Christmas, and I can read that right down cold, no problem.

Playing the ESOS show live is dangerous for the guitarist's cardiac health...imagine a ski run that's super steep, super narrow, has house-sized moguls and a line of lift towers going up the center. No matter how good you are, you're in survival mode in such terrain (you may recognize the voice of experience). Playing one of Ross's ESOS charts is like that. Playing the whole show is a long, very burly roller coaster ride. We'd end one tune and I'd feel a massive rush of relief as I exhaled, allowing myself a brief smile in self-congratulation for not totally screwing the pooch or going into cardiac arrest. Then I'd turn the page, glance at the next chart and scream "OH, FUCK!!!" inside my head. At least, I think it was inside my head. Shows were 90 minutes of that, one after another after another, followed by a drive home feeling like I had just climbed out of a tumble drier.

But here's the thing: The camaraderie. To be asked to play such a body of work is a high honor, to say nothing of doing it with such a collection of talent. And if I'm being honest, the thrill ride—the fight for survival, the wild pin-balling through the book—is snot-slinging fun. You can't buy that for any amount of money. So for all my whining about playing things that were never meant for guitar—or maybe they're simply over my head—the truth is that I love playing that book a little more than I hate it. It's an abusive, co-dependent relationship.

I'm one of probably very few guitarists who have been on stage playing an electric guitar in the middle of an orchestra during the opening stanza of Orff's "Carmina Burana". If you know the piece, you'll be aware that it's one of the biggest and most iconic noises an orchestra and choir can possibly make. And I've been in the middle of that incredible melee playing rock power chords on a Strat. It felt like lightning bolts were shooting out of me and everyone around me. It literally raises the hair on the back of my neck even thinking about it. You can't buy a ride like that.

Blending an electric guitar with an orchestra is difficult, to say the least. There is no shortage of attempts that have been made, from some of the fifties-era guitar crooner instrumentals to Moody Blues, ELO, Zeppelin--any comprehensive list would be too long to actually set down here. But until recently, nobody ever made it sound right: An electric guitar isn't an acoustic instrument, and in an orchestral setting it inherently sounds like a bull in a china shop or a skill saw among the natural noises of a farm in the 1700s.

Then Jeff Beck cracked the puzzle. It makes perfect sense that it would be him—he who contributed an entire career of groundbreaking, pioneering pushing of the envelope, coming up with one unique trademark technique after another, not the least of which was his capacity to get such incredible tones. Of course it would be him to solve the great orchestral quandary.

If you haven't heard his album "Emotion and Commotion", you should fix that. You'll hear an electric guitar laying so naturally, beautifully and brilliantly into an orchestral setting, it's like it was born there. And sure, the engineering and mix is a massive part of the puzzle, and prerequisite to success. But the man's delivery of an exposed melody is second to none, and combined with his mastery of tone, his gift for delivery made him the one—the only one—to finally get the thing to work. Like any guitarist worth his or her salt, I've made a lifelong pursuit of getting useful tone, hopefully beautiful tone. And I have no idea how he did it. None whatsoever. I don't know if anyone does, and the great Mr. Beck has left the room, so he ain't talkin'.

* * *

Speaking of British pioneers with otherworldly talent, Keith Emerson gave us the honor of playing some of his orchestral pieces, and he in turn played in the rhythm section. So I got to be in the rhythm section with him for multiple rehearsals and shows, not to mention some nice after-the-show hangs at local pubs. He was a very humble, friendly guy—just a normal, pleasant hang. During one show at Catalina Jazz Club on Sunset, he improvised a "Happy Birthday" solo to his lady on the acoustic grand, playing the "Birthday" melody with his right hand and the bass line from "Tarkus" with his left. Try doing that sometime. What an incredible badass he was.

I couldn't care less about his fame, though packing 60,000-seat arenas with a keyboard trio is no mean feat. What got me—what has always gotten me—was the man's inhuman talent. I've been in awe of his chops and sensibilities ever since early adolescence, and saw ELP live many times in the glory days, so I know from first-hand experience how real and viscerally powerful his actual ability was. It was like staring at the sun. The added perspective of passing time only makes it seem more so. And I know I'm not the only person who was ever in his orbit to feel this way upon his leaving us, but: Had I only known the pain he was in. Fuck.

* * *

The stage plot of a professional orchestra is a high-stakes obstacle course. The chairs and music stands are sometimes so tightly packed, you find yourself high-stepping around them on tiptoes like you're in a snake pit. The instruments are variously perched on stands or balanced on the chairs, and they are exquisitely expensive. For a guitarist, four thousand dollars is an expensive axe. For a good professional string player, an instrument runs between forty and over a hundred thousand dollars. If you're a big name, your instrument might be worth over a million.

One of the more unlikely displays of physical coordination I ever saw was performed by one of ESOS's horn players getting to his chair, right in the middle of the orchestra, on an especially tight stage. The man weighed 375 pounds if he was an ounce, and his only possible way in was right through the violins. I couldn't look, but I couldn't look away. It was like watching a semi truck gracefully pirouetting across a coffee table full of priceless delicate figurines, in slow motion. The performance always took several excruciating minutes, and he always made it. I don't know how, but he never touched a thing other than the floor and his own chair.

* * *

A few weeks before this writing, after almost three decades fronting the melee, The Fabulous Miss Thing gave her swan song performance with ESOS. It was a poignant show, a brilliant show, and marked the end of an era. Angela dug deep and left it all on the field. If Ross is the father, Angela is the founding mother. The show won't be the same without her.

I wasn't playing, but I made damn sure to be there. The band, for its part, was in stellar form. Jeff Miley did a truly fantastic job of playing the guitar book—he told me after the show that he had basically spent the last fifteen days shedding the thing. I especially relished watching him wrestle and slug it out with the dragons, while I daintily sipped perfectly brewed coffee from the comfort of the audience, pinky extended.

The show was also the maiden voyage of the new front lady heiress-apparent: Doctor Thu (pronounced "Two"), a superbly talented soprano who shows every promise of ringing in the new era in great form, whatever its nature may be. I know that change is the only constant in this universe, and it's vital to embrace it in all areas of living, but I'll always miss The Fabulous Miss Thing. Hats off to Dr. Thu for having the courage to follow in the footsteps of such a one. I look forward to seeing what's 'round the next bend.

The first time I ever heard that band it hit me as the hippest and most absurdly cool thing I had ever witnessed. Wherever it goes from here, I doubt I'll ever feel any other way about it.

Chapter 38
Clinicians, Commissions and Unleashing the Pen

For any musician, there will be slow years. When that happens, it's important to be able to reach out to new contacts, bravely infecting new areas like a pathogen mutating around an antibiotic. You must be the tick, attacking a new host for tastier blood. And when needed, you need to be versatile enough to go zoonotic and invade other species entirely.

It was with that mentality that I approached things when, in 2013, my booking calendar looked as open as the Wendover salt flats of western Utah. I went on the hunt for bookings as a clinician, and discovered that contrary to all likelihood, I had done enough musically cool stuff for my input to have value to the world around me.

Booking clinics at colleges is a complicated dance with department heads, your own calendar, the school's academic calendar and—most importantly—the timing of the school's budgetary disbursements. In other words, at some point Lady Luck just has to smile on you. The challenge is getting the timing right: there's a window of about five minutes between a school's music department receiving its budgetary allotment and when the clinics have all been booked for the coming year. To make it more of a challenge, every school's budgetary and booking schedule is a bit different.

You won't get rich doing it, but it's important work. The voice of experience and nuts-and-bolts reality from inside the industry is badly needed inside the isolation of academia. Teaching the students how the things that they're learning will actually be applied in the wild is usually a valued thing, and important to any school who holds the students' interests highly enough. The exception is when a school is too deeply mired in that old academic feedback loop, creating more professors of 1700s doctrine like so many museum curators, holding on to their traditions with white knuckles.

After a hundred hours on the phone and writing emails, follow-up emails and confirmation emails, then no small amount of paperwork to assuage the gods of government and school bureaucracy, I managed to book a clinic tour through UC Colorado campuses and Colorado State Universities along the Front Range towns. It was the first of several. If I account for all the time it took to set up the first tour at the hourly I like to get for my time, it didn't quite break even. But since I love Colorado, her people and her culture, it went in the 'win' column. I also taught a lot of clinics around SoCal, mostly at high schools, which are far simpler to deal with.

* * *

There's a big band in Long Beach that's so good, they've competed nationally and won 1st place multiple times. If you close your eyes and listen, you hear the sound of seasoned professionals working their magic, sweeping you off into a realm of sonic finery, reminiscent of when popular music was opulent and glistened with everything musically excellent. If you open your eyes, you'll see the players in their element and their...acne. It's a high school band.

High School Bands are an important part of the journey for most up-and-comers, and this book wouldn't be complete without my shining a light thataway for a moment.

Many members of Long Beach Poly Technic High School's "Jazz A" lineup are too young to drive or shave, but on a good year they comprise one of the best high school bands in the country, and sound even better than some of the professional outfits I've played with. If you're lucky enough to catch a performance, it'll screw with your head to try to match the sophisticated, polished sounds you're hearing with the kids that you're seeing on stage.

It's all to the credit of Chris Stevens, the driving force behind it all. As band director at Long Beach Poly Jazz, he has poured his love and energy into that school and that band for twenty eight years, building it into the powerhouse that it is. Like every high school band director I've dealt with as a clinician, Chris is a living saint: a walking cornucopia of encouragement, accountability, learning and realization of goals for the kids who pass through his program.

If you haven't yet today, look up your local high school band director and buy him or her a beer, or a car or something. They'll probably tell you that what they really need is reeds, or drumsticks, or maybe music stands. Maybe the instruments themselves. They probably need some help with the bake sale that they hope will replace the funding that got diverted to athletics. I wish to hell I was kidding.

Make no mistake: High School Band Directors earn and occupy hallowed ground in the karmic strata, way up there in the thin air with dogs. Without their tireless and selfless efforts to overcome itinerant budgetary shortfalls, musical education in this country would come to a standstill. Do what you can to help them out.

It's been my honor to teach clinics to the talented young fiends at LBPTHS many times, and to have been tapped by Chris to compose and arrange several pieces for them. The last one I wrote was especially poignant: It marked Chris's finally retiring— just a few months prior to this writing—and moving on to rejoin the musical workforce in SoCal as a mallet player and percussionist. I named it "Farewell New Brigade". Hats off to whoever follows in his footsteps, because those are some truly massive shoes to fill.

* * *

Not long after going zoonotic to escape the calendrical salt flats, I also reached the professionally hallowed ground of getting commissions as a composer. To put a finer point on what that means, to me anyway: it's not the same thing as being hired to compose for TV or Film, or being a songwriter, or an arranger / producer. What the commissions meant to me was that I had somehow managed to make my wiles as a composer valuable enough to the world around me that I was being hired to compose music solely for music's sake. I find that a high honor. It was one thing to have been given that honor in Bishop with my first symphony, but in LA--with the talent pool hereabouts--it truly humbled me.

As I discovered with my first symphony, the reason a commission is such a cool thing is the creative freedom. Having spent so much of my career on gigs where I'd be fired if I expressed myself too freely, now I was actually being paid to do it. It's a feeling I hope you get to experience someday.

Cobbling my calendar together between commissions, teaching and clinics, arranging and production clients, and artists hiring me to arrange and record guitarish things on their projects, things were okay. It wasn't pay dirt or the motherlode, but it was a living. And it was definitely preferable to the "workaday" type of gigs that had played such a disproportionately large role in my past...I hadn't played a truly hate-worthy gig in years, and I still haven't. Somewhere along the line, I just started saying no:

No more playing for club owners whose moral bankruptcy made me wonder how they hadn't met with a violent demise; no more playing for drunken geniuses bellowing at the top of their lungs with the vocabulary of a six-year-old; no more finding myself on stage while a drummer counted off a tune that would make me want to throw up into the back of my mouth; no more trying to identify the genesis of gooey globs on a stage under my pedals and cabling. With any luck, I had replaced the "gutter gigs" with better work. Better late than never.

California College of Music in Pasadena hired me on as a part-time teacher, and the clinician bookings started building a head of steam as well. I usually had at least one client in the work queue for guitar tracks or arranging and production, and a handful of choice private online students. Gigs and recording sessions were light and high-quality, more like things to celebrate than to dread, and I did what I could to keep things that way.

The lesson here is that you have to keep tossing baited hooks into the water. Keep reaching out, make the calls, go to the hangs, keep getting your face out there and network. The world doesn't see you if you're sitting at home.

Chapter 39
Of NAMMsong and Wizards

"Fercrissake Fry, don't be such a friggin' luddite. Think of what your competition is doing." The voice was my own, the words flitting through my head in the background of the unbridled cacophony and surreal chaos of the L.A. NAMM show's 3-ring melee. Thomas Nordegg and Don Ramsay had rendezvoused with me at the Bogner Amplifiers booth to hand me a guitar that compared to everything else I'd ever played about like a Formula One racer compared to my '67 Mustang. Tom and Don are pretty high-profile guitar design luminaries, whose work is responsible for much of the ground-breaking technology used so well by Steve Vai, as well as several other big-name players.

I thought my custom FrankenStrat was high-performance tech, but the axe they handed me flew, dove underwater, fired lasers, gathered intel from orbit, cooked food, controlled world politics remotely at 2.4 GHZ and foresaw my creative ideas based on its telepathic reading and interpretation of my dreams. It played incredibly well, it was bewildering, titillating, disturbing, enthralling and liberating. It dared me to even try to find its limits.

The guitar was one of Steve Vai's personal weapons, called Samoht. It sported what I thought was highly-customized, prototypical madness you couldn't just buy off the shelf, but it turns out that most of the techery was (more or less) on the market. Here's what Samoht was sporting that week, in case you're a guitar geek--and even if you're not, you might want to read this, because it'll surprise you what can be done with a guitar these days:

- The Ramsay Linear Tremolo, which will hopefully go into production and be available soon. It's a major revolution in guitar tremolo design, solving several inherent tremolo issues we've all suffered along with for generations. It employs a moveable fulcrum point, above which the rocking motion of the tremolo arm is transformed—magically, it seems—into smooth, frictionless, linear, planar motion of a non-rocking bridge plate. It just floats back and forth along the longitudinal axis of the strings, in evident defiance of physics. Depending on how you have it set up, its motion can be as gentle as a Bigsby or more aggressive than a Floyd. It returns much more completely to pitch from above or below than physics would allow any conventional (rocking) tremolo to do.

- Antares Auto-Tune for Guitar (created by Dr. Andy Hildebrand and master luthier Henrik Bridger) will shift up or down chromatically ("Capo Mode"), to an octave above or below; it will change your tuning to Drop D, Open D, Open G, Open E, 12-string or Standard Tuning--every chord you play being turned into natural-sounding but perfectly-tempered bliss, all without touching the tuners. Bends, vibrato and tremolo use are all unaffected and completely normal, which is freaky. The pitch-shifting is multi-timbral and polyphonic, each string being processed independently and transparently, with no perceivable lag. It all comes out of the guitar's audio output (1/4" or 13-pin) just like the normal sound. Exit 'digital mode' and auto-tune goes away--your guitar is its normal self again.

- Revpad is a kidney-shaped controller touchpad that velcros to your guitar about where the pick guard would go if it was an acoustic, and reads your fingertips for X,Y and Z-axis control of an accompanying multi-FX unit. It's 2.4GHZ wireless, range 65 feet. Cool sounds, new possibilities.

- Steinberger Gearless 40:1 Tuners are sadly no longer on the market, having been bought out by Gibson and shelved, whatever that's about. But they're incredible. They'd be on every one of my "A" axes if it were possible, but last I checked they're unobtainable. And I'd be remiss not to include the following information from Don Ramsay, if only to provide a delightful glimpse into an engineer's mind: He points out that the 40:1 number isn't actually a ratio: "The worm gear tuners do have a ratio. The Steinberger simply uses a common fine micrometer thread of 40 threads to the inch, or .025" of barrel travel per revolution. A comparison (of actual string travel) with geared tuners takes measuring the post diameter x pi (3.14156) = travel of one "wrap" divided by the worm gear ratio. For example, a .187" diameter post = .587 string travel per turn of the post, divided by the gear ratio (i.e.: 18:1) = .0326" string travel per turn on the tuner key." Got all that? Good.

The Trev Wilkinson 'Jeff Beck' Roller Nut is a must-have if you want a headstock that stays in tune with aggressive use of a whammy. The detractor is that you can't change the string spacing or fretboard radius--you have to go with the nut's existing specs. But having played the thing, to me it's worth it. It's unfortunately a hard item to find, as Trev evidently doesn't make them anymore.

TimeSpeed Lectronix Accelerometer Power Switch, for guitars that have active electronics, turns the guitar off two minutes after you set it down. It powers back up the instant it's moved. Same tech as in the Line6 wireless transmitter (one of which is set neatly into a cavity in the back of the guitar).

I also played another one of Steve Vai's axes, and a brand-new custom build of the same design for Richie Sambora, who hadn't even seen or played it yet himself. While all this was happening at the Bogner booth, I found myself the focus of a scrum of people and the ubiquitous, ever-present cell phone cameras recording me, immutably and for all time, as I got my wheedly-wheedlies on and floundered with the bewildering technology while plugged into a well-heeled Bogner Ecstasy.

All of this was the upshot of my recently making the acquaintance of Don Ramsay— a very gentlemanly, unassuming and soft-spoken mechanical genius—who in turn introduced me to Thomas, the mad wizard of audacious guitar technology. Thomas is partnered with Don and guitar wiring guru Eddie Clothier, who had a hand in installing this hi-tech weaponry in the amazingly fine axes that they kept handing me, built to their specs by the master Austrian luthier Michael Spalt. Thomas was ceaselessly flipping switches and changing sounds on the axes as I played. I found myself trying to play during a long sequence of rapid-fire changes of sound that were so extreme, it was truly jarring: Various open tunings, to 12-string acoustic, to a hippopotamus coughing out a hit from a bong, to a peacock, to a howler monkey, to a piccolo mating with a canary. I was so far outside my comfort zone I couldn't even see it from where I was.

These guys occupy the headwaters of the guitar invention river and the tip of the spearhead. Like me, they have a healthy and complete disregard for tradition, so I was happy to become a guinea pig for their inventions. I've been over to Thomas's pad many times since then as a test pilot for this and that, playing Samoht, Evo II and some other innovative machinery, usually through Thomas's famous master rig, which he calls Sonica. As far as I can tell, Sonica consists of every piece of guitar processing gear that he's ever used, invented, postulated or, for that matter, has ever existed. I have no idea how many pedals and controllers for outboard gear are in the floor unit, but as a knee-jerk guess, I'd just say "All of 'em." My own pedal board is a couple of feet by 18 inches or so. A large one might be four feet from left to right. Sonica's footprint occupies roughly half of Thomas's entire living room.

As I play, Thomas ceaselessly darts from device to device like Dr. Frankenstein, tweaking knobs and flipping switches. My voice is transubstantiated through a dizzying array of radically different sounds, never more than a second or two for each one.

Thomas's professionalism makes it impossible for him to ever supply anything but the absolute latest, greatest and most advanced tech to his clients and their guitars. If it doesn't work perfectly at all times, it goes right out the window in ongoing defense against any degree, whatsoever, of errant technology. You may laugh, but it's a serious thing at the top: besides Steve Vai and Richie Sambora, his technology and audacity has enabled Frank Zappa, Dweezil Zappa, Steve Lukather, Jimmy Page, Yngwie Malmsteen and several other luminaries to push the envelope. Like so many ace pilots, they carve their vapor trails across the sky with unlikely and unique noises—as well as visual weaponry like guitar-mounted lasers and the like—with the help of Thomas, Don, Michael, Eddie and Steve.

Before guitar manufacturers even consider whether or not something is possible or affordable, whether it makes sense or is ethically right or whether it's maybe just too audacious for the world of guitar retail to accept, these guys have already put it on an axe, on a pedal board or in a rack, tweaked it until it works better than anything that has gone before it, and placed it in the right hands to blow minds and raise the bar.

It occurs to me, having written this, that I'm overdue for a visit to Mr. Wizard.

* * *

Pre-pandemic NAMM shows were truly proud. "NAMM" stands for National Association of Music

Merchants--an oddly boring monicker for what it actually is. If you've never attended one, just imagine fifty thousand or so partying visitors from every area of musical enterprise—rock stars, inventors, sales reps, music store owners, manufacturers, artist relations people, techs and roadies, circus performers-on-stilts and stripper / models in lingerie, world-famous musicians, rank-and-file musicians and the occasional paparazzi—all ceaselessly milling, mingling, staggering and eddying in currents around each others' elbows. Put that in the massive space of the Anaheim Convention Center, bursting at the seams in every hall and every annex building with twenty five hundred booths of musical merchandise proudly being unveiled for the following year.

There is of course no crowd on this planet more difficult to impress than musicians, so presentations are a bit over the top, adding to the circus atmosphere. Some of the world's best and most respected players are featured performers for the companies whose products they endorse, and they bring their A-games. Many musicians watching these displays of virtuosity put on a finely-manicured air of practiced boredom, as though to say "I could do that better." But it's worth mentioning that the best players watching a show never say that, nor do they feel that way.

In every booth that carries musical instruments, they're being played. And the booths aren't enclosed, so the collective sound defies description. One year I was visiting a booth in the back row of the main hall to keep an endorsement alive, when there was a spontaneous and alarming ramp-up in the noise, and something that sounded for all the world like a freight train was rumbling right through the center of the hall. I could feel the floor shaking and large random sound waves thumping me in the chest. I looked at the vendor I was talking to, raised an eyebrow and yelled over the din, "What the hell?"

He just smiled knowingly and yelled, "NAMMsong."

Distributorship deals are cut between retailers and manufacturers, endorsement deals are brokered between musicians and manufacturers, and other endorsements kept alive as players poke their heads into their endorsee's booths to shower them with praise on their merchandise. The universal language spoken by all is the finely-tuned, nonchalant aggrandizement of promotion. Most of the deals won't be brought into fruition on paper until weeks later, when the carnival has packed up and gone home, the dust has settled and people have had a chance to catch up on correspondence.

It's a frothing, fire-breathing, foaming frenzy of fanaticism for anything and everything that makes money by making noise. Amid all the hype, hoopla and hubbub, the saving grace that keeps things grounded is the humanity: old friends who haven't seen each other in years catching up on news, players falling into jam sessions with other players everywhere, and musicians meeting new musicians to forge relationships that could lead to anything in the coming years and decades.

Chapter 40
Hunting With the Beast

Every good musician has a beast inside, and it has to be fed. If it doesn't get fed it either dies, or it dies and takes the musician with it. Feeding it is easily accomplished if you have the right company around you, and it's similar to what working out in a gym is to an athlete. Only louder.

For a player, work is almost always a matter of playing the simple and mundane in such a sparkling way that it becomes magic. That's no small trick as far as it goes, and it's actually really gratifying when it all comes together. But to be able to play it in such a sparkling way, you have to have the chops of doom. And you can't have those chops when you have a bunch of carbon buildup in your cylinders. Besides, the same inactivity that leads to carbon buildup also leads to a buildup of bent-out-of-shape creative energy, which can come busting out in any number of miscreant ways. It's hard to 'suave a groove' on a pretty ballad when your beast is gnawing at your guts, wanting to go out on a hunt. It all has to balance.

In the early-mid teens of this century, I needed a musical outlet that would keep me honest, strong and honed—ideally some challenging, high-RPM stuff that would keep my cylinders clean. So I called my good brother Jay Setar, the inhumanly good drummer I had met at Magruder's. When putting a band together I always start with the drums, in the same way that I almost always start with a clave and rhythmic groove when I'm writing or arranging a piece of music. After all, if there's no temporal premise, when is anything supposed to happen?

For bass we tapped a very talented player named Chris Buck, who has an impressive resume and cred as an indie Prog artist. We called the thing "Tribus", and spent many fun afternoons playing far too many notes in Jay's studio. After spending an unjustifiable duration rehearsing the unlikelihoods that Chris and I wrote, we were the featured performers at a special concert event at the last remaining Carvin store. It was a lot of fun, and was videotaped. Not long after, Chris moved east of the Mississippi.

Our beastly cravings far from sated, Jay and I went on the prowl and targeted bassist Mark Corradetti as the next victim to sucker into our dubious enterprise. He lived in Malibu and worked steadily in the talent stable and studio of Alan Parsons. We added my old friend and brother-in-arms Bob Luna on keys—one of LA's finest, he's played with everybody up to and including Paul McCartney—to make it a four-piece called "Smarticus". We played at NAMM, to a room full of drunk musicians. We had a great showing as players and were well received, despite our performance being beset with so many tech glitches, it was like we were playing on top deck of a cruise ship. Nonetheless, it was fun. Not long after, Mark moved east of the Mississippi. Spinal Tap has exploding drummers, we have migratory bass players.

For most humans, listening to rhythmically mathy and technical progressive fusion is not a gratifying experience; it's just annoying. Fortunately I have yet to learn that lesson, despite the many situations in my past that blatantly presented the opportunity. I can only hope that someday I manage to record an album of beastfood that's well-written enough for me to actually enjoy listening to it. As any musician will tell you, that's a lot to hope for.

As happens from time to time, in 2014 arranging and production work slowed to a trickle, along with recording work. I still had some students, but I didn't want to rebuild that into a full-time thing, and the slow suicide of sitting for long hours every day.

So for the first time in a decade, I rejoined Musicians Contact Service, solemnly swearing a blood oath to myself not to resume work in bars. I joined more or less on a lark and because my old buddy Sterling, the proprietor, is such a cool guy. But I also joined because on occasion, there are indeed great gigs listed there. Thus did I find myself, not long afterwards, wearing a suit and a headset mic while playing a solo for a screaming crowd of thousands.

Chapter 41
Bus Life and Related Perpetuities

Imagine a day when the world falls on its side, spectacles akimbo and halfway off its head. Everything is seen through a distorted funhouse mirror-like lens, as though from underwater. The wowed perspectives enable the stretching of norms, and society accepts all manner of unlikelihoods.

That day is here, and the beneficiary is an odd phenomenon called a "tribute band". I had played in a few of these over the years, and it always struck me as too myopic to limit a cover band's entire song list to one artist's catalogue, unless that writing is incredibly good. People forget that writing is always the main factor in the success or failure of any musical enterprise.

There are precious few recording acts whose songwriting is so good that I wouldn't mind playing an entire show—or tour—of nothing but their material. It probably goes without saying that at the top of that list is The Beatles.

Another is The Eagles. I've used their songs in teaching lyric writing in clinics for many years, and their list of hits is more homeric than any I can think of, excepting of course the lads from Liverpool. The Eagles' melodies are so strong they're built from bricks, and the chord progressions are simple enough to have a timeless strength to them. They run a pretty good gamut stylistically—a little something for everyone—and I've always been impressed by their productions, as well as the fantastic vocals of the band.

I really had no idea how thriving the business can be for the top feeders in the tribute band world. Hotel California is among the top handful of tribute acts in the country. They own their own Prevost H3, the largest tour bus on the road, and they play 120 to 150 shows a year, mostly to small theaters that seat 1,000 to 3,500—always sold out or close to it—and occasionally to festival crowds of over ten thousand. They've been around for decades, since long before the tribute band craze. There are a lot of Eagles tribute acts, but Hotel California is pretty much THE Eagles Tribute Band, if there can be such a thing. It's like saying "THE copy".

The cool thing about the band is that it's not a straight tribute, as their ringleader George is quick to point out. It's more of a salute. There's no role playing, or trying to look like the real guys, and the song list is open enough to include things that are only loosely associated with The Eagles, like James Gang and Joe Walsh hits. There's also some musical interpretation that's allowed, and the players bring their own personal mojo and personality to the songs and to the stage, which gives the thing more believability and dimension. Overall, it's just a really good show, and at the end of the day that's all that really matters. It's easy to understand why they're so popular.

Having seen their listing on MCS, I auditioned and got the field narrowed down from 50 guys to one other guy and me, and they hired the other guy. He had stronger pipes, and it's nothing if not an intensely vocal gig. Then after about three weeks he washed out, and I was in.

If you sing, or want to sing, you should know that singing is not like riding a bike, or even like playing an instrument. If you stop singing for years like I had, your pipes will go away and turn into a weak and yodely, nasal, reedy noise that you won't even want people to hear. Such was my situation when I started the rehearsals. I wanted to open my mouth and hear Tom Jones, or Steve Walsh...or Don Henley for that matter, what pipes on that guy! Alas, all I got was Alfalfa, from that old black and white TV show "Our Gang". My voice gradually came back to about two thirds of its former strength and I had to make do with that. The missing strength I compensated for with mic-pre settings and EQ. In other words, technological crutches.

* * *

On my first "out" with the guys, the tour bus grunted away from SoCal with five miscreant ogres, a soundman and enough instruments and gear in the belly to start a revolution. Food and baggage of every metaphorical ilk was onboard, along with hierarchies that emerged as I familiarized myself with the band. I stowed my gear and grub without running afowl of any turf wars, and heard the age-old "rule number one on the bus" speech. It's a tenet all musicians know and the violation of which, as of this writing, I believe myself to be the solitary innocent ogre: "Never shit on the bus."

The bus became a long-standing second home, where we spent more time than we did with our families. For the three years I was touring with Hotel Cal, I averaged about 300 days out per year. We all had good familiarity with The Machine and were a pretty solid traveling team.

The steadiness of the gig played a big part in putting my wife through nursing school, and the band understood that as soon as she graduated, I'd be leaving. That one gig left very little room for anything else, and as fun as it was, I didn't want to make a career out of it. Besides, nursing shifts are twelve hours, more like thirteen or fourteen if you factor in drive time, and we always have a lot of animals. It's a high-maintenance house and I'd have to be home, simple as that.

There were a few projects I did manage to keep my hand in while being with Hotel Cal: I still played shows with Orchestre Surreal, when the schedule allowed.

The two occupy opposite extremities of the complexity spectrum, and just the mental pendulum swing between the two was an E-ticket ride. I also did some musical odd-jobs, like transcribing noteworthy jazz guitarist Ron Echete's playing for an e-zine while riding on the bus. And of course, playing with my fusion buddies was always fun during the breaks.

The band knew how to put in the miles: It was late Tuesday afternoon when we pulled away from Ontario, CA...the first gig of the tour was in Buffalo that Friday. Cali, Nevada, Arizona and Utah all blurred by outside as The Machine was kept going and we all took breaks onboard, relieving ourselves, eating, stretching, napping, switching drivers every four hours. As was custom, we pulled off somewhere and napped a few hours in the middle of the night, the generator's drone vibrating my dental work loose. In the morning, I was halfway to the zombie state that I would fully achieve by Friday, but Wyoming's transfixing views flowing past the picture windows, combined with Copland on my headphones, restored my mojo. Then Nebraska and an incredible nighttime lightning show from Ma Nature as we powered through a large band of tornado-wielding super cells. Then Iowa, Illinois, Indiana, Ohio...I was experiencing what marathoners and other endurance athletes call relentless forward motion. The difference was that I wasn't burning a single calorie...I was just sitting on my ass for durations that can only be called injurious.

Preparing coffee, tea or food on board is a delicate dance that breaks the monotony, requiring a mix of balance, dexterity, invention and prescience for what the road is about to do. The floor and walls are alive at all times.

The coffins are 22 inches tall and disguised as bunks. Surprisingly, I discovered that it was pretty comfortable in there, despite the length being a few inches shy of my height. By the second week, I had switched coffins with the drummer so I wasn't over the generator: hey presto, I was sleeping on the bus. I was getting sucked into The Machine—there was a tangible feeling of assimilation.

For three years we criss-crossed the country constantly, perpetually, endlessly. It seems like we played every town in it--over four hundred shows on my watch. It added up. The calendar favored the Southern US in the summer, with many shows being outside. The bus's AC had an impish personality and kept quiting, just to prank us. The other ogres had gotten used to it, but heatstroke was always nipping at my heels...color me a snowflake.

We played a couple of rock cruises—those familiar shebangs where a promoter books some faded-glory rock stars from the 70s and a few tribute acts on a chartered cruise ship for a week. It was strikingly different from doing a "real" cruise ship gig: we each had our own passenger cabin, and we were there and gone in a week. The gear we played through was also just visiting the ship, provided and run by professional audio companies, so it wasn't festooned with barnacles and it actually worked. If you're going to play a cruise ship, that's the way to do it.

In the towns we played, we occasionally taught clinics for local colleges, did occasional terrestrial radio interviews and podcasts, and were commonly wined and dined by mayors, city councilmen, mover-shakers and local business mucky-mucks. At one show in SoCal, the local law enforcement running security had taken a shine to us and provided us with a wild, adrenaline-packed code-three motorcade escort that included some airborne time over some swales in the road, to get us from the middle of a fair out to the highway, so that we could make the airport in time for a flight to the next show. "No shit, there I was, riding in my second motorcade..."

Overall, it was more like touring with a major act than can be justified, replete with autograph signings, meet-and-greets, and dedicated fans driving across several states to see a show. And it's not like it isn't an honor: some of the fans I came to know remain valued friends, and there's nothing about that that isn't real. At the end of the day the efficacy of the whole concept is arrived at according to the almighty metric of business economics.

You'd be forgiven for feeling that it's weird to see a cover band, however good their show is, playing on Saturday in an amphitheater packed with thousands, followed the next Saturday at the same venue by Ringo Starr and his All Starr Band.

This is not to disregard the very real mojo of the performers or the management. Some of these tribute acts are extremely good, and pay the bills for the families involved—no mean feat in today's landscape. You'll find the math understandable, even if the reasoning behind the deification is elusive.

Personally, I don't get the practice of elevating a human, or group of humans, to vaulted status. From a homeless, wounded war veteran to the president, we're all here to do what we can to get by, and we all hope to have a good place to lay our heads at night. And if our heads are in the right place, we're helping the world in whatever way we can. So I've never understood the deification of the actual stars themselves.

For my money, I'd rather hear something more personal and genuine, like a talented busker on a street corner. Something real, something organic. But by now you probably know that my tastes aren't representative of the general public.

* * *

It's worth pointing out that music is truth, it's alive, it's expression. A tribute band is basically required to take a great song and chain it down to the way it happened to go down one day in a studio. To me, that's just a portrayal of somebody else's still life, and it flies in the face of expression. All of the best bands I play with set the songs free to be whatever we think Calliope wants them to be that night, and sometimes we break out the stave paper and re-invent things completely. If the song has good bones—strong root movement, good melody, definitive chords—it'll fly with any treatment thrown at it.

The mass hysteria of a hit—the concept that that piece must always be that way—results from nothing more than familiarity, bolstered by a consensus so large that it's on a societal level. That's too strong a current for most people to overcome.

Thus a specific version of a song becomes cemented into a place of honor on high, glowing in the firmament of the zeitgeist. It has nothing to do with propriety, or what is actually possible, and worst of all it kills reinvention. As an arranger / composer / producer, I'm literally in the business of reinvention, and constantly looking for possibilities. Music is to me a lot like scientific exploration, and the deeply spiritual quest that drives it. One of my favorite quotes, from Carl Sagan, is "I'd rather have questions that cannot be answered than answers that cannot be questioned."

Music is sculpting sound against a framework of time. There are countless sculptures that I love, productions whose playback will never grow old for me. I fully get the love of a single, solitary way that a thing went down one particular day, and I thank the heroes of human invention for the fact that we can save great performances through recording technology, and that the technology of production itself has become such an incredibly cool artistic medium.

Remember, that wasn't the case for the vast majority of human history. Until the late 1800s, music came solely in printed form, published so that people could read it and interpret it in their own performance. The paradigm shift that occurred when we started selling recordings had to have been seismically massive.

The masses' familiarity with a hit recording shouldn't dampen enthusiasm for other possibilities. It shouldn't have to always be THAT way, however great. Every production of Shakespeare is different, and nobody says "Hey, that ain't how so-and-so's movie did it!"

For a fan of a tribute band, though, precisely none of that matters. For someone who works like a dog through the week for their family and fights their own battles, like we all do, all of this is over-thinking it. They just want a little break, to go out and see a great band play some of their favorite music and bring back memories of their glory days. There's definitely nothing wrong with that, and from that perspective, providing that musical service is an honorable thing.

A talent buyer can get a high-quality tribute act for a fraction of what the real thing would cost, making it possible to present that music in fairly good form to some folks who otherwise wouldn't have the opportunity or dough to see the real thing. That's definitely a win.

* * *

If you haven't lived the musical road warrior lifestyle, you don't know about Mom. Mom is that selfless, kind, giving soul who sets the tone of and runs the hospitality area backstage at most major venues, lavishing warmth and sustenance upon the musicians and crew.

Mom is usually a lone woman, usually a retiree, and usually does it as a volunteer. Often she has a team. Usually, her kids have long since grown and gone and sometimes she's a widow. But always, there's a vacancy in her heart and she adopts us all, collectively, as her family. She always does it with, and in the name of, love and art.

Typically elderly, born in a more civil and less abrasive time, she is surrounded by stage and venue managers, crew, promotors, agents, musicians and other jaded types who tend to be crass and take her for granted. But though Mom usually doesn't know it, she gives the venue its soul. A handshake for Mom is like a cold slap in the face to her. The currency she deals in, invariably, is hugs.

I can't count the times my life was saved by the right home-cooked generosity at the right time, when I had been going too far, too hard and for too long. When there was a packed house and an important show to do—as of there's any other kind—a mom somewhere would see that I was about to keel over for lack of simply sitting down and refueling in the presence of some human kindness, dignity and warmth. Sometimes she cooks and sometimes she delegates that task, but she always serves, she cares, she lavishes, she sets the tone and she provides the love.

Many of these spiritual benefactors literally go by the name "Mom", and her presence has usually shaped the venue's interior feeling and spirit. In some places she's been at her post for over 25 years and in that time she's taken care of everyone passing through that venue. It always comprises a very impressive list of dignitaries, and she has the attendant stories to tell. And though you really ain't squat compared to the legends she's fed and cared for, she treats you with a level of kindness and warmth that makes you feel like a king. Her stories also serve as a gentle conveyance of humility, gently toppling prima donnas from high-horses in a way that inspires them to give their best when they go on.

I remember one time just as I was catching a cold at the beginning of a bus tour of 4 shows in 4 states in 4 days—all of which were to be under cold, midwest winter storm conditions—the mom at the first venue served me home-made chicken-vegetable soup. It was mind-bendingly good. I had been eating truck stop road kill for 3 solid days to that point, and my body had nothing to go on. My throat was sore, I felt feverish, it hurt to talk, I had travel fatigue and was probably headed toward a lousy showing on all four shows. At that pivotal moment, that soup was a magical salvation for my body, soul and spirit. I have no doubt that it turned around the whole tour for me.

One night in Warren Michigan, we left after the show with the fridge packed to the gills with a home-cooked Thanksgiving dinner from Mom. I can't give you her real name because everyone knows her simply as Mom, but she must be an octogenarian. She's always there, making the place go. Like moms everywhere, she's the beating heart under the hood, driving the whole Macomb Performing Arts Center. Some may think it's the artists, the crew, the gear, the promotors and the like, but don't you believe it. It's Mom.

That Thanksgiving feast provided soulful warmth for our travels as we made our way past all the jack-knifed big rigs and spun-out cars along I-80 in the aftermath of a massive storm, west and homeward-bound through the truck stop and junk food culture of the American highway.

* * *

"The president has just told a joke. Everyone please laugh."

Thus spake then-President Jimmy Carter's Chinese translator to a large gathering in Beijing during Carter's diplomatic visit to further develop the recently-opened U.S.-Sinai relations. Carter had just told a joke that was innocent to Americans but would be very offensive in Chinese culture. It was a deft, astute move on the part of the translator in the face of such pomp and potential circumstance, and it's one of Jimmy's favorite stories from his time in office.

To any musical act playing venues that require big P.A. systems, the soundman is The Translator, and the final hands through which your performance passes on its way to the audience. In short, he has at least as much an effect on the success or failure of your show as any musician in the band. Yet he rarely gets his due.

While you're up on stage enjoying the bewildering and improbable adulation of a frenzied crowd who is deifying you like you're a god because—well, who the hell knows—the soundman is making all of that possible through constant changes to everything from levels to EQ to pans to effects and much more, in an effort to hit the constantly-moving targets that minimize the 'nasty' while emphasizing the 'sweet'.

It is a difficult, thankless job requiring many, many years of experience, great ears, lightning reflexes, a sixth sense for the technologies involved, otherworldly memory for their different interfaces—which are very advanced these days—great understanding of acoustics, Apollo 13-level troubleshooting chops and at times, perhaps most importantly, the ability to appear genuinely supportive of a diva's drama. And all of this while the industry and the public blithely minimize the imperative nature of what the soundman does, whether out of ignorance or actual disrespect.

Rich Picard, the soundman for Hotel California for my first year or so with them, was every bit as much of an artist as anyone in the band. He was just as involved and invested in, and vital to, the moment-to-moment doings of a show as anyone on stage. We'd have been immediately and unequivocally dead in the water without him, as is commonly the case with well-developed shows.

I can't count the number of gigs I've been on where the talent was less talented than the soundman, but still put on airs and treated him with disrespect, even delivering the odd temper tantrum. So whether you're a touring musician, a fan, a manager, booking agent, venue owner or a plumber, please take a moment to appreciate The Great Translator—he or she without whose tireless, selfless efforts the music would quickly sour and render us all penniless, homeless and on the streets.

* * *

There are musicians who wouldn't be bothered by playing the exact same show the exact same way more than four hundred times. As you've probably figured out, I'm not one of them. So during my time with Hotel Cal, I made a point of doing what I could not only to avoid burnout, but to reconnect with the passion—the magic—of what live performance really is. I'm happy to say I succeeded. I'm not sure why, but I did, and I guess the most tenable explanation is that I just decided to. The best illustration of what that looked like, from between my ears, is a Knucklehead's Log entry I wrote about it at the time:

The band makes no noise. I move to center stage on cue. The follow-spot reflects off of my Strat's hardware, shooting beams of light over expectant faces, as the crowd falls silent. There's a hush of "...Well?"

Every generation contributes some performances that remain in the collective conscience, glistening above the waves of fading history like blazing gemstones, accenting the shadowy hallways of the human journey. The Beatles on Ed Sullivan, Jimi at Monterey and at Woodstock, Jaco at Montreux, the riot-inducing premier of Rites of Spring in Paris, 1917. I seriously doubt I'll ever make a contribution so important that it will ring down through the halls of history, but so be it. Any performer worth his or her salt knows that the mission is to die trying.

Some say that being on stage alone in front of several thousand people is the loneliest thing a soul can experience. To me it just feels exposed...and like the cosmos are inviting me to see what I can pull off.

Absorbed in the technical moment-to-moment, I glance at my pedals and the settings on my axe, adjust a thing or two, look out at the expectant crowd, clear my head and prepare to launch off into the unknown...

This is the part of the show where I get to go off-script and express myself alone on stage in a natural, spontaneous way—the little moment of musical authenticity for me on this tour. It's the water my thirsty soul craves. I never know what I'm about to do, but I always take an honest run at it and the results will be exactly what I can make it. How well it flies will be in direct proportion to how sincere my love is, and how disciplined my craft. I'll get what I deserve, no more no less. But will the audience? We're about to go exploring together, up into the thin air, where we'll find out...

I unexpectedly lock eyes with a small child in one of the front rows. The sudden shift to my context is jarring...time stands still and breathless as I blink, suddenly yanked out of my technical minutiae and into the moment...she's such a potent reminder of why I'm here, I may as well have been slapped in the face. I realize my mouth is hanging ajar, and close it. I smile and wink at the child, who smiles and hides her head in her Mom's bosom. And I let it hit me: what I do is sort of amazing.

That is to say, my job is to amaze. And that's amazing. I sometimes lose track of that. I can remember some pivotal concerts I saw when I was young, which filled me with The Awe and The Wonder; I can remember keenly the passion I felt while witnessing master practitioners of The Craft performing in their hour of greatness, and the limitless possibility I saw for myself. The future was lifting Her cosmic skirt and beckoning; we were going to be the greatest love in history, Music and I. Had someone told the young, aspiring me that I would someday be struggling with burnout, I'd have laughed. Yet struggle I have, lo these many years gone by.

And I'm not alone. It's not like the musical workplace doesn't encourage cynicism, given the shock-and-awe spectacles that have come to be expected of musical performance these days, our ranks consequently swelling with posers, over-blown computer jockeys and talent-free, promo-savvy opportunists. How does the actual voice of music—that fragile, nuanced connection between artist and art—survive in such an alienating, roiling circus of sense-stunning effects, over-the-top volume and visual diversion? This is to say nothing of yapping bandleaders, technical directors and other workplace insect authorities who try to get the most out of performers by badgering them with obvious minutiae or dazzling them with displays of clinical psychosis.

If you're a player, you know that of which I speak. The causes are real, they're digging under your skin all the time and it can all get to be an irritating rash that's hard to ignore.

But: From the crowd's perspective, exactly none of that exists. They cared enough to leave the comfort of their home—some driving for hours through bad weather—just to honor you with their presence, and that's as real as human love and support gets. It ain't about you, the performer. It's about them, those expectant souls in the seats, having schlepped all the way out to your show, in hopes of being amazed—in hopes of having their lives brightened and having something to talk about on Monday morning.

The good news is that musical authenticity and crowd pleasing are not mutually exclusive. It's up to the performer to make both happen. As a humble servant to Music, my job is to be true to Her and to do Her bidding. She didn't put me on Her path in order to make me rich; this is a high honor. And while a performer's emotional baggage is out of place here on stage, that baggage is a large part of what makes us who we musically are. We have to be able to draw from it without letting it dampen the delivery, and that requires mental, emotional and spiritual duality.

But I find that when my head is in the right place, I can lose myself, my ego and the baggage, tune out the chattering insects and become the blank canvas. Then, if the wind is from the right quarter of the sky, I can hear what wants to be. And if I can block out the chatter, if my love is pure, if my discipline is worthy of the craft and if I can play it true and sincere, it will get traction and mean something...I...will mean something.

If my performance is sincere and I say what I mean, then all of us—the audience, the musicians, the crew and maybe even the lighting director—will leave with a pleasant glow in our spirits.

I play an idea. I hear it echoing off the back walls during the pause afterwards. "Once upon a time..."

I build on the idea, trying somehow to appease the laws of musical composition and thematic development, while at the same time appeasing the necessities of theatrical presentation. Toward the end, pushing the idea towards its hole in the clouds, the audience and I ride a surging, bucking probability into the final intensity. I catch the child's eye again. This time, she doesn't hide in her Mom's bosom. She smiles openly, right at me. And I know I've won the day.

* * *

People will always love great live performance. The human connection between audience and performer hasn't been effectively digitized, so the sales of tickets is one of the most viable remaining areas of musical enterprise: Robots and holograms aren't far enough along or cost effective enough to compete with live performance (yet).

A.I. is here and we're tackling it head-on in typical fashion: asleep at the wheel and too slow to muster a defense against a three-thousand foot tsunami that can wash the industry into the sea for good. Yet for all that, I doubt if even AI can do anything to threaten ticket sales.

Streaming royalties and download sales will never buy you a house, unless your project has already achieved orbital velocity and you have your own line of perfume coming out, own an island somewhere and no longer care about such things.

Song placement on film and TV is a numbers game against tall odds for those outside the circles of production, and even if you're lucky enough to get a good placement, that's not likely to be more than a few months' decent income.

That leaves ticket sales and a merch table as your most reliable friends. So if you're a musician wanting to work, don't be afraid of the road. And if you're an indie recording artist, the road is your most viable way to make life pencil out without a day gig.

The good news is that there's a pretty well-defined path to getting booked above the nightclub level if your live act is really good, and you can be on that path for a fee that will pay for itself with the first few bookings. It's not the only way, but it's the most direct way that I'm aware of. I've mentioned APAP in Manhattan, and Western Arts Showcase, which I've seen happen in Kansas City and in Downtown LA. I've played all three multiple times. IEBA in Nashville is also a good one.

These are basically like the NAMM show, but instead of musical gear manufacturers exhibiting their stuff to retailers, it's touring acts and agents putting their best foot forward for promotors, talent buyers and venue owner / operators from all over the planet. It's a huge affair and costs the acts a good deal of dough to perform there, so consequently the acts who appear—mostly tributes, but some are the real thing—have their I's dotted and their T's crossed. The quality of performance is between great and truly amazing.

The fee is stiff, so don't pursue this unless you know your showcase set is "undeniable". Hang out for a few days prior so you can network, press flesh and pepper the place with handouts and other promo material, to get people to your showcase.

Promoters and buyers will want you to be popular in your own part of the world, and it's typical to start with grass roots, farming your own back yard. This is where you build your core fan base, doing local arts showcases, the local fairs and such. Then, when you know you've got a race-ready car, do what you can to muster the entry fee for the big meet. You'll find yourself surrounded by dizzying talent and opportunities, making important liaisons.

* * *

It's a fact that cities have personalities, and no one city's character is exactly like any other. New York is of course vividly, unabashedly alive, radiating fast-paced energy at all times, her arteries aflow not only with commerce, but with art and culture. Rampant, robust, unfettered, unapologetic celebration of expression is everywhere. Floods of it. It's clearly a matter of great civic pride, and I like that about the place.

It was in this setting and against this backdrop that I found myself in Manhattan with Hotel California every January playing APAP (Association of Performing Arts Presenters), which encompassed about one thousand shows in all, most of which were at the midtown Hilton.

And it's an interesting scene: Describing it to my fiance on the phone went thus: "Cher's down the hall dressed in black lingerie next to Stevie Nicks, who is practicing her pirouettes. Janis Joplin just killed it in the room we're playing later, Michael Jackson's kicking back on a bench, Abba just delivered compliments to my playing, I exchanged five fist bumps with The Temptations on the escalator and there goes Paul McCartney." But the dancers, acrobats and other circus performers lend the coolest elements. Something about a lavishly made-up and costumed human on stilts walking next to a befeathered little person just makes me smile.

In stark contrast to all of that, the entire fourth floor was set aside exclusively for Jazz and related substances, providing calm refuge from the melee and cacophony of the other floors. It was there that I had the honor of getting demoralized and inspired by a great Brazilian Jazz guitarist named Diego Figueiredo. Being a Jazz hang, everyone was dressed in the muted colors and studied understatement of the urban sophisticate's uniform. Except for me, of course. I wore my customary and beloved military cargo pants, T-shirt and hoodie everywhere I went, lest my crass disregard for the aesthetic come under scrutiny.

I saw some amazing talent at the convention every day, almost all of whom were visiting from elsewhere. The violinist and cellist accompanying an acrobatic troupe were as good as any I've ever heard (a string duo is very exposed and had better be damn good). There was a progressive avant garde fusion big band from Norway that absolutely astounded me. It was reminiscent of, and almost on the level of, "Wide Angles", by the Michael Brecker Quindectet. A man by the name of Brian Owens, out of Missouri, can SANG like nothing you've ever heard. He does a Marvin Gaye tribute, but he could probably make Take6 into Take7.

WAR performed—the actual band—and I got some good hang time with them, as we shared a green room. And as much as I love WAR, the highlight of the whole thing for me was an explosively, deliriously brilliant act out of Minneapolis called "Rhythmic Circus". All were kids between 20 and 30: five-man rhythm (keys, bass, guitar, drums and percussion), alto sax, trumpet and 4 fantastic tap dancers. The percussionist was also an amazing beatboxer and vocal sound effects guy. They didn't do any covers. They had great music, great dance, and the auditory spectacle of "Heatbox"—the percussionist / beatboxer—trading fours with mega-talented tapdancers was hilarious, blindingly brilliant and above all, it was FUN. Everyone I spoke to about them agreed that they took the cake of the entire shindig.

The energy on the streets of Manhattan is vibrant to some, manic to others and famously very high at any time, day or night. Like everybody else I charged everywhere I went, unable to walk at a reasonable, normal pace. Looking up at the ribbon of sky from the bottom of the deep, narrow corridors of commerce gave me a strong sense of being in an ant colony, assimilated into a frenzied collective driving the thriving, striving machinery of economics, following the commandments of bright ads for the latest chic, garishly displayed on 80-foot tall LED screens affixed to buildings. All the while, the soundtracks my head generated were high-energy.

Our huge tour bus had no business trying to negotiate Manhattan and no place to park, so we were commuting in from Jersey each day in a rented vehicle. On a good day, the traffic was on a par with LA's worst, and sometimes it was just a parking lot. Viewed from the spot where we'd been sitting in traffic for half an hour, a sign proudly advertising "one-bedroom condos for 1.1 million and up" made me ponder what unlikely paradigm might explain humanity's pricing index.

But I have to set the record straight about something: New Yorkers are not rude. That stereotype needs to go away. Without exception everyone I talked to, everywhere I went, was friendly and helpful. Ditto the experiences of everyone in the band: not one of us had a negative interaction the entire time, neither in Jersey nor in Manhattan. Some great visits with my old friends Barry Danielian (he of the Emmanuel tour, and as of this writing playing trumpet with Springsteen) and Rod Ossa (stage manager from the Emmanuel tour, now doing lots of big-time live sound gigs) were good for the soul as well. And I met a new friend I had known only from facebook, who's a singer-songwriter and runs an arial photography business. He faced the challenges of getting into Manhattan to meet in person and take in the show, for which I was honored and humbled. I also bumped into Ross Wright, aka Elvis Schoenberg, who was there just doing some reconnaissance. The dichotomy wasn't lost on me of hanging with Ross while showcasing with a band playing four-chord, campfire-friendly pop.

At one point, having changed into show attire in the first stall of a very busy men's room in the middle of APAP's main floor melee, I left my reading glasses and bluetooth (a nice one) perched on the TP dispenser housing. Realizing my mistake 90 minutes later, I made my way back there to find them undisturbed. "Touche, New York, touche", I thought to myself. Despite my preconceptions and precocities, I found myself opening up to the good things the place has to offer.

And I started to get it, I started to understand the allure of New York. She's a beloved and priceless history for many whose families landed here, she's a beautifully designed building, she's a skater in Central Park, she's Wall Street power-brokering the entire planet. She's that homeless lady bundled up and asleep on the sidewalk in 12 degrees under that overpass, she's Lady Liberty and the United Nations Headquarters, she's a songwriter with a world-changing imagination, she's a bass player wheeling his upright down the street to the next gig. She's tacky industrial sculpture and some of the world's finest art, she's ugliness and beauty, she's sticky, stinky and delicious, she's The Halal Guys serving up chicken over rice faster than people can even pronounce it. She's as unforgiving a mistress as a Himalayan mountain if you don't have your shit together, and like any city, she kills people all the time.

But more than anything, New York is culture. And her culture springs primarily from her art. I've often said that if I were asked to justify the grievous crimes of humankind to any intelligent non-human species, I'd point to the London Philharmonic playing Stravinski, Debussy or Ravel's Bolero...I'd point to Jimi Hendrix, to Michael Brecker, to Allan Holdsworth...but art, in New York or anywhere, is more than humankind's saving grace.

Art's higher purpose is a sharing, among humans, of the best things humanity has to offer to humanity, to the future and to the cosmos. The collective experience, not just among artists but with the audience too, builds the zeit and is a part of the thing. As a musician and as a human, I derive much spiritual nourishment from "sharing the things I know and love with those of my kind", to quote the Walter Becker lyric from Deacon Blue. For me, the interaction between musicians is the whole point—that's probably why I'm a composer / arranger—and when that interaction is missing from my life or is at too base a level, it's unhealthy. It's no secret that many of the world's greatest living musicians are in New York City, and I enjoyed dipping my feet and ears into that flood of rampant, robust, unfettered, unapologetic expression.

* * *

You can look up the management for Western Arts Showcases and APAP online, and pay your dough to book a slot. Just know that if it's going to pay off, you need to bring your A-game. Here's your context:

Audacity and perfection. Think of what needs to happen on stage, viewed from the perspective of a jaded talent buyer watching a 20-minute showcase by total strangers, in order for that buyer to have absolutely no choice but to book it. If you can make that happen reliably, you're all set.

And I hate to say it, but the world expects shock and awe. If you want to compete at the level of other acts playing theaters and venues, you need that level of presentation: A custom video show playing behind your heads while you're performing is pretty much a must. There's usually a house lighting tech, but as is the case on tour, don't be surprised if they combine all the colors and just leave them all on, resulting in a perpetual whitewash for your show, rather than anything artistically useful. Some of the acts at these showcases bring their own lighting and visual effects, and fog machines might or might not be provided. But that's the kind of stuff you'll need if your shows are going to compete.

* * *

Before you ink the bookings, you'll need to know some things about deal-making and the art of negotiation as it pertains to this particular wing of the industry.

The success of Hotel California as a touring entity is due, in its entirety, to the efforts of George Dickinson. He's a perpetual force of nature on the phone, as well as being the band's frontman, leader and one of the lead guitarists. On the bus it was impossible not to overhear his end of conversations as he cut deals and laid bookings, usually six months to a year ahead. He's been doing it for decades, and has built an agreeable reputation for Hotel Cal as being a *dependable* band, who is *easy to deal with*, has its shit together *technically* and always puts on a *great show*. The italics are to highlight each of those aspects of the band's reputation, because each one is priceless. Between his relationships with buyers all over the country, his contact list and that reputation, it's not difficult for him to be booking a year ahead.

The band also has a long-standing relationship, as do I, with a great agent named Jerry Ross. Yes, they do indeed exist, and Jerry has been a hard-working, honorable presence in that scene for decades. Hotel Cal is probably the 15th or 20th band I've been in that was booked at least partially by him. Between the combined bookings and leads from George, Jerry and a couple of other agencies, the calendar is pretty crowded terrain, but it's worth pointing out that George does more of the bookings than all the agents combined. That's a hint.

If you want a well-booked calendar, you're going to have to blow up the phone and make it happen yourself, and you should consider giving the agent who handles that room his or her cut, so you don't burn that bridge. Remember, relationships make the world go around, not gigs. Gigs come and go.

George is on the phone many hours of every day, applying the things he's learned about the art of negotiation in his relaxed, soft-spoken and polite southern drawl, and I gotta say: It's impressive to watch the guy work. He's returning inquiries but also cold-calling people, which is a numbers game of course. But once you've got a reputation and track record as solid as the one he's built, the numbers are definitely in your favor.

Here are some helpful tips and tenets for dealing with promoters and talent buyers, some of which I gleaned from watching George suave the calendar:

First off, everybody wins. Whatever the deal is, it has to work so that nobody walks away unhappy. The entire time I was in that band, every place we played, the customer was happy. We invariably had venues that were 90% or more full, and that helps a lot. But I suspect that's more a matter of playing places with good advertising in place, and providing them with great looking promo materials.

Be flexible, and let it be known that you are. Whether it's a buyout (playing for a fixed sum, regardless of how well or poorly the house does, such as the way fairs and festivals work), or a split (splitting the ticket sales) or a split with a guarantee (a base sum you're guaranteed, that will hopefully at least allow you to break even, and a split of ticket sales past a certain benchmark), there's always a way to make it work so that everybody's minimizing risk and maximizing gain. Once in a while, a call would end with "Well, Ah guess we're jus' too fahr apart on the numbers, then. Darn, it woulda been nahss. Maybe next tahm, though! You've got mah number, so please don't hesitate t' call..." followed by the usual niceties and very politely ending the conversation. And that, children, is how you allow the other party to save face, and leave the door open.

With splits, you have to be certain that the promoter has a good PR and advertising pipeline in place, and a solid track record selling tickets. You also have to be able to discern when that's not the case, like when you're dealing with a less experienced party. Until you're experienced enough to be able to judge how good or established a promoter is, you might consider taking buyouts to minimize your risk while you familiarize yourself with the whole scene and the people in it. Call it getting your chops.

George was comfortable, casual and matter-of-fact when throwing around numbers. He's dealing with people who are also that way—that's just the nature of the waters they swim in every day—so it gets to be a friendly, nuts-and-bolts, matter-of-fact back and forth.

You might consider making your merch table a sweetening point. If you don't travel with someone to run it, you can let the house staff it and cut generous, house-friendly deals regarding the split of the bank. It'll help build that "easy to work with" reputation, and get your promo material out into the world. Also, some artists charge for meet-and-greets, and you can split that in a friendly way for the house. The premium tickets (first two rows, say) might get a gift bag with your CD or something.

Know your input list and backline needs, and have them sitting in a document you can easily send to people. Arranging the logistics and technical end of things for a show is called advancing. Learn about the process and have your technical shit together. Venue staff will require that you do, in order for shows to go smoothly. Often enough, you'll be dealing with venue staff who don't have their shit together—that is what it is, and there's very little you can do about it. Just don't let the unqualified one be you.

***

The touring sector has done us all proud, rising like a phoenix from the ashes of the Pandemic. It took some bad lumps like everything and everybody did, but never underestimate what we humans and our moxie can overcome, whether driven by love of music, or of celebration, or our primal need for gathering. And of course the need to resume the business of "making music make money" is a factor, but probably it's all of the above. Thus the slumbering giant reawakens, staggers to its feet and resumes its pitching and stumbling progress into the familiar and the unknown. The show must go on.

Hotel California is still out there, perpetuating a road of their own making. As of this writing I'm teaching two extremely talented young fiends in the band, via zoom. The band's personnel spans multiple generations, so who knows how long it can go on.

The bus does its part in The Greater Mechanism, the band and everyone in it doing theirs, as do agents, promoters, venue staff and fans. A piston goes down and sucks in fuel, the right note is played at the right time, the soundman moves a fader, a phone rings and another gig gets booked over a year away. The Greater Mechanism has been built over decades, and is now an endless dance feeding its own perpetuity: pistons, gears, wheels, phone calls, notes, input lists, load in, soundcheck, show, meet-and-greet, eating—all components moving in precise accordance with their scheduled roles, propelling them all into the future on time, laying down a highway paved with bookings so that The Machine doesn't run out of road.

Valves in the engine, valves in their amps, valves in their hearts. They feed and obey The Greater Mechanism as it feeds and obeys them. It will continue its waltz across the American dance floor with diligence and obedience until the wrong valve inevitably fails, in the meantime now and then a component asking who the hell shat on the bus.

Chapter 42
The Unpredictably Predictable

I think most musicians will tell you that it's kind of incredible, the way the future in music is always shaky, but something always comes through. The timing of gigs in my career has been so consistently freaky for so many years, it's like I've spent decades running across a huge lake while stepping stones just magically pop up out of the water right where my foot is coming down. Most of society thinks of a job as a path. For a musician, one job is never more than a stepping stone.

I don't believe in anything not scientifically proven. On the other hand, I enthusiastically admit there are plenty of things about how this universe works that our science can't yet explain, and I cannot scientifically disbelieve in the unknown. Viva l'exploration.

I can't explain the eerie regularity with which the next gig always comes along, but it always does. Those closest to me--family, girlfriends and the like--have never been able to accept it, it's unnerving for them and I can't point to any solid math that'll reassure them. It's easy to understand why this running across a lake has cost several relationships, but it is what it is and I am what I am. Back when Roni and I were first getting serious, I told her "I've gotta warn you, I'm a musician. It's just the way I was born, and that won't change."

She just looked me in the eye and said, "Well, I come with a poodle." Thus had I met my match, in several ways.

In late 2017 Roni graduated nursing school, heralding the end of the Hotel Cal gig. I had no idea what would be next for me, but I was looking forward to swinging the pinata stick around town to see what kind of work I could knock out of the sky as arranger / producer. Thus did I put that energy out into the universe, and just a couple of days later my old buddy Steve Kramer came to see a Hotel Cal show at the Orange County fair, and asked me if I'd be interested in doing some arranging and producing of his material. It eventually led to my doing over 60 full-blown arrangements and productions for Steve, spanning six years so far. It was budgeted well enough for me to use my A-list cats for horns, winds, strings, vocals, drums, percussion and the like. We started work in late 2017. I eased out of Hotel California in a way that worked for everyone—APAP in January '18 was my last show with them.

Within a few months, all the sitting on my butt wearing the arranger / producer cap made me itchy to play some more challenging music with scary monsters. After three years on a tour bus playing Eagles music, I needed to dust the cobwebs off my chops and burn some carbon out of the cylinders. Rehearsing the fusion thing with Jay Setar, Mark Corradetti and Bob Luna and then playing NAMM was fun, but I wanted to be gigging out and playing with 'live bullets' more often. Thus did I put that energy out into the universe, and the response was a call from Jerry Salas, lead singer with El Chicano. He was doing a Gino Vannelli tribute around town when not touring with El Chicano. Ronnie Ciago was drummer, Larry Antonino was bass and Bob Luna was keyboards. Some combination of those three monsters had recommended me, and after an audition I was in. The four of us have been the rhythm section on so many projects, I've honestly lost count. We make a great team, and it was incredible fun to play the Gino Vannelli book with such great cats and friends. Gino's charts (actually written by his brother and MD, Ross Vannelli) manage to be a unique mixture of hip fusion and hit songwriting. It's very well written and arranged, and makes a lot of sense. I spent a little time with it in the woodshed, simply because it was such a joy to play. Gino's music and band has a well-earned reputation in a good way, and commands great respect among great players. Jerry is a really cool guy and enjoyed being frontman on those gigs, encouraging us to stretch a bit and have fun as we played the best listening rooms in SoCal.

    I had a great balance between arranging and producing for Steve, grooving and stretching with the guys on the Gino show and with the fusion lineup with Jay, Bob and Mark. I booked Smarticus into Alva's Showroom, and The Baked Potato wanted to book us. Life was good.

Chapter 43
There be Monsters

In December of 2018, not long after starting a nursing job, Roni was diagnosed with cancer. Trying to breathe after all the air had been sucked out of the room by the doctor's words, we got the contact info for the next doc and a STAT referral. Driving away, I remember hearing myself say for the first of a million times: "We'll get you through this, my love. I don't know how, but we will. We're gonna beat this."

Over the next week or two of prioritized testing, a picture quickly emerged: it was aggressive, it was fairly rare—so they didn't have all the statistics to draw from that they really needed—and we caught it a little late. Eventually, her particular case presented a long cascade of deadly complications that were so bad, for a while the complications were a bigger threat than the cancer itself.

I cleared my calendar of everything but working for Steve, and became a full-time caregiver. I ran my ass off from my waking moment until falling into the sack at night, taking care of her while ceaselessly shuttling information from medical team to medical team, because the right hand in medicine never knows what the left is doing. She was put on sick leave with her medical benefits intact—thank the stars—and laid in bed in perpetual agony that I could do nothing about. All she could do was lie there and softly cry in pain, sometimes not so softly, for many months. I have never felt so fucking helpless. I wanted so badly to get my hands on that goddamned disease and wring its fucking neck, I almost broke my teeth gnashing them. My jaw muscles perpetually hurt.

Suddenly cast into the deepest, darkest woods of her life, she was staring at the likelihood of dying within months, and much of her energy and mine went into insisting that we'd get her through it. We both just set our jaws and refused to give in. I didn't want to even think about what losing that battle would look like. The darkest moments for me, by far, were when the battle was just too damned hard, and she wanted to give up.

After the initial round of chemo and radiation, she went into remission and a rubber stamp of approval returned her to work. A few months later, it came back.

Roni and I both made a point of becoming as knowledgeable as possible about every aspect of her cancer and its treatment, until she became too incapacitated and was admitted. Then it was down to me. At that point I was perpetually chasing down and badgering doctors to keep the ball rolling, to stay out ahead of things and not to write her off, which some of them were starting to do. It took long hours every day for months, running around the hospital. I put so many miles on my dogs that my legs actually started to get built up.

Until that time, I had spent my entire life being happily impervious to stress. My 'stress generator' was just broken at birth I guess, and I never really felt it. But I was feeling it now, in no uncertain terms. It manifested mentally, emotionally and physically. What the hell was this "stress" beast? Is this what people around me had been talking about this whole time? Shit, no wonder girlfriends had broken up with me over financial uncertainty, if it made them feel this.

It never let up. It was there in my every waking moment and in my dreams. It felt like the air was full of tiny needles...hot and close, like being in a hyperbaric chamber with a thousand pounds per square inch of pressure, from all sides, at all times. Every day was a fresh hell, bringing new things trying to kill her...a whole team of monsters killing the love of my life. She was in agony, she was losing and there was nothing—nothing—I could do to directly battle the thing. She's such a better human than me, I'd have given anything to just trade places so that she could have a full life. I'd be lying if I said it didn't take a toll. The world became a hot, prickly blanket pressing on me from the outside, while inside I was perpetually fighting an explosion.

I had so much pent-up rage, it felt like a roaring monster was in me that I could just barely control. I sometimes felt like I'd just as soon kill somebody as look at them. I had to acknowledge the uncomfortable truth that sometimes I didn't feel completely stable, and that I might actually be getting a bit dangerous. If some guy had given me the wrong look at the wrong moment—pacifist and child of the sixties that I am—I might be in prison now, rubbing elbows with those I used to teach and direct in the bands as a contract artist. But I couldn't just bug out and go into the woods to pound my forehead into a tree trunk until I felt better: Roni would die if I did. So I turned into a walking bomb containment unit, absorbing the detonations that occurred inside me every day.

Working in my favor was the fact that nothing I've ever done with my time on planet Earth ever felt as right as saving Roni, so resolve was never an issue. We might both die doing it, but we never doubted that giving it whatever it took was the right thing to do, viewed from any point of the compass, regardless of the toll. It was that simple.

One of the most remarkable things was that when it dropped out of the sky on us, there were zero resources that I could find to help me become an effective caregiver and advocate—nothing about any of it, whatsoever. I eventually discovered caregiver.com, but not until I didn't have much need of it. It would have been great to have had that as a resource at the time.

I had my closest brothers who I could call when things were looking especially dark, and call I did. Several times I was talked off the ledge by a patient brother. As unimaginably horrible as her battle was, people on the medical team were warning me not to underestimate the toll an ordeal like hers takes on the caregiver. They weren't wrong.

Ultimately, more things went right than went wrong, and we won. It still amazes us. But it was a years-long, horrible fucking nightmare that left us both permanently changed, and more than one doctor on her team has mentioned writing a paper about her having survived, and why—HOW—she even did.

The science of it explains it I guess, but how that science was brought to bear was through a string of extraordinary unlikelihoods and coincidences that was stranger and more consistent than any stepping stones popping up out of a lake.

Without her rock star oncologist, she would have died. The radiation machine that they had was the best, one of only five in the entire country. Without that particular machine she would have died. Without a personal connection between her brother and a childhood buddy who had become the president of one of the national medical boards in an area pertaining to her case, she would have died. Without an incredible home health care nurse named Brenda, she would have died. Without her being an RN at that hospital and getting fast-tracked VIP treatment, she would have died. Without that gucci health coverage, she would have died. Without having a bullheaded, aggressive advocate who perpetually had at least one boot up the ass of at least one doctor, she would have died. Without a consulting doctor at the tip of the cannabinoid research spearhead to guide us through the bewildering maze of products, enabling her to stop taking opiates, she would have died. Without the valuable advice of our great friend Carolyn Tiernan, she would have died. Without a lady who was in charge of appeals at the insurance company's HQ, who was solidly on our team and threw some pivotal bureaucratic switches at pivotal life-and-death moments, she would have died. Without my wonderful friend and client Steve Kramer keeping the work load sitting there so I could just walk from the bedroom into the studio and earn enough money to keep the roof over our heads, whenever and at whatever pace I needed, we would've lost the place and she would have died. Hell, for much of the time during her ordeal, things were so close to the edge that if there had been a bad enough earthquake, she would have died. The list goes on and on and on.

But more than anything, without her incredible stamina and determination, without what she understands medically and how intelligently she attacked it, she would have died. The single most important member of any medical team is of course the patient, and she was steadfast to the science of it.

I did what I could to learn, and despite having the wrong background I actually caught a lot of things the docs were overlooking, just because I was paying attention to what seemed obvious, and dealing with only one patient. But it was Roni whose research turned up many things that saved her, most importantly a brand new immunotherapy treatment. Its inventor had won the Nobel for it, and we introduced her oncologist to it. It ultimately saved her life, and without it—you guessed it—she would have died.

But before she got better, she got worse. Much worse. Once things had progressed to where she was laying in a hospital bed, incapacitated and fighting for her life, it was on me and my dogged efforts to keep the team engaged. At one point she became an unresponsive skeleton with gray skin, and the docs were telling me that what might happen soon is that her organs would start shutting down. You might recognize that as medical code-speak for death. At that point, three things saved her: One was her innately solid physical machinery and another was her gloriously stubborn refusal to give up the fight. The last was that we were just freakishly lucky. The sheer number of happy accidents the universe dumped on us to save her life astounds us both to this day.

One fine sunny day I finally brought her home, barely able to stand or walk. She very gradually and steadily restrengthened, and returned to living. After many more months, she was far enough out of the woods for me to trust her to the care of home health nurses for a few days, and it was time for me to handle some overdue business I had with myself. I called a good friend named Jack Jacobsen who lives up in North Cal. A seriously excellent keyboardist, he had been with Huey Lewis and the News through the heyday years, we had had some serious fun playing together on a couple of occasions, and he had me provide remotely recorded guitars on a very cool project of his.

Jack had recently invited me up to his property in the redwoods north of the Bay for a visit, mentioning conversationally that he had a big pile of madrone rounds that he needed to chop, and wasn't looking forward to doing it. Madrone is pretty hard stuff and chopping firewood was exactly the kind of thing I needed to do, so I told him to hold off and let me do it. I tossed a couple of axes in the car and drove all the way up there to exorcise the ragebomb out of me in a way that wouldn't damage anything, in the service of a needed physical task, wherein that kind of energy wouldn't get me arrested. Jack, bless his open mind, seemed to understand.

On a gorgeous afternoon at his compound in the redwoods outside of Bodega, for about ninety minutes I let my ferocity off leash and went through those rounds like they were balsa wood. The visceral, snot-slinging animal satisfaction of wreaking physical havoc and making something fly apart was exactly what I needed. As I attacked that wood, I felt so much rage leaving my body that it was "like a tyrannosaurus jumping out of a flea", to quote John Long. I drove back to LA a couple of days later no longer feeling like an unstable pile of dynamite, Jack and I had gotten in a great visit, and he had a cord of Madrone ready for the fireplace. Win-win-win.

* * *

As of this writing, next month marks the magic five-year anniversary since Roni's last treatment, when statistics indicate that we can start breathing normally again. It's one thing to love your spouse so much that you married the person, but seeing them almost die, start to slip from your grasp and then come back against such tall odds will change how you value your time with them. Every second I can spend with her now is priceless.

The effect this has had on my musical doings is in line with the new norms that were imposed on the world a few years ago, in a way that's as fortunate for me as it is unfortunate for the world: While millions were dying and humanity struggled with the jarring lifestyle changes accompanying the deadliest pandemic in a century, I discovered an upside to being employed full-time working at home, not needing to leave the house, while caring for someone who couldn't. Other than the challenges that faced everyone in procuring food, the lockdown didn't really change anything in our daily lives. And we now had a name for the lifestyle we had already been living for a couple of years: "Shelter in place".

Other than a token Orchestre Surreal show and a few other choice noiselettings, I put the kibosh on playing live in tight spaces for a few years.

Chapter 44
Of Balance and Balrogs

A career in music takes everything you've got and demands more. If you're wired to answer the call no matter what, as most are, this can get dangerous. Earlier this year, my good brother Steve contracted me to retool my arrangements of thirteen of his songs for a live show (live arrangements are a bit different from studio arrangements), and to contract an 11-piece lineup of top-shelf studio cats and vocalists—mostly the same people who had recorded them in the studio version—to perform the show under my direction. All well and good. We locked out one of LA's premier soundstage facilities, in the same room where Paul McCartney puts his shows together. The songs were great, the budget penciled out, so what could possibly be the downside?

Retooling the arrangements for live was the easy part, if you can call it an easy thing to amend 13 scores to new instrumentation, adjust existing parts for live performance, then extract and lay out over 430 pages of new player's parts. It was a lot of work, but it's smack-dab in the middle of my wheelhouse, so no problem there.

The contracting, on the other hand, was more like trying to juggle globs of jello while balancing on a beach ball and rendering psychological services in several languages. It covered a lot of sectors and took a surprising amount of focused, unceasing effort to choose and contract everything and everyone. Besides needing the right facility and the right backline, we needed the right technical director for lighting, video, recorded audio and live audio. My hope was to find one person to be TD and oversee his own contracting and delegation for each of those areas. Then there were the cats. The studio productions are heavy on guitar parts (go figure), so I needed two additional guitarists who could read well, play chords literately, groove, balance their volume, AND rock their asses off when needed. That's a combination that doesn't grow on trees, even in LA. Contracting the right singer for one of the slots presented a homeric odyssey in itself.

    I saw a video once of kids trying to catch greased pigs for a county fair competition. It's a pretty hilarious thing if you're not a pig, and exactly the way I felt trying to get things in place and stable. If I could get everything lined up and everyone covering their own sectors, I just might be able to concentrate on mine. Alas, as most MDs will tell you, that's not what directing usually looks like.

    After a few months of increasingly intense prep, we took it all into the soundstage where the show would go down, and rehearsed the whole band for five hours every day for four days. Between the rhythm section, the vocals and the guitars, I also had to run two additional 90-minute sectional rehearsals each day, one before and one after the full band rehearsal. On the fifth day, after another sectional, we did a final run-through and then that night was the show. The mission was to play it live while videotaping and recording audio to multitrack, with family and friends serving as the audience. Steve had a lot of money riding on my pulling this off in good form, and I couldn't let him down.

    I had been so busy that I hadn't had time to run the math on just how busy I had been: by downbeat I had been driving myself doggedly into the ground in deadline mode from the moment I woke up until I fell into bed--usually 18 or more hours later--for 57 solid days. Roni had been mentioning this for weeks: "You need to slow down and get some rest. You're going too hard. I'm worried about you."

I brushed it aside in typical form, tossing out the usual assurances: "I'm fine, I'm superman, this is what I do. And it's gotta be done. It's ALL gotta be done." All of which was true, except for the superman part.

When the fifth night arrived and we hit downbeat, the cats were incredible, the arrangements were fine and the show was fine—except for the MD. I could barely stand, and felt like hammered dogshit. I had the show, eight video cameras and a client all needing me to be 200% alive and all bouncy and bright-eyed, at precisely the time when the effort required just to remain upright felt like a losing battle against gravity.

I tried my best to rally, but of course to try is to fail. I looked haggard on camera. And as is common with directing a show, getting everyone else ready had required so much of my time and energy that I hadn't been able to shed my own parts, so my attention was glued to the music stand in front of me. Fortunately, I was surrounded by blinding talent on stage, and they brought it all home in excellent form.

I got home after the show using the tattered remnants of survival mode energy, flopped face-down into bed and went very quickly downhill from there. I woke up the next day sicker than I had been in over a decade. We made sure it wasn't covid, but whatever it was, it was a large fire-breathing monster...maybe the Balrog of Morgoth that Gandalf fought in the Tolkien movie. It just knocked on the door, smiled and handed my ass to me in a garbage bag, then walked in and got comfortable in the corner of the bedroom and laughed at me for over a week as I lay in bed. I deserved it. With the 20/20 vision of hindsight, I looked at the calendar and saw what I had done--I could have given myself a heart attack with a load like that. Steve didn't set that schedule, I did. What the hell was I even thinking?

That's the problem, of course: We don't think. Duty calls and hey presto, we're superman or superwoman, just try telling us differently. The lesson here is to learn to pace yourself, because the industry sure as hell won't do that for you.

I'm happy to say I'm fine and all I needed was rest to overcome the Balrog, but it took a lot of it. It was three weeks before I started to feel my energy returning, and almost two months before I was one hundred percent. I'm not the sickly type at all, and for me to have run myself so far into the ground that my immune system was actually weak is a bit scary. If I was thirty years younger it might not have phased me—but then if I was thirty years younger, I would've missed all the cool music that made me who I am. Neener-neener, kiddies.

* * *

Aging in this industry is interesting. I'm no longer the prodigal golden boy, the adonis, the desirable. And I always expected to be out of the running for most things past the age of forty or so, but that hasn't happened at all. I think this is because of boomers having pioneered the majority of the popular musical forms that are now in place. Stages all around me are exhibiting the unlikely spectacle of melba toast-gumming old farts performing music, and the level of acceptance they receive from all ages is downright encouraging.

But the industry is less kind and forgiving of the aging process if you're female. Chalk that up to women's roles in entertainment itinerantly being that of sex objects, as if the creative contribution of an entire gender doesn't exist. This runs so deep that even now, not many people think of Charro (for instance) as the musical badass she really is. She knew which side of the bread had the butter, and broke onto the public scene by presenting herself to the world as the coquettish "Cuchi-cuchi" girl. The persona is fetching to the eye, and that's as far as the public was ever asked to think. But her musical chops stand up to scrutiny when compared to any of the world's greatest flamenco players. It pisses me off, on her behalf.

Things are improving for women in arts and entertainment, but far too slowly. Overall it remains a male-dominated industry, and women aren't allowed to age with the same impunity as men.

David Bowie once said "Aging is the process of becoming the person you should have been all along." I wholeheartedly agree, and I'll add that it's also the process of bringing more and more valuable experience and musical ability to the table while being seen as less and less valid.

But regardless of your age or your X/Y chromosome, you ignore your body's needs at your peril. There's a reason I call sitting for long hours every day a slow suicide, and if you add deadline pressure and heavy mental tasking, you're in dangerous territory whether you acknowledge it or not. Musicians are nutjobs, and you need to respect what your nuttiness can make you do. We're so driven by our art that when we're in the middle of a project we feel like health is irrelevant, or protected by some sort of higher-calling fairy bullshit. For me, having a dog that requires me to be outside a lot is a very good thing. Our Jesse is no fool.

The art of making this career balance with your life requires its own skill set. And not to put too fine a point on it, but it also requires that you remain among the living. At some point, a situation will demand so much of you that the challenge won't be technical or musical: it'll be admitting to the limits of your own humanity, the alternative being to join the ranks of those who have worked themselves to death. As I keep discovering, being self-employed doesn't mean you don't work for an idiotic dickhead.

Chapter 45
Bon Vivant Confidante

As widely varied as all the genres and their inhabitants are, in society's eyes all musicians, from the lowest to the highest strata, are assumed to be "cool". It doesn't mean that we're as acceptable as normal folks or that people want to date one of us, or would want us going out with their son or daughter...and it definitely doesn't mean they want their son or daughter to be a musician. It's just assumed that we're cool, like we're all in on a great secret and can be trusted with yours.

I've been automatically granted all-access passes to the inner sanctum of strangers' personal lives everywhere I've gone on gigs. Often it's a warm-hearted invitation into someone's home to meet the family, and I'm made to feel like an honored guest. At other times, I've been tapped to be in on a shenanigan, or let in on some dirty dark secret or local gossip like I'm running a confessional booth. On big tours, the band might get taken out on a yacht owned by some local bigwig, where all the local politics and personalities are laid bare over icy beverages.

It's assumed that we like to party and kick up our heels in our little secret musician underground, and we find ourselves being invited to backyard shindigs just for the entertainment of it, so that people can introduce us to their friends, or show us how hard they can party.

One night in the summer of '86, I was playing a biker bar in Page, Arizona—a tiny desert town providing life support for the Glen Canyon Dam and Lake Powell—and two Arizona state troopers on vacation for the weekend were hammering whiskey and pitchers of beer. Having decided they were adopting the drummer and me into their weekend bender, they kept sending up shot after shot, and we didn't want to be rude by not drinking. By the end of the night, we were all listing to port and starboard as we walked the one block to the cinderblock motel where we were all staying. The party continued in one of our rooms with a case of beer. By and by one shitfaced trooper asked, "You guys ever been waddershkiin'? We've godda boad..."

"Yeah, I been a few times, in my teens" I slurred, "I'm not very good". The room was starting to spin.

"I've been too, I'm good enough for one ski" said the drummer, trying and failing not to appear drunk.

"Well, we're takin' you two oud on th' lage tomorrrroo..." the trooper's eyes were starting to cross. The other trooper could only laugh.

By halfway through that case of beer, it had become an especially good idea to get an early start by waking up at 05:00, just a little over two hours away. And so it was that we found ourselves in a 20-foot twin outboard ski boat, bucking around on whitecaps in the blazing sun with no drinking water, only cases of Budweiser to drink, pounding beers and getting pounded on water skis for several hours. Whenever they traded boat-driving duty, the troopers made a great drunken show of performing field sobriety checks on each other, one guy waving his index finger right and left in front of the other's eyes:

"Follow my finger."

The other trooper's eyes were visibly jerking and not pointing in quite the same direction as the finger.

"Ee-yep, yer drunk. You drive."

That night in the bar, the bikers were treated to an exciting new look on stage, as the band featured the lambent green faces of the guitarist and drummer. Those troopers—looking no worse for wear—had felt like they had to show the musicians how the law parties. This was to become a repeated experience in my life. Trust me when I tell you: If you're ever invited to party with law enforcement, don't say no—that would be rude—but bring your A-game and some drinking water. In all my travels, I've never met any cadre who parties as hard as law enforcement.

* * *

Such is music's amazing ability to bridge gaps. It can even enable a man to communicate with a woman in a way that she understands, in a medium that includes words, which are normally a dangerous thing for a man to use when communicating with the smarter sex.

Music is communication, it is expression. It supersedes words and language, like life and death. It brings people from different countries, cultures, races religions and generations together in a way that can cause spontaneous celebration, and the pagan ritual we call dance—this in a time when we're hesitant to even look at the car next to us at a stop light. It even unites people from different centuries, sharing an experience across the boundaries of time itself.

Music has shaped civilizations, by inspiring conversion to this or that religion. In fact, many of our proudest musical achievements have been in the name of religion. I can understand how some might be converted to faith by music alone.

In Barcelona every Saturday in the summer of '03 on that cruise ship gig, I loved to wander the dark gray stone labyrinth of medieval alleys around the Gothic Cathedral, where fantastic classical musicians from all over Europe are known to set up in the alcoves and corners and play the masterpieces, usually Bach. His angular lines cry despair and desire, the dark strains of tension and resolution marrying with the dark gothic stone architecture.

Standing there and listening, the combined magic was so heady, I could imagine my cynical self being a pauper in the 1700's, surrounded by famine and disease, beset with injustice all around, and the exaltation that that music would offer to my body and soul as it led my spirit up the soaring gray walls and flying buttresses toward the sky and glorious salvation—a stronger force than any words.

Only a fool or a sociopath could fail to realize the spiritual power music has over us all. There is music with beautiful spirit and music with ugly spirit, and our children are assaulted every day with far too much ugly-spirited music. I worry about the effect this will have down the line. Our kids don't know any better than to swallow whatever dreck the world's playlist is shoving down their throats, as has always been the case.

When I hear the genius and passion that went into Bach's double-choir motet "Trestes Est, A Ni Ma Mea" ("Be not afraid, I am with thee"), or Mozart's Requiem, or Ave Maria—all very powerful, very religious masterpieces—cynic and atheist that I am, yea, and calloused, jaded musician too, I am moved sometimes to tears. Much of the music I hear on the world's playlist these days moves me to tears too, but more in the way a dentists' drill does. The same way I might be moved to tears by the downfall of a once-great civilization.

I think of the famous story of American and German soldiers in WWII, joining together in song across a field from each other, singing Christmas carols. I think of the story that one of my inmate students told me when I was a contract artist: During a lockdown on their yard, everyone was escorted outside and made to sit around on the lawn in the heat of the summer sun in Lancaster for many hours. Impatience grew, things got tense and tempers heated up continually, until my student knew the situation was about to ignite. He happened to have his guitar with him and was sitting right in the middle of the lawn, so he jumped to his feet and sang "La Bamba" at the top of his voice. Everyone started joining in. He said the levity diffused the situation so effectively, the correctional officers didn't even tell him to sit back down.

As history shows, when people are stripped of dignity, freedom, food, water and clothing, even stripped of civilization itself by war—when all we have is our naked shivering asses and our wits, our ferocity, our love and our courage—we still sing, and we still dance. When it all goes to hell someday, song and dance will be our last remaining refuge.

Music has shown itself to be the only unifying factor that truly reaches across the barriers of culture, politics, religion and war. It is, literally, the only thing that I see as being capable of saving the world from the follies of humankind. If we ever do manage to live as the single species we actually are, floating here on this pale blue dot in the middle of the interstellar void, music will play a big role in that unification.

I hear the immensity of music's power when I listen, and feel it coming through me when I play or write. Whether or not any humble contribution of mine can nudge humanity's cosmic scale toward the positive, Her capacity for changing our zeitgeist keeps me hopeful. I'm humbled and honored to spend my time here on Earth in Her service.

It's a life well spent.

Epilogue

I hope this has been useful to you, these things I've learned over the course of my experience so far. Looking forward from here, time and humanity will continue to lurch forward from fiasco to fiasco, as will music and I. Hopefully you too.

As I write these words, my desk is juggling the post-production of that live show that almost got the better of me, doing pre-production on a song for another client and friend named Jeff Hobbs, and I just got in from the first day of a two-day, 11-song recording session in Silver Lake at Daniel Fabiano's studio. Today there was a 4.4 magnitude earthquake epicentered less than five miles away that shook that studio fairly hard. I was right in the middle of a take and just kept playing...the part that I was recording went on for another minute or so and the take was good. Thus did Mother Earth become a collaborative element, as if it could ever be otherwise.

I'll continue to make music as long as I breathe. I always welcome the calls to do more noiseletting live and on recordings, and at some point in the coming year I'll be in front of Greg Beaton's camera, doing another interview for his brilliant documentary on the life of Allan Holdsworth. My next album has been impatiently clearing its throat at me from the corner for some time, and who knows: maybe this year I'll be able to answer its call.

Meantime, as always, our dog Jesse needs to be walked.

The End

Whatever you do or don't know about being a musician, this no-holds-barred tour through the hilarious and brutal realities of life inside the music industry is as informative as it is entertaining. Written for musicians and general public alike, Byron Fry's story imparts hard-learned, hard-hitting truths from his wild ride through life as a musical pinball.

His journey is a dizzying study of how many hats one person can wear, and he places each of them on your head. Incredible stories and adventures range through dozens of strikingly different musical disciplines and worlds, delivering priceless tips and perspectives from every strata of the food chain.

From playing the seediest dives and living on potato buds to riding in motorcades and working with multi-grammy-winning artists alongside world-famous musicians, Byron's bumpy trajectory navigates musical training, poverty, alcoholism, life-changing injuries and relationships, a beautiful collision with fatherhood, and validation. The story is one of friendship, healing, adaptation, love, and the most important thing for **any musician:**

An unflinching, sardonic sense of humor.

www.ingramcontent.com/pod-product-compliance
Lightning Source LLC
Chambersburg PA
CBHW051417290426
44109CB00016B/1330